The Attractive Empire

The Attractive Empire

Transnational Film Culture
in Imperial Japan

Michael Baskett

University of Hawai'i Press
Honolulu

© 2008 University of Hawai'i Press
All rights reserved
Printed in the United States of America
13 12 11 10 09 08   6 5 4 3 2 1

Library of Congress Cataloging-in-Publication Data
Baskett, Michael.
The attractive empire : transnational film culture in
imperial Japan / Michael Baskett.
p. cm.
Includes bibliographical references and index.
ISBN 978-0-8248-3163-9 (hardcover : alk. paper)
ISBN 978-0-8248-3223-0 (pbk. : alk. paper)
1. Motion pictures, Japanese—Asia—History.
2. Motion pictures—Japan—History.   I. Title.
PN1993.5.J3B38   2008
791.430952—dc22   2007043305

University of Hawai'i Press books are printed on acid-free
paper and meet the guidelines for permanence and durability
of the Council on Library Resources.

Designed by April Leidig-Higgins

Printed by The Maple-Vail Book Manufacturing Group

Contents

Acknowledgments

My earliest research into the subject of this book began more than twenty years ago. This book was made possible by the generous and tireless assistance of the staff of many libraries and collections including: the Special Collections and Theater Libraries at the University of California at Los Angeles, the University of California at Los Angeles Film and Television Archive, the Tsubouchi Memorial Theatre Museum (Waseda University), the Kawakita Memorial Film Institute, the Makino Collection, the Film Center Library at the National Museum of Modern Art, Tokyo, the Margaret Herrick Library of the Academy of Motion Picture Arts and Sciences, the Louis B. Mayer Library of the American Film Institute, the Cinematic Arts Library of the University of Southern California, Shochiku Studios Library, the Japanese National Diet Library, the Library of Congress, the Chinese Taipei Film Archive Library, the Hong Kong Film Archive Library, The Museum of Kyoto, and Planet Bibliotheque de Cinema.

Over the years, many people have supported this project in various ways providing useful criticisms as well as welcome advice. In Japan I would like to thank Hosokawa Shuhei, Iwamoto Kenji, Kano Masanao, the late Kurosawa Akira, Makino Mamoru, Nogami Teruyo, Sato Masaharu, the late Shimizu Akira, Tajima Ryoichi, the late Tsukada Yoshinobu, Yoshimi Shunya, and Yoshitsuru Yoshimitsu for selflessly sharing their time and insight with me. Outside Japan I would like to thank Nick Browne, Darrell Davis, the late William Everson, Elyssa Faison, Poshek Fu, James Goodwin, the late John Hampton, Jan-Christopher Horak, Iwasaki Shoichi, Joo Soowan, Kim Minkyu, Kim Soyoung, Thomas Lahusen, Sheldon Lu, Todd Mittleman, Mizuno Hiromi, Abe Mark Nornes, Remco Rabin, David Shepard, Mariko Tamanoi, Alan Tansman, and William Tsutsui. I wish to express my deepest thanks to Miriam Silverberg, Seiji Lippit, Carol Gluck, and Madge Huntington, who were always there to guide and support me in this project from the dissertation stage through to publication. My valued friend and colleague Barak Kushner of Cambridge University has been an invaluable influence on this project sharing both his expansive knowledge and humor to make writing this book a far more enjoyable and worthwhile process that it might have been.

At several stages the work was supported by a generous fellowship from the

Fulbright Foundation allowing me to conduct research in Japan, a summer grant from the University of Oregon, a Hall Center Fellowship and two travel grants from the University of Kansas, and three academic fellowships from the University of California at Los Angeles. I am very grateful to the film directors Hal Hartley and Mabel Cheung for giving me the opportunity of working as an assistant director and for their friendship. I would also like to thank my colleagues in the Department of Theatre and Film at the University of Kansas for their support. I also want to thank my graduate and undergraduate students who helped me think through many of the issues that I presented in the book.

This book never would have been completed without the love and support of my families. In Japan, Hideo and Tomoko Kuroda were and are a constant source of much needed love, encouragement, and trust. Their spiritual and material support made all of this possible. In the United States, Don and Joyce Baskett also supported, encouraged, and in many ways inspired this project by instilling a deep love of film in me when I was a child. Throughout all of this Dariko has always supported me in every way and at all times. Over the years and through every challenge we have faced together her love and companionship have been the greatest constant in my life, inspiring me to want to become both a better person and a better scholar. Doriko, you'll never know how glad I am that I met you.

Finally, I wish to express my sincere gratitude to Patricia Crosby of the University of Hawai'i Press for believing in and guiding this project through to completion. In addition, I wish to thank Margaret Black and Cheri Dunn and the two anonymous readers for their immeasurable patience and professionalism in helping me publish this during what turned out to be a particularly challenging time. While these people and institutions (and many more that I am unable to name for reasons of space) have contributed to this project, only I am responsible for any mistakes or errors in this work.

Earlier versions of portions of chapter 4 have been previously published in different forms in the following: "Dying for a Laugh: Post-1945 Japanese Service Comedies," *Historical Journal of Film, Radio and Television* 23, no. 4 (October 2003): 291–310; and "Goodwill Hunting: Rediscovering and Remembering Manchukuo in Japanese 'Goodwill Films,'" in Mariko Asano Tamanoi ed. *Crossed Histories: Manchuria in the Age of Empire* (University of Hawai'i Press, 2005): 120–149.

Lost Histories

In 2002, the fourth highest grossing film in South Korea was a big-budget science fiction epic directed by Lee Si-Myung entitled 2009: *Lost Memories*. Based on a bestselling novel by Bok Geo-il, the film poses the intriguing question: "What if Japan had never lost its empire?"[1] *Lost Memories* offers viewers an alternate history in which Korean nationalist Ahn Jung-geun (a real-life figure who assassinated Japanese Resident-General of Korea Ito Hirobumi in 1909) fails to assassinate Ito, with the result that Japan is not defeated in World War II but fights with the United States against Nazi Germany. Atomic bombs are dropped on Berlin, ending the war, and Japan retains its Asian empire intact. In 2009, Seoul is the third largest city in the Japanese empire, a high-tech postmodern metropolis awash with Japanese billboards, stores, and cars. The Japanese Bureau of Investigation (JBI) maintains colonial order, which is challenged only by an underground Korean resistance movement known as the *furei senjin*.[2] The two main protagonists, Korean JBI agent Sakamoto (played by Korean actor Jang Dong-Gun) and Japanese agent Saigo (played by the Japanese actor Nakamura Toru), learn the truth about this false history late in the film.

> Japan has tampered with the history that you know. In 2008, North and South Korea united after sixty years of separation to be reborn into a mighty East Asian nation with a stable economy and a powerful military. At that time, a movement started to take back land that once belonged to ancient Korea (Goguryeo).[3] You may not know this, but all of the territory around Manchuria belonged to our ancestors. Naturally, the Chinese government denied any access to the area, but with persistence, [China] finally admitted a joint research team of Korea, China, and Japan. [The Japanese] discovered a doorway in time [that they used] to escape the shame of defeat in the Pacific War and Hiroshima and Nagasaki. A Japanese right-wing extremist group sent an assassin back a hundred years in time to change history. This was the start of our unfortunate history.[4]

Lost Memories concerns us because it is not simply anti-Japanese Korean nationalist propaganda. It is important to consider that *Lost Memories* was a mainstream box-office hit and not a documentary or art-house film produced for a limited audience. Equally intriguing is why the film's producers found the subject of Japanese empire to be commercially viable for both South Korean and Japanese film audiences. The casting of a well-known Japanese actor in a leading role and extensive use of the Japanese dialogue for most of the film acknowledges the producers' conscious targeting of the Japanese market. This was a shrewd business decision in a year when the last barriers banning the importation of Japanese cultural products into the South Korean market were removed, and liberalization of the Korean market inspired a boom of interest in Korean cultural products in Japan.[5] *Lost Memories*' subplot of nascent Korean expansionist desires in China suggests that the attraction of empire is not limited to imperial Japan but may even be found in countries like contemporary South Korea, which not only did not possess colonies but were themselves the victims of colonialism. Even the film's anti-imperialist resistance leaders cling to the notion that Korea once had an empire of its own and will actively seek to regain it in the future.[6]

Lost Memories alerts us to the fact that over half a century after its official demise the cultural legacy of Japanese imperialism remains a heated and unresolved topic. A growing number of South Korean mainstream films[7] like *Lost Memories* are popular responses to tensions created in part by official and semiofficial Japanese statements such as Tokyo Metropolitan Governor Ishihara Shintaro's claim that Japan never invaded Korea,[8] Japanese politicians' quasi-official visits to the Yasukuni Shrine for Japan's war dead, the ongoing debates over Japanese history textbooks, and the comfort women issue, as well as the deployment of Japanese Self-Defense Forces to Iraq. Similarly, a steady flow of recent Japanese films such as *Lorelei* and *Merdeka* [Indonesian for "independence"] 17805 (*Murudeka 17805*) have fueled fears across Asia because they depict a rearmed, hypernationalist Japan as well as for their historical amnesia. That these films speak to political and historical issues, as well as to each other, should remind us that official histories are always and intimately linked with popular culture. In this sense, we should regard South Korean films as being not only in a dialogue with Japanese films but also as part of a broader international context of mainstream films emanating from East and Southeast Asia that are all attempting to rewrite their own histories of Japanese imperialism that were similarly "tampered with" or reinterpreted by the Japanese.[9]

These films fully illustrate what cultural critics have been warning for years, that "we need to take stock of the nostalgia for empire, as well as the anger and resentment it provokes in those who were ruled, and we must try to look carefully at the culture that nurtured the sentiment, rationale, and above all the imagination of empire."[10] We need to understand that films about empire have a specific history, one that originated in what historians have called the "age of empire." As filmmaking becomes increasingly dependent on globalized capital and the need to appeal to transnational audiences, we are witnessing a proliferation of "Pan-

Asian" coproductions that often recycle themes and images from their shared colonial history. This broader colonial history links the development of cinema in East and Southeast Asia, for Japanese imperialism either launched the film industry there or at the very least significantly transformed it.

Imperial Japanese Film Culture

Film played a crucial part in the promotion and expansion of the Japanese empire in Asia from the first motion picture screening in Japan in 1896 right through the end of the Pacific War in 1945. We do not usually associate Japan's film industry with either imperialism or the domination of world markets, and yet as early as 1905, Japanese cameramen were filming newsreels of the Russo-Japanese War in China for export around the world. Exotic thrillers like *The Village at Twilight* (*Yuhi no mura*, 1921) established Manchuria as a popular, accessible space to Japanese audiences a full decade before the Manchurian Incident. Filmmakers from Korea, China, Burma, and Taiwan traveled to Japan during the 1920s and 1930s to train in Japanese film studios. By 1937, Japan became one of the most prolific film industries in the world, out-producing even the United States.[11] By 1943, Greater Japan was massive—covering most of Asia from the Aleutian Islands to Australia, to Midway Island, to India. With each Japanese military victory, Japanese film culture expanded its sphere of influence deeper into Asia, ultimately replacing Hollywood as the main source of news, education, and entertainment for the millions living under Japanese rule. Imperial Japanese film culture was far more than just the production of films set in exotic imperial locations. It was a complex network of interrelated media that included magazines, journals, advertising, songs, posters, and films. At the same time, imperial film culture was also a way of looking at empire. It presented the attitudes, ideals, and myths of Japanese imperialism as an appealing alternative to Western colonialism and Asian provinciality. Japan envisioned that its attractive empire would unify the heterogeneous cultures of Asia together in support of a "Greater East Asian Film Sphere" in which colonizer and colonized alike participated.

This book is the first comprehensive study of imperial Japanese film culture in Asia from its unapologetically colonial roots in Taiwan and Korea, to its more subtly masked semicolonial markets in Manchuria and Shanghai, and to the occupied territories of Southeast Asia. In my research, I have made three assumptions. First, I break with conventional film scholarship by recognizing the fact that Japan *had* a cinema of empire and that its film culture should be analyzed in its entirety. It is crucial to understand that the Japanese film industry was integral to Japan's imperial enterprise from 1895 to 1945 and not simply a byproduct of mobilization for Japan's wars in Asia. This relationship illuminates how film functioned outside the context of war in such areas as colonial management,

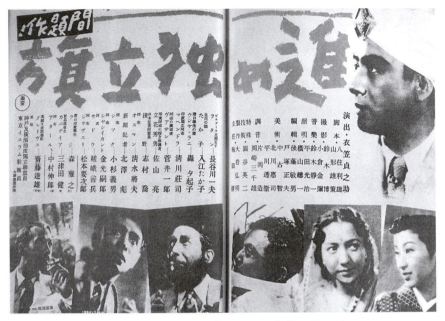

Japanese actor Hasegawa Kazuo as an Indian liberation
activist in *Forward Flag of Independence* (1943).

mass Japanese emigration in Asia, and the opening of semicolonial markets like
Manchuria. Shifting our perspective from war to empire also realigns our vision
of film culture at that time and how contemporary Asian audiences saw it—as
part of an imperial enterprise.

Second, I contend that both in concept and reality Asia was central to the
construction of Japan's collective national identity. I agree with cultural historian Iwabuchi Koichi that Japan's national identity has always been imagined in
an "asymmetrical totalizing triad" among Japan, Asia, and the West. Japanese
ideologues devoted enormous energy to the question of Japan's identity vis-à-vis
that of other Asian nations. Throughout the imperial era, Japanese filmmakers
produced films that placed Japan both in proximity and in contradistinction to
various parts of Asia, alternately emphasizing or deemphasizing Japan's Asian-
ness according to the situation. Whether its image was positive or negative, Asia
was the lynchpin for Greater Japan (and later, Greater East Asia) ideologically,
industrially, aesthetically, and strategically. Japanese ideologues often claimed
the colonial film markets of Taiwan and Korea as evidence of the modernizing
and civilizing effects of Japanese imperialism that legitimized Japanese rule and
simultaneously placed Japan on a par with other industrialized, film-producing
nations. The promise of working in semicolonial film markets such as Shanghai
and Manchuria became literal lifelines to Japanese film personnel unable to find

work in the Japanese homeland. The idea that Asia was an exotic Japanese space for adventure became a staple in the creation of an imperial Japanese worldview in which Japanese audiences situated themselves at the top of a hierarchy of East Asian co-prosperity.

Third, this book assumes that film cultures, like empires, are popular projects that cannot exist on terror alone but depend on and gain reciprocal participation on all levels and not simply from the top down. This book examines a broad range of participation in empire through the concept of imperial Japanese film culture, which I define as an integrated system of film-related processes including legislation, production, distribution, exhibition, criticism, and reception. This approach replicates how films actually circulate within any film culture. Imperial film culture was not dictated solely by what ideologues legislated or the personal vision of individual directors. The visions of empire that circulated throughout imperial Japanese film culture were by necessity *attractive*. As a multicultural, multilingual, multi-industrial enterprise, imperial Japanese film culture wove together a wide fabric of participants who brought with them any number of motivations—patriotism for some, opportunism for others, independence for still others, and so on. Images of Japan's attractive empire were meant to inspire voluntary participation in the imperial project through what contemporary political scientists have called "soft power."[12] As opposed to military or hard power, soft power is the process of rendering a state's culture and ideology attractive so that others will follow. This is not to deny the violence inherent in colonialism: imperial film culture was brutal, at times even deadly, to those involved with it. Participation in Japanese imperial film culture, however, was complex, and we must not limit our discussion to terms of either collaboration or resistance.

The notion of imperial film culture poses troubling questions that cannot be easily answered by national cinema paradigms that call attention to gaps and contradictions in existing film histories. For example, examining the origins of colonial filmmaking in Taiwan and Korea immediately raises questions of collaboration and resistance to Japanese rule: What constitutes "Korean" within the context of Japanese colonialism? Who financed, directed, distributed, and produced films and for what types of audiences? How does one discuss the concept of influence within a colonial or semicolonial context? Perhaps more importantly, which films remain unclaimed by Japanese and native film historians and why? If early films produced in Korea like *Arirang* (1926, dir. Na Ungyu) and *You and I* (*Kimi to boku*, 1941, dir. Hae Young) were both made during the "dark" era of colonialism by Korean directors and multiethnic crews, why is the former hailed as a classic example of "pure" Korean cinema, while the latter remains missing from filmographies of Korean film? Conversely, if film producers Zhang Shankun and Wang Qingshu both openly worked in Shanghai under the Japanese, why is the former regularly mentioned in contemporary Chinese film histories, while the latter is entirely ignored? The answers are far more cumbersome than simply evaluating the post-1945 legacy of either film or director; they go straight to the need to reexamine this period from the point of view of imperialism. Imperial Japanese film culture did not exist in isolation; it was very much part of an international fraternity of film imperialists.

Film and Imperialism

Two of the most significant events of the nineteenth century were the advent of industrial technologies and the rise of the "new" imperialism that would ultimately dominate and exploit most of the territories in Africa, Asia, and the Pacific. Some contemporary historians argue that the real triumph of imperialism was essentially one of technology rather than ideology.[13] That is, after all the rhetoric of empire has been forgotten, what will remain are technologies—medicine, transportation, communication. The development and employment of these industrial technologies must not be considered as separate but rather understood as having developed simultaneously within an imperial context.

French cultural critic Paul Virilio maintains that out of the countless technologies invented and developed in the nineteenth century, two in particular—visual and military technologies—are crucial to understanding the establishment of the power base of modern nation states.[14] The symbiotic relation between visual and military technologies is both material and ideological in nature. Taking into consideration the fact that an army cannot destroy what it cannot see, the need for military progress spurs the development of visual technologies and vice versa. Advances in film lens technologies were reintegrated into military technology to create better gun sights. The military depended on advances in visual technologies, which adapted faster film stocks, for example, to enhance aerial reconnaissance. Likewise, the film industry grew exponentially with each new technical advance—the timing mechanisms that made airplane-mounted machine guns a reality were incorporated into early film camera motors. The possession of these advanced technologies was, by itself, an ideological power that divided those nations able to wage modern warfare from those that could not. Moreover, the technology that enabled these twin enterprises of expansionism was also used to justify the use of national might, that is, they both supported a worldview as seen by the colonizer. Materially, film and military technologies enabled armies to fight wars against enemies of far greater number and in distant lands. Ideologically, the possession of film and military technologies demarked "advanced" nations from "underdeveloped" ones, and the power of the images created by these technologies in large part helped regimes consolidate and maintain power at home and abroad. The same technologies needed to wage wars also made the logistics of empire building a reality.

Media scholars remind us that the largest film-producing nations of the late nineteenth and early twentieth centuries also "happened" to be "among the leading imperialist countries in whose clear interest it was to laud the colonial enterprise."[15] Almost immediately after the Lumière brothers first projected films on screen in 1895, British, French, and German imperialists set to work applying the new technology of film to the ethnographic classification of indigenous peoples as part of the imperial reordering of the world.[16] In 1897, just two years after Japan gained its first colonies after the Sino-Japanese War, Constant Girel, a cameraman for Lumière, screened the first motion pictures in Osaka, Japan.[17] The twenty-three films represented the world as Western imperialists saw it—a virtual catalog of modern technology ranging from state-of-the-art trains to factories and bridges. These films unequivocally illustrated that it was the royalty, aristocracy, and military of the world's advanced nations that controlled these new technologies. The stark contrast between the onscreen images of wealthy abundance in places such as London, New York or Paris and the squalor of the underdeveloped countries staggered viewers. Japan's newly won status as a colonial power notwithstanding, the West generally categorized Japan as underdeveloped and did not consider it an empire of equal standing. Lumière films such as *The Ainu of Ezo* [Hokkaido] (*Les ainu a yeso*, 1897), *Japanese Fencing* (*Escrime au sabre japonais*, 1897), *Japanese Actors* (*Acteurs japonais*, 1898), and *Geisha Riding in Rickshaws* (*Geishas en jinrikisha*, 1898) focused on Japanese exotica—the performance arts, "primitive" martial arts, and the indigenous aboriginal population.[18]

Imperial Japan understood the ideological value of modern technology and quickly took steps towards controlling its own imperial image. In 1900, during the Boxer Rebellion, the Imperial Japanese Army dispatched the first Japanese newsreel cameramen to China along with the Fifth Regiment.[19] In 1904, the Imperial Japanese Army again dispatched newsreel cameramen to film the Russo-Japanese War, this time alongside their counterparts from the Lumière, Pathé, and Edison companies. Japanese newsreels of this time showed Japan's well-trained modern infantry and navy using the latest technology to fight and beat the Russian army—images that troubled many in the West. British propaganda scholar John MacKenzie describes British film audiences at that time who found themselves inundated by newsreels about "[t]he Boxer rising in China, the developing industrial and naval might of Japan, and the battles of the Russo-Japanese War . . . the latter conflict helped to spread the many false perceptions, both professional and popular, of the nature of the twentieth-century warfare, and fueled the naval race which was kept prominently in the public eye by repeated newsreels and of the launchings and dreadnaughts."[20] Among modern nations, the Japanese were the first to use searchlights during the battle of Port Arthur in 1905, prefiguring the target acquisition technology of modern warfare.[21] In the space of just under four decades since the opening of Japan to the West, Japan had gained sufficient technological and military power to militarily conquer a Western nation and become part of the imperial world order.

Images of a modern Asian nation defeating a Western empire promised hope to many throughout Asia of liberation from Western colonial rule. The Japanese model of empire was an attractive alternative to Western modes of imperialism, at least initially, due to the fact that Japan had itself only narrowly escaped Western colonization, and many believed its success could be replicated. This resulted is what some historians have called a "trawling" of Japanese culture by other Asian nations eager to discover elements that they might import and adapt to modernize their own societies. This realization is similar to what Einstein called an "information explosion" and helps explain in part why Japanese Pan-Asianist slogans such as "Asia for the Asians" initially did not fall on deaf ears.[22]

Because Japanese expansion was often opportunistic, improvised, or in response to a crisis rather than motivated by grand ideologies or powerful cultural forces, Greater Japan came to mean a project of civilization and assimilation of diverse Asian cultures. Japanese films legitimized Japanese imperial expansionism sometimes even before the fact; newsreels such as *The Korean Crown Prince at Oiso Beach* (*Oiso kaigan no kankoku kotaishi*, 1908) or travelogues like *A Trip around Korea* (*Kankoku isshu*, 1908) naturalized the presence of Korean royalty traveling to Japan or future Japanese Resident-General Ito Hirobumi's tour of Korea a full two years before Japanese annexation of Korea.[23] Likewise, Japanese-sponsored films presented Japan's empire in its own image, as an Asian success story. Films depicting Japanese-built, state-of-the-art bridges in Taiwan, factories in Korea, and trains in Manchuria were an important part of the construction of an attractive modernist vision of empire, where indigenous populations were presented as living in co-prosperity, ethnic harmony, and material abundance. Japanese imperialism was the logical extension of the Meiji era ideology of "blending Japanese spirit with Western technology" (*wakon yosai*) and these films were its fulfillment.[24]

Filmmakers may have presented Japanese imperial rule as a modernizing force, but they also showed the antiquated and sometimes contradictory elements of the imperial project. Empire always involved ethnic, cultural, and linguistic diversity. Diversity was one way that Japanese ideologues justified their conquest of non-Japanese populations as a civilizing mission. Japan's status as a modern empire was based precisely on its difference from subjugated or "backward" Asian cultures.[25] By the 1940s and the rise of Japanese Pan-Asian rhetoric, the real paradoxes of Japan as the only Asian nation to hold colonies, while simultaneously presenting itself as a liberator of Asia from Western colonial oppression, blemished nearly every aspect of Japan's imperial ideology. Therefore, it was entirely consistent to hear politicians, critics, and filmmakers state that they were opposed to imperialism, but a friend to the Japanese empire. Despite these contradictions and paradoxes, interaction within the rubric of empire inevitably made various kinds of cultural exchange possible.

This book aims to explore more fully how imperial film culture represented the idea of an attractive Japanese empire to Asian subjects as well as to Japanese audiences both at home and abroad. It is this idealized notion of Japan's empire in Asia rather than any preexisting "reality" that is implied in the title of this book. Similarly, it was precisely the notion of Asia—rather than its physical reality—that was important for most Japanese of this period.

The Historiography of Japan's Cinema of Empire

There is no complete history of Japan's cinema of empire. Sources before 1945, such as Ichikawa Sai's *The Creation and Construction of Asian Film* (1941), Hazumi Tsuneo's *Fifty Year History of Japanese Film* (1942), Tsumura Hideo's *Film War* (1944), or Shibata Yoshio's *World Film War* (1944), all portrayed Japan as a massive transnational film network with a dominating presence throughout most of the film markets in Asia—but the specific term empire was only rarely used.[26] Much like popular writers of fiction in Britain after World War I, Japanese film critics and historians appear to have been "covert in their fables of imperialism."[27] For Japanese filmmakers, too, avoided the term imperialism, reserving it for use against their (usually Western) enemies. Japanese film journalism, unique prior to 1945, is perhaps unique in its obsession with chronicling the history of individual territories. Film journals such as *Motion Picture Times* (*Kinema junpo*) and *Film Criticism* (*Eiga hyoron*) often ran stories on the histories of film production in individual territories such as China, Korea, Taiwan, and the Philippines. The writing of history then, as now, was a powerful way to naturalize the hierarchy of authority. Just because Japan's empire did not always call itself an empire does not mean it did not exist. More often than not, what functioned as the idea of empire was an uncritically accepted notion of Asia as simply being Japan's "place in the modern world system."[28]

References to Korea, Taiwan, and Karafuto (Sakhalin) as colonial markets (*shokuminchi*) gradually disappear by the 1930s. The nature of colonial discourse was changing at this time in Japan, just as it was throughout the world. After the Japanese military's massive sweep throughout Asia and the Pacific and then following December 7, 1941, discussions of Japan's film activities in Greater East Asia gradually slip into the discourse of war with the United States.

Film histories written after 1945 have largely ignored or obscured the history of empire. In 1955, film critic Iijima Tadashi's two-volume *Japanese Film History* offered only the following two sentences on Japan's film activities in Asia: "Along with the Japanese army's advance into Manchuria, China, and Southeast Asia, film construction in the outposts of empire, which had been implemented from

before, became more active and local film production companies were established in each territory. Japanese production personnel from the home islands
were sent to each of those areas for that purpose."[29] The following year, leading
film historian Tanaka Junichiro devoted one intriguing chapter in his five-volume
Developmental History of Japanese Film to film production in Japan's "overseas
territories."[30] While Tanaka's knowledge is encyclopedic, and he offers an institutional history of most of Japan's film territories, he does not consider them to
be linked to each other in any significant way. Neither Iijima nor Tanaka can be
accused of ignorance of this system, for both lived in Shanghai and Mainland
China at various times during the 1940s and were active participants in imperial
film culture. Apparently what these critics failed to appreciate was the depth and
breadth of imperial film culture from the 1910s throughout the 1940s, a culture
that included film-related books, music, radio programs, magazines, museum
exhibits, exchange programs, talent contests, and traveling projection units. The
commitment by powerful official and private interests to Japan's imperial film
culture legitimized its existence.

There is a growing body of film scholarship on Japan's film activities in individual territories such as Manchuria and Korea, but most stop short of linking
these territories into the Japanese imperial project or the world film order of the
time.[31] Part of the problem lies in the fact that the Japanese film industry, for all
its output, never developed to the point of being able to absorb films produced
in its newly acquired markets or to supply those markets with enough films to
sustain demand. But comparisons with Hollywood always unfairly characterize
Japan's cinema of empire in terms of failure both industrially and ideologically.
Another reason that the cinema of empire has not been studied has to do with
the discourse of war itself. After defeat and decolonization in 1945, that Japanese
audiences defined the preceding decades of violent struggle solely in terms of
war and not empire suggests a desire for closure for many to decades of imperial expansion. By subsuming the discourse of empire into that of war, Japanese
defeat in the Pacific War marked an end for any need to reexamine the causes
and tensions that led to all of the wars fought until that time on behalf of the
Japanese empire.[32]

Surprisingly, however, popular images of Japan's imperial project did not disappear from Japanese screens after defeat and decolonization in 1945. Despite official U.S. Occupation directives prohibiting the production of films set in Japan's
former empire, exotic melodramas like *Bengawan River* (*Bungawan Soro*, 1951,
dir. Ichikawa Kon) and *Woman of Shanghai* (*Shanhai no onna*,1952, dir. Inagaki
Hiroshi) were huge hits with Japanese audiences. Directors such as Inagaki Hiroshi and Ichikawa Kon, who began their careers in the imperial era, made several
films after 1945 that were critical of the war but benignly sympathetic to the imperial impulses that motivated it. Yamamoto Satsuo is representative of another

group of directors who lamented being coerced into collaborating with Japan's *wartime* regime, but almost never questioned their own participation in empire. In post-1945 narratives, the war was coercion, but empire was a separate matter.

Attractive Empire

This book is broken into four chapters that examine Japanese imperial film culture's collective significance and cumulative impact on the creation of a transnational empire in Asia as an ideological construct.[33]

Chapter one charts the development of film institutions within the formal colonies of Taiwan and Korea and its extension to the semicolonial film market of Manchuria. I detail how legislation, production, exhibition, and reception conditions differed in each territory and document salient shifts in official and popular perceptions by Japanese film journalists and filmmakers. How the nature and vocabulary of colonialism changed is illustrated in the attitudes of people like Manchurian Film Studios chief Amakasu Masahiko, who said: "We must never forget that our focus is the Manchurians, and after we make headway nothing should stop us from producing films for Japan."[34] Amakasu was a strong advocate of independence from the Japanese film industry, which challenged his authority, and he maintained that the Manchurian film market was a separate but equal member of the empire.

Chapter two surveys three areas of imperial film culture—*manga*, popular music, and film journals—in order to analyze how film interacted with a variety of media. Each of these media attracted audiences that were not necessarily dedicated film audiences and crossover appeal was not simply the result of government consolidation but grew out of a complex interplay of official and unofficial interests. The result was the development of a mass audience linked together through filmic discourses over a variety of media all supporting the representation and consumption of Asia.

Chapter three analyzes Japanese assumptions about Chinese, Korean, and Southeast Asian difference through elements of mise-en-scène, specifically, acting styles, gestures, makeup, and dialogue in specific feature films. My analysis centers on Japanese representations of culture, ethnicity, and language, and the ways in which they masked Asian difference in order to construct a seamless and attractive image of an idealized Pan-Asian subject. I focus on how the Japanese filmmakers producing these films attempted to represent what properly assimilated Asian subjects looked, acted, and spoke like. We need to remember that for most of the nineteenth and even well into the early twentieth century, assimilation was an idea not always considered taboo and frequently encouraged. Assimilation was the goal for vast numbers of colonial elites educated in the colonial system.[35] In this chapter, I discuss non-Japanese reception of Japanese performances of Asian identity in order to examine schisms between Japanese and non-Japanese imperial subjects.

Chapter four analyzes Japan's struggle to create and define its empire as a unique entity vis-à-vis the West. In the first half of the chapter I examine how Japan clashed with Hollywood for market domination and the "hearts and minds" of Asians. The rise of Japan's imperial power in Asia threatened American film dominance there and led to a film war. Japan restricted access to Asian markets, censored or banned American films, and finally conducted a comprehensive embargo on all Hollywood films. This prohibition led to secret meetings among Japanese film industry representatives, Hollywood representatives, and the U.S. Department of Commerce in which the United States threatened to stain Japan's national reputation by making Japanese villains in American films. The second half of the chapter interrogates Japan's paradoxical status as a member nation of the Axis at a time when it was preaching anti-Westernism throughout Asia. Although Japan presented itself to the world as a liberator in Asia, ironically, Japan could emphasize little in common with its Axis allies other than the fact that they all shared the status of colony-holding empires. This chapter discusses a broad range of the film interactions among the cinemas of imperial Japan, Nazi Germany, and Fascist Italy on the legislative, distribution, and exhibition levels.

Finally, chapter five highlights connections between pre- and postimperial Japanese film culture with regard to a longing for empire. I examine two films produced after 1945 and set in the final days of empire that replicate verbatim the structure of the imperial era "goodwill" films. Not only does the desire for empire that remains in postwar Japanese society warrant our attention, but also the representation of hierarchies of power link back to Japan's imperial past and suggest areas for further study.

CHAPTER ONE

From Film Colony to Film Sphere

Imperial Japanese film culture was complex—its influence extended to practically every area of the empire. In the case of Taiwan, I consider the ways in which the colonial government used film education programs to assimilate indigenous Taiwanese populations while at the same time combating the undermining influence of Chinese films. For Korea, I investigate the role of colonial film censorship in the struggle to maintain social order and also analyze popular Japanese perceptions of the Korean film industry in the domestic Japanese market. In the case of Manchuria, I argue that the local film industry actively sought out ways, industrial and aesthetic, to distance itself from the Japanese film industry rather than to merge with it. Finally, I consider how in the film *Vow in the Desert* (*Nessa no chikai*, 1940) ideology shifted away from organized institutional concepts of Japanese empire to the decidedly more indeterminate idea of the Greater East Asian Film Sphere. My approach assumes that imperial film culture consisted of a broad range of participants and was not dictated solely by either the whims of Japanese ideologues or the personal visions of individual directors.

Taiwan

In 1901 Japanese film exhibitor Takamatsu Yujiro traveled to Taipei and established a small film company to promote Japanese culture among the island's indigenous population. Importing Japanese talent from Japan, Takamatsu also created theater, dance, *rakugo* comedy, and *Naniwa bushi* (a narrative genre accompanied by a stringed instrument) troupes that precipitated a boom in local interest in Japanese entertainment. In 1905 Takamatsu raised over 10,000 yen in donations for the Japanese military through his screenings of short films about the Russo-Japanese War. Colonial authorities, together with the Taiwan chapter of the Japanese women's group the Women's Patriotic Association (*aikoku fujinkai*), used newsreels of the Russo-Japanese War to persuade the unbelieving indigenous population that

Japan was actually defeating a Western imperial power. Increasing local interest in film stimulated exhibition and sparked construction of film theaters from
1905 until around 1917. During that time each of the major Japanese film studios
established flagship theaters in Taiwan, and by the end of World War I there were
sixteen permanent theaters in Taipei alone. Until the 1920s, however, many Japanese distributors considered the island colony to be little more than a peripheral
market for Japanese films.[1]

In the early 1910s, Taiwan Colonial Government officials and independent
distributors and exhibitors like Takamatsu believed that film should be used to
improve the lives of the indigenous population by educating them about modern
life in Japan. To that end, both the colonial government and distributors and
exhibitors collaborated on the production of educational films from 1904 to 1905.
These films dovetailed with the Japanese assimilation policies first instituted in
1896 by Vice Minister of Foreign Affairs (and later Japanese Prime Minister) Hara
Kei. Taiwan Colonial Governor Goto Shimpei would later successfully implement these policies for the purpose of "imperializing" (kominka) the Taiwanese.
Initially based on French models, Goto's administration transformed assimilation
policies into "extension of Japan" (naichi encho-shugi) policies intended to link
Taiwan as closely as possible to Japan. From 1921 colonial authorities believed
that one way to "raise the cultural level" of the Taiwanese was to produce short
instructional films.[2]

Nearly every major Japanese film studio established branch offices in Taipei
because they expected to expand their share of the Taiwan market. However,
feature film production never managed to develop to any significant degree here.
Only a handful of Japanese feature films, such as The Eye of Buddha (Buddha no
hitomi, production data unknown), Whose Mistake? (Dare no kashitsu (production data unknown), and Song of Sadness were shot on location in Taiwan; and
this was mainly for "color," utilizing the local landscape as little more than an
exotic backdrop.[3]

Taiwan never became a hub of colonial film production in the way that Manchuria did, perhaps due to its comparatively claustrophobic scenery—Taiwan's
narrow island vistas failed to capture the Japanese imagination the way China's
vast plains and romantic frontiers had. A Japanese film critic in 1942 wrote that
the problem with Taiwan was that it was geographically and culturally too close
to the Japanese homeland to be interesting.[4]

Takamatsu noted that Japanese perceptions of Taiwan ran to opposite extremes.
For the average Japanese, Taiwan elicited lurid images of malaria-infested swamps
teeming with murderous natives. Early films manipulated these fears by churning
out exploitative titles such as Current State of Conquering Taiwan's Native Rebels
(Taiwan dohi seibatsu no jikyo, 1910) and Heroes of the Taiwan Extermination
Squad (Taiwan tobatsutai no yushi, 1910).[5] On the other hand, Taiwan was also

Kawata Kimiko as a Taiwanese "aborigine" in *Song of Sadness* (1919).

viewed as a model colony. Takamatsu and others wanted to educate Japanese audiences of this latter image, but even the decades of successful colonial modernization policies that improved Taiwan's infrastructure, economy, and education
could not easily dispel the general perception in Japan that Taiwan was a savage
island wilderness fraught with danger. As late as 1942, actor Sawamura Kunitaro
described the dread he felt of going to Taiwan to star in the Japanese feature film
Clan of the Sea (*Umi no gozoku*):

> Shooting on location during a time of crisis caused considerable worry. Every
> one of our stereotypes about Taiwan—the aborigines, poisonous snakes, ma-
> laria, etc.—all came rushing before our eyes as if in a big close-up. We made

sure to fill our suitcases with medicine. We filmed mostly in the mountains of Garanbi on the southern part of the island—the sort of a place that made you think that *something bad is going to happen.*[6]

Japanese like Sawamura felt conspicuously distanced from Taiwan and inferred that for many in Japan Taiwan felt more like a foreign country than a Japanese colony. The article points out, however, that Sawamura and the rest of the crew eventually realized that Taiwan was not as dangerous as they had believed it to be. For example, Sawamura was astonished at the fact that the local people were nowhere near the "ignorant savages" he imagined. He praised the Taiwanese cast and crew members for being able to take direction, perform competently, and, above all, speak Japanese. Sawamura wanted magazine readers in Japan to know: "This is one example of just how mistaken our cultural knowledge of Taiwan really was. I'm embarrassed to admit it but you would need to talk to the local police there if you really want to learn how Japanified the Taiwanese have become."[7] Film magazine articles like this hinted that it was the Japanese who needed to foster a greater understanding of the Taiwanese, but this was quite rare in the 1940s. Film journalism in the form of magazines, newspapers, and criticism usually took the opposite approach, that the Taiwanese needed to assimilate, and it was the colonial government's job to make sure they did as quickly and effectively as possible.[8]

The Taiwan Colonial Government believed that of all the modern technologies, film was the most effective medium for transforming indigenous Taiwanese into properly educated imperial Japanese subjects. The authorities were fascinated by the prospect of mechanically reproducing a single film ad infinitum and projecting it to vast audiences in multiple locations simultaneously. Film, unlike theater, dance, or literature, did not require an advanced education or linguistic skills to be understood, making it an ideal medium for disseminating ideological messages to a mass populace. Taiwan colonial administrators took their cues on how best to implement film programs from Japan's Ministry of Education. Using Japanese models, the Taiwan Colonial Government subsidized film screenings in schools and at regional facilities in order to educate, edify, and socialize the Taiwanese.[9]

Colonial authorities actively encouraged educational committees throughout the island to integrate film into their educational systems and offered government subsidies to those organizations that held officially sponsored film lectures. Typically, screenings consisted of two types: public lectures and classroom screenings. School administrators worked in collaboration with government officials to conduct classroom screenings for students in large lecture halls in public schools. Government officials considered these screenings one way to protect children from "the harmful influences of vulgar films and the film theater environment."[10]

These screenings resembled the "balanced program" format, which generally started with the screening of an educational film (*kyoiku eiga*), followed by a how-to film (*jitsuyo eiga*), and subsequently a feature film (*geki eiga*). Film distributors in Taiwan imported a variety of Japanese educational films that included such films as *Cherry Blossoms* (*Sakura*), *Nara, Talking about Volcanoes* (*Kazan no hanashi*), *Kamakura and Enoshima, Tokyo*, and *Our National Anthem* (*Kokka*), all of which taught local audiences what Japanese life and culture actually looked like.[11] Classroom screenings also focused on specific school subjects such as spelling, ethics, and geography. As one colonial administrator stated, educational films helped make "curricula that were difficult to explain verbally easier to understand through film images."[12]

Various social organizations organized lecture screenings, often employing traveling projection units, a system that was also widely used throughout rural Japan as well as the Chinese interior. Before a screening, short lectures instructed viewers on how to properly interpret the film. After the screening, the government lecturers conducted short discussions in order to gauge audience reaction and ascertain whether the film had been understood properly. Colonial administrators placed a high value on lecture screenings and classroom screenings, for they believed these were the most effective ways to reach audiences like children, farmers, and peasants, who normally would not or could not attend screenings in regular film theaters.

Films about daily colonial life, such as *Japanese Police Supervise a Taiwanese Village* (*Nihon keikan no hansha shisatsu*, 1935), were constructed very much in the vein of early Lumière films. These films normalized colonial power structures by presenting figures of authority, like teachers and colonial police, as civilizing forces who educated the masses and held real power.[13] In both content and form these films linked the Japanese empire to its Euro-American counterparts, but Japanese films were not just imitations of those produced in the West. Japanese films about the Japanese empire clearly presented Japan as a "civilizing" presence, but they lacked much of the blatant racism found in Western colonial ideology. Edification and socialization were two key themes in the proper imperialization of Japanese subjects, who, when they had become imperialized, would gladly fight and die for Japan's empire.

Taiwan Colonial Government officials felt that assimilation programs were especially necessary in Taiwan where Chinese influence had begun earlier and was far more prevalent than Japan's. Colonial administrators hoped that institutionalizing policies of imperialization—or Japanization (*nihonka*) as the evolving concept would later be named—would deter Taiwanese interest in Chinese culture and bring the local population into closer proximity with Japan. The idea that Taiwanese needed to be assimilated into Japanese culture gained wide credence in Japan, and by the late 1930s Japanese film industry leaders also began to take more serious notice of Taiwan as a prospective market. The thought of Chinese culture possibly overwhelming Japanese culture troubled both government and industry officials and had the effect of galvanizing them in opposition to the Chinese "threat."

Japanese film distributor Ichikawa Sai speculated that the Taiwanese preference for Chinese culture was a "natural result" of colonization by both Fujian and Guangdong provinces in China.[14] Ichikawa's interpretation of the historical presence of China in Taiwan is instructive because it imagined Chinese immigration to Taiwan in the language of the current vernacular of colonialism. Ichikawa was only one of many in Japan who deemphasized the Chinese influence in Taiwan by claiming that the Chinese had exercised remarkably little official interest in or control over Taiwan until the late 1880s when France and Japan began to vie for the island. Ichikawa claimed that many Chinese immigrants came to Taiwan to escape crop failures on the mainland rather than as part of any formal plan to colonize the islands. Ichikawa dehistoricizes China's loose colonization of Taiwan by characterizing the Chinese model of empire as antiquated and obsolete and validates Japanese colonialism as a modern enterprise that will, along with European models, inevitably replace the old world order.

Japanese colonial administrators in Taiwan specifically singled out Chinese film as a barometer signaling the extent to which Taiwanese preferred Chinese culture. These officials considered Chinese film a significant obstacle to the smooth Japanese imperialization of Taiwan and were shocked to think that local audiences might actually prefer Chinese films to Japanese ones. The threat of a film war in Taiwan is another reason why colonial officials supported official film programs. Film in colonial Taiwan was more than just an effective medium to instruct and socialize, it was also a cultural weapon manipulated by the colonizers to defend the indigenous population against the transnational flow of Chinese culture and thought.[15]

At the time the Chinese were beginning to produce films in 1905, the Japanese had already tightened their grip over film distribution on Taiwan, making it impossible for Chinese film studios to vertically integrate their operations as smoothly as they had in Hong Kong or Singapore. However, Taiwan became a lucrative exhibition market for Chinese films after 1924, and local Taiwanese audiences preferred Chinese-produced films to Japanese ones almost from the beginning. Colonial administrators and local Japanese exhibitors found the prospect of Japanese films being shut out of their own market a continued source of vexation. By the end of the 1920s, colonial officials who had at first worried only very generally about the effects of Chinese culture on the Taiwanese now had to deal with the potentially catastrophic impact of a burgeoning Chinese film culture. Film often portrays language, fashions, lifestyles, music, and assumptions about authority. Partially due to the popularity of Chinese films, it became a fashionable trend in Taiwan from the late 1920s to wear Chinese-style clothes. The problem, as the Japanese saw it, was deeper than either fashion or film. The Japanese feared that unless it was countered, the onslaught of Chinese culture would undermine the entire base of Japanese colonialism that Goto and other colonial administrators had established. In a roundtable discussion on the topic, Japanese film promoter Fuchigami Sansei commented on Taiwanese dress and acting Chinese: "These people are not Chinese, they are Japanese. Obviously we didn't force them to Japanize their dress, speech, or all matters of good taste in their everyday lives—we bestowed all of these things to them as a privilege."[16]

After the 1931 Manchurian Incident, and especially the 1932 Shanghai Incident, Chinese films, especially those produced in Shanghai, became more overtly anti-Japanese in tone. Taiwan distributors imported some of these films and screened them together with other mainstream Chinese feature films. Taiwan colonial officials immediately took three steps to halt the flow of these ideologically "dangerous" films. First, they drastically reduced the number of Chinese films that could be imported. Second, officials implemented a mandatory "reeducation" program for everyone who imported films. Last, the colonial government exercised its official and informal clout to quash any advertising for the Chinese films that still managed to enter the market. Officials made the already oppressive film censorship procedures even more arduous by raising censorship fees and complicating bureaucratic red tape. The colonial government also drastically consolidated the entire film industry in Taiwan, taking steps to keep anyone they had not approved from working in the film industry in any capacity.

Even with such formidable barriers and increased stringency, the colonial government was unable to shut Chinese film out of the Taiwan market entirely, where it retained an audience despite its being officially branded as "enemy cinema" by the Japanese in the 1930s. This does not necessarily indicate that Taiwanese audiences preferred Chinese films over Japanese ones for any qualitative reasons. It is quite possible that many Taiwanese simply could understand films in Chinese better than those in Japanese. Japanese officials in Taiwan sometimes screened Japanese-language films without Chinese subtitles to encourage the study of Japanese. The idea was that audiences frustrated with the inability to understand the plot would naturally seek out Japanese language instruction. It was not until the last two years of the Pacific War, when either pressure applied by the Japanese colonial authorities or poor business management shut down most of Taiwan's local theaters, that colonial administrators were finally freed of the Chinese film threat.[17]

That the Japanese would spend untold hours fretting about the corrosive influence of Chinese films is intriguing when we consider that the number of Hollywood films shown in Taiwan actually outnumbered Chinese films. After the entry of the American film studios into the Taiwan film market in the 1920s, an

Table 1: Source of Films Screened in Taiwan

Year	Japan %	America %	China %
1925–1928	70	25	4
1929	80	14	4
1930	78	10	10
1931	83	10	5
1932	78	10	10
1933	75	15	8
1934	70	19	9
1935	63	18	6
Total %	over 60	under 30	under 10

Source: Ya-wen Hung, "Taiwan sotokufu ni yoru eiga seisaku," *Eiga gaku*, no. 12 (1998): 135.

American film invasion seemed far more imminent than a Chinese one[18] (see Table 1).

Ironically, since the end of colonialism and especially since the 1980s it has been Taiwan's film industry that has offered some of the more positive representations of Japan's imperial legacy. Hou Hsiao Hsien, one of Taiwan's leading directors, frequently cites his admiration of Japanese filmmaking in general and the works of director Ozu Yasujiro in particular. In 1994 New Taiwan Cinema director Wu Nien-Jen produced *A Borrowed Life* (*Duo-sang*, 1994), a powerful, semiautobiographical depiction of the lingering influence that the Japanese empire had on the daily lives of an entire generation of Taiwanese. Directors like Hou and Wu are speaking directly to the experience of colonialism and indicate that the long-term effects of imperial Japanese film culture were wide-ranging, although they varied by region and over time.

Korea (Chosen)

The Korean colonial film market differed from that in Taiwan because Korea had an indigenous film distribution system before Japanese annexation in 1910. Due to this precolonial history Korean film historians claim that Japan hijacked the normal developmental trajectory of Korean film. Nationalist Korean film historians also maintain that throughout the colonial era Korean film personnel actively resisted attempts by the Korean Colonial Government to create a pro-Japanese film culture. Film historians also disagree as to who the first person was who introduced motion pictures to Korea, but sources clearly show that as early as 1903 Japanese film promotion companies like Yoshizawa Shoten actively competed with Western film studios in Korea.[19]

Japanese interest in Korea peaked during the Russo-Japanese War when tens of thousands of Japanese fought in and around the peninsula. Newsreel exhibition in Korea was commonplace by the time of the 1905 Portsmouth Treaty, which announced Russia's defeat. Five years later, when Japan formally colonized Korea, film audiences across the empire clamored for films about Korea. Increased interest in Korea inspired the major Japanese film studios to begin constructing theaters there, which further strengthened the vertical integration of these companies. The major Japanese film studios took a far more active role in Korea than they had in Taiwan, quickly establishing branch offices in Seoul to handle film exhibition, distribution, and later production. Nikkatsu was the first to establish its branch office in 1918, followed by Shochiku in 1920, and Teikine in 1921.[20]

Japanese film companies faced formidable competition from foreign, mostly American, films. The Korean Colonial Government was slow to enact official film legislation, and film imports remained unregulated until 1916, when the first censorship laws were created. The authorities enacted nationwide censorship laws in part to curb unsupervised film censorship by local and regional colonial police agencies. Officials implemented the new laws to help contain a growing tide of illegal film imports. Colonial officials eventually realized, however, that consolidation of the film industry, which had been an effective means of control in the Japanese home islands, was a far more effective way of gaining and maintaining control over film production. They hoped that by strictly limiting the importation, distribution, and exhibition of films to those who were licensed by the Korean Colonial Government to distribute and exhibit films that the number of "undesirable" films entering the colony would decline. As in the case of Taiwan, however, it became apparent that even the most stringent legislative measures were no guarantee against film serving as a source of conflict and contestation.[21]

One site of conflict occurred in a Seoul film theater just two years after Japanese annexation in 1912. The program consisted of several short films, including travelogues and military parades, but the main feature was a match between a Western boxer and a Japanese judo wrestler. The 600-seat theater was divided into two sections—the Japanese sat on cushions on matted floors in the balcony, while the Koreans sat in chairs on the first floor. Many in the audience had come to listen to the performance of the Korean *pyon'sa*, or film narrator, who was often as popular or even more so than the film itself.[22] *Pyon'sa* performances were more than narration. The most effective performances added an emotion and excitement to onscreen events that produced a fervor hard for modern audiences to imagine. The *pyon'sa*'s passionate oration was a key factor in polarizing the audience into two factions: Koreans, who supported the Western boxer, and

Japanese, who supported the judo wrestler. The Korean half of the audience cheered when the judo wrestler was knocked down by a punch, but the Japanese went wild when the judo wrestler recovered, threw the boxer down, and won the match. This turnaround of events sparked a violent exchange. From the balcony, Japanese hurled seat cushions and food at the Koreans, and the Koreans threw chairs back at the Japanese. The struggle spilled out into the main lobby where both sides beat each other with wooden sandals, walking sticks, and broken furniture until the colonial police were called to put an end to the violence.[23]

This instance embodies the volatility of colonial film exhibition and suggests that colonial authorities, undoubtedly aware of the ideological implications of the film's outcome, completely misread the Korean audience and its capacity to be willingly "edified" by such displays of Japanese strength. Authorities and audiences found that harmless entertainment was never harmless, especially in a colonial space. The power of audacious propaganda could be dissipated by the conditions of reception, and benign topics might transform into potent symbols of anticolonial, national, or regional identity. Colonial censorship could limit the number and type of films that entered the country, but even films that had passed these safeguards carried the potential to provide violence and even insurrection, depending on the cultural and political context in which they were shown. A similar instance occurred in the early 1930s during a screening of the American silent film *Ben-Hur*. In a scene where Ben-Hur, a galley slave on a Roman ship, confronts a Roman soldier (and oppressor), the film's intertitle reads: "This moment for you Romans means one hundred years of trial for us Jews!" Both Koreans and Japanese in the audience recognized the obvious parallels between the conditions of the Jews and those of the Koreans under Japanese colonial rule, and the film set off a near riot. The local colonial police put down the disturbance, and *Ben-Hur* went back to the censor's office to be drastically recut.[24] Seen from the viewpoint of the colonial government, instances like these seemed to justify measures giving the government near total control to regulate every part of the film process, from preproduction through to reception.

Few in the Korean Colonial Government, however, believed that prevention was enough. Colonial ideologues demonstrated an almost absolute belief in the power of film to indoctrinate subjects and spent great time and effort promoting the production and promulgation of films that would properly educate and assimilate Koreans as imperial Japanese subjects. One such attempt was the establishment of the Korean Colonial Cinema Unit (KCCU) (*Chosen sotokufu kinema*), an agency that produced and distributed short films on Korean and Japanese customs. In short, the KCCU existed to protect and manage colonial Korea's image both domestically and abroad. It described the comprehensive nature of its mission in a promotional booklet:

The Korean Colonial Government established this motion picture unit in order to introduce conditions in Korea to a mass audience in Japan as well as conditions in Japan to Korean audiences. By capturing Korea on film, this unit is part of an effort to spread a correct understanding of the region to Japan while at the same time making the mother country familiar to Koreans by introducing them to Japanese scenery.[25]

Films produced by the KCCU were screened across the colony. Traveling projection units, like those used in the lecture screenings in Taiwan, served difficult-to-reach places and rural areas without electricity. In 1934 the Korean Colonial Government passed a law mandating the screening of KCCU-produced films at every film program across the colony. Until the China Incident in 1937, the KCCU's average output was a modest two films per month. After that time, however, increased audience demand for films about events in China brought a spike in production. These films were obviously ideological in nature and were produced in order to "guide Korea to properly prepare itself as part of the [Japanese] homeland."[26]

The presence of Japanese colonial authority in the film industry could also be felt in other, less tangible ways. As filmmaking is dependant on capital, many of the fifty production companies operating in Korea in 1922 found themselves funded either wholly or in part by Japanese investors.[27] In addition to funding, the Japanese provided a transfer of technology, for the Japanese film studios were superior to those in Korea. Japanese film studios became a mecca for many Koreans (and Chinese) hoping to learn their trade and gain experience working with the newest technology. Yun Baek-nam, who would later become the director of the first full-length Korean feature film, *Oath Under the Moon* (*Mingjun gukdan*, 1923), traveled to Japan to study at Waseda University while working as an apprentice in the Japanese film industry. Yi Pil-u, the cinematographer for *Oath Under the Moon*, had also worked as an intern at the Tenkatsu Kosaka Studios in Osaka.[28] By all accounts, most Koreans were not welcomed into the Japanese film industry but endured great hardship and prejudice. Some even concealed their Korean background out of fear of deportation. One Korean who successfully "passed" as Japanese in Japan, under the name of Hinatsu Eitaro, eventually became a well-known screenwriter and director.

The desire to practice their craft not only drew Korean film personnel to Japan, but many Japanese also found work in the colonies. As material conditions in Japan worsened in the 1940s, some Japanese stayed to work in the fledgling Korean film industry or moved on to Manchuria, which boasted the most modern film facilities in all of Asia. Conditions in Korea were often better than those in the Japanese homeland, and the wealth of experience that these Japanese craftsmen brought with them definitely left an impact on filmmaking in Korea.

Scholars generally agree that the first type of Korean-produced film was a kino-drama *Loyal Revenge* (*Uirijok gutu*), in 1919. This film was inspired in part by a Japanese kino-drama (*Rensa geki*) performed in Seoul the preceding year.[29] Kino-dramas were immediately successful in Korea, inspiring a production boom in the genre that became a catalyst for the production of the first feature-length Korean film, *Oath Under the Moon*. Korea's relatively autonomous, production-based film industry made it unique among Japan's other colonial film markets. By the mid 1920s Korean directors had produced a string of domestic hits that included *Arirang* (1926), *An Ambitious Boy* (*Pungun-a*, 1926), and *Goldfish* (*Gumbung-o*, 1927). Contemporary film critics in Korea and Japan hailed these films as classics in their day. The first two were even exported to Japan where they had a limited release. Generally, however, Korean feature films never penetrated the Japanese domestic film market in large numbers, in part because of their content.[30] Throughout the 1920s Korean filmmakers managed to produce films with themes that promoted their distinct ethnic identity as Koreans and not just as assimilated Japanese despite the intense scrutiny of the Korean Colonial Government.[31]

No prints of *Arirang* or *Pungun-a* exist, but the scripts have survived, and together with firsthand accounts recorded by spectators who saw these films during their initial release, everything suggests that the anti-Japanese themes in the film are subtle but unmistakable. How were these films funded? Why were they produced? Why were they exported to Japan? Given the draconian nature of film production in Korea the success of *Arirang* raises more questions than answers. One contemporary Japanese film critic argues that *Arirang*'s director/writer Na Un-gyu initially had to submit the script under the name of a Japanese coworker, Tsumori Hidekazu, to get permission to start production. The same historian surmises that colonial officials probably believed that this was a Japanese production and not a Korean one, given the fact that the production company (Chosen Kinema) was run by Japanese and the film's cinematographer was Japanese. Such coproductions were common in Korea and elsewhere in the Japanese film empire. But even if this is true, it explains only how such a film could be produced, not how it was exported to Japan, where censorship laws were far more rigorous than in Korea. Curiously, although *Arirang* is listed in the Japanese censorship records, which offer detailed entries on the length and content of every feature and short film submitted for censorship between 1926 and 1944 (whether banned or not), there is no mention of any material being cut from it.[32] This is remarkable for a film touted as being an obvious and remarkable example of Korean resistance.[33] *Arirang* opened in Japan in 1926 to positive critical acclaim in the Japanese film press. Japanese film distributor Ichikawa Sai's comments are indicative of the overall reception of this film in Japan:

Arirang touches the true emotions, thoughts, and lives that are characteristic of the Korean people. Skillfully depicting the atmosphere and institutions of the period, it expresses for the first time on film many long-held emotions. The film satisfies because it shows us the simple Korean people and their landscape. *Arirang* has raised the standard set by earlier Korean films both in content and technology, and anyone who goes to see this out of curiosity or simply wanting a spectacle will be unexpectedly surprised.[34]

Uncharacteristically for Ichikawa, while praising *Arirang* as a benchmark of Korean film, he provided no synopsis or summary of the film's plot. This does not seem to be an oversight on his part and suggests that any anti-Japanese content in the film may have been removed or far less obvious than scholars now claim.[35] The Japanese reception of *Arirang*, however, appears to be an exception. Reviewers did not devote the same amount of attention to any other Korean films exported to Japan. In fact, the Japanese film press in general did not display great interest in Korean films and often harshly criticized their production values. Educational films produced by the Korean Colonial Government did not fare much better. When Japanese critics did cover short films and newsreels about, say, a member of the Japanese imperial family visiting Korea, industrial/agricultural developments, or Korean folk art, it was only as topical news and quickly forgotten.[36]

The Korean peninsula was only marginally more appealing to Japanese audiences than Taiwan. With a few notable exceptions, Japanese feature films shot in Korea rarely enjoyed long runs in Japan. Again, despite the supposedly shared interests that Japanese Pan-Asianists claimed linked the races of East Asia, when it came to films Asia was distinctly not "one." Japanese film journals offer every indication that the "characteristically Korean emotions" (*Chosen no koyuteki na kanjo*) critics like Ichikawa praised were precisely the sort of thing that did not interest Japanese audiences. In light of rising Pan-Asianism in the 1940s, a growing perception in Japan of Japanese disinterest in Korea was presented as an ideological problem in the Japanese film trades. A 1941 advertisement in *Film Criticism* (*Eiga hyoron*) asks its readers: "Are you apathetic about films from the peninsula? Since the first were produced twenty years ago, they have continued their brave struggle amidst poor conditions. Now is the time [that we Japanese] should watch these films in the spirit of understanding and cooperation."[37] With no mention of what it is selling, this advertisement assumes that Japanese audiences were once interested in Korean films but are now somehow bored with them, a claim that neither *Film Criticism* nor other contemporary Japanese film journals ever truly proved. With few notable exceptions, Korean film was more interesting to intellectuals as an ideological topic—the promise of what an overseas Japanese film market could mean in the face of the threat of Hollywood—rather than a source of intrinsic interest.

Even when veteran Japanese comedy-film director Saito Torajiro traveled to Korea to scout for possible locations, the Japanese film press gave the story only minimal attention. Saito lamented the dearth of Japanese films set in Korea in a 1941 article for the film magazine *Film* (*Eiga*). He wrote that compared to the relatively large number of films set in Manchuria, Korea was almost never represented in mainstream Japanese feature films. Part of the blame, he suggested, lay with the media, which had pushed Korea into the "shadowy recesses of print journalism" after the China Incident (as they would again later after Pearl Harbor). Saito strongly urged politicians, scholars, businessmen, men of letters, and film people each do their part to "rekindle interest in Korea."[38] Saito claimed that he had chosen Korea as the setting of his newest film comedy, *A Wonderful Gold-mine* (*Subarashiki kinko*), about the lives of Korean farmers. Since the script was written entirely in Japan, Saito explained, he wanted to go to Korea to personally experience how authentic Korean farmers actually lived. However, once there, the experience of observing their struggle against the harsh elements firsthand seemed to have had a destabilizing effect on him, for it caused him to write:

> I initially came here with the goal of shooting a comedy . . . but after stand-ing on the wide open red earth, everything I saw and heard caused me to wax melancholy, lyrical, and sentimental. Of course one can find comedy in lyricism and sentimentality, but the sights that I saw pierced right through me, dulling their comic impact.[39]

Saito experienced the same "murky" feeling toward Korea that he claimed kept other directors from choosing it as a setting for their films. In addition, Saito's impressions of the material conditions for filmmaking in Korea were undoubtedly influenced by the fact that his visit coincided with some of the harshest consoli-dations to ever affect the Korean film industry. Saito would eventually make his film, but his tone laments the loss of relative autonomy while foreseeing a plum-met in film output. Soon after the Korean Colonial Government commandeered raw film stock as a necessary resource for the war effort, and the next step was the consolidation of the entire film industry in Korea into ten film companies.[40]

Japanese author Niwa Fumio had a slightly different view of Korea. He dis-missed the idea that Korea had been completely forgotten in Japan and pointed out that other directors were making feature films about life in Korea all along. The real danger, he added, was not the lack of representations of Korea in Japan but rather the misguided exoticization of the colony. Niwa criticized films like *Friends* (*Tomodachi*, 1937) because he thought they did not express any true Ko-rean emotions but only projected Japanese sentiments unmodified onto Korean actors. Niwa offered *School Fees* (*Suopryo*, 1940) and *Homeless Angels* (*Jipopnun*

chonsa, 1941) as examples of recent Korean films screened in Japan that com-
municated a far more "authentic" sense of Korea. His only criticism was that
Homeless Angels used Japanese actors, which he thought was unnecessary. Niwa
advocated that "peninsula films" be made only by Korean, not Japanese, directors.
If the Japanese were to be involved at all, he thought they should be restricted
to minor supporting roles. And even then they should be used only when their
presence was absolutely necessary to make the plot "easier for audiences in Japan
to comprehend." Ultimately, Niwa saw that Japan's total control over nearly every
aspect of the Korean cinema was artistically and commercially harmful.[41]

Korean author Jeong Hyakuchu, whose novel was adapted into the first Korean
talking motion picture *Tale of Chunhyang* (*Chunhyang jeon*, 1935), wrote in the
Japanese film journal *Film Friend* (*Eiga no tomo*) about his misgivings over the exoticism he so often found in Korean films produced under the Japanese: "Frankly,
I had never seen a Korean film until now that didn't leave me with a sick feeling
of embarrassment—a feeling similar to that of having some dark family secret
discovered by a stranger. For me, all Korean films seemed to contain this fatal
flaw whether they were produced for audiences in Japan or not."[42] Jeong claimed
that *School Fees* enjoyed greater success than other Korean films due to its purity, which Jeong thought lent it authenticity and moved him to tears. Ironically,
Jeong was unable to define purity other than by comparing its effect to a Japanese
film entitled *Children in the Storm* (*Kaze no naka no kodomo*,1937). Jeong's high
praise for the film's moving portrayal of "Korean emotions" was countered by his
criticism of the acting in the film *School Fees*, which he called "primitive" and
"inferior" to the level displayed in Japanese films. "First and foremost, [the film]
reeked of amateurism. Maruyama Kaoru said that he thought the film had a
documentary-like feel to it, but I think that was due to their using rank amateurs.
However, when one considers the absolute dearth of child actors in the Korean
cinema, one probably could not expect much more talent than that."[43]

Jeong was a member of a minority of Japanese-educated elite Koreans. His
ability to understand the Japanese and communicate in their language was one
reason why his article on Korean perspectives on Korean film was even published
alongside Japanese perspectives on Korean film. As part of the colonial elite,
Jeong took up the position of a properly assimilated imperial Japanese subject
by sharing the sentiments of Japanese critics. Jeong critiqued Korean tradition
from a carefully calculated distance, choosing to never associate himself with
any Korean traditions. At the same time, however, he claimed that his ethnic
authenticity gave him an innate ability to recognize the Korean purity of spirit.
His dualism—both adhering to and deviating from "Japaneseness"—is itself a
reflection of the state of Korean film under the Japanese. Jeong's voice is divided,
claiming native authenticity at the same time he speaks out in the language of
and on behalf of the colonizers: "Films have graduated from relying on *exoticism*

or adding *local color*, but stopping at mere sweetness suggests that they have not completely shed their first stage."[44]

Japan maintained only two colonial film markets—Taiwan and Korea.[45] With the creation of Manchukuo, the Japanese-supported puppet regime established in northeastern China, the Japanese exhibited an entirely different set of assumptions about the legitimacy of colonialism. By the late 1920s and early 1930s, worldwide changes regarding "commonsense colonialism" drastically affected how imperial Japanese film culture represented itself to the world. Manchuria was a test case in a new semicolonial style of imperial film market, quite different from the formal colonial film markets of Taiwan and Korea.

Manchuria (Manchukuo)

In 1921, when Japanese director and cinematographer "Henry" Kotani took a film crew to Manchuria to shoot the exotic thriller *The Village at Twilight*, feature films set on mainland China were still rare. The plot concerns a young Japanese man who is captured by bandits (*bazoku*) in Manchuria and saved from execution only when the bandit leader's daughter sacrifices herself to free him.[46] If the plot sounds like it came from Hollywood, it probably did. Kotani had just returned to Japan after working seven years in Hollywood, first with Thomas Ince and later with Cecil B. DeMille at Paramount. After returning to Japan in 1920, he entered Shochiku studios, where his bosses expected that his experience abroad would "modernize" production. In this sense Kotani's choice to set his action-melodrama in an exotic locale may not be unusual; this was, after all, the same year that similarly exotic fare as *The Sheik* (United States), *Queen of Atlantis* (*L'Atlantide*, France), *The Indian Tomb* (*Das Indische grabmal*, Germany), and many others were released to wide acclaim.[47] The heightened interest of imperialist film-producing nations in "exotic" subjugated cultures becomes significant when we consider that a full decade before the 1931 Manchurian Incident, the Japanese regarded Manchuria as something more than just another battlefield. Kotani brought Manchuria into reach for mainstream Japanese audiences in much the same way that John Ford popularized the American West in the United States, Jacques Feyder visualized the French Maghreb in France, and Alexander Korda mythologized India in Great Britain. Kotani knew that Manchuria's wide, romantic plains struck a chord deep in the Japanese collective imagination, making it a potent symbol of an imperial frontier that "belonged" to Japanese audiences. Japanese imperial subjects could project their imperialist fantasies onto Manchuria, just as their Western counterparts had done with their colonies.

Manchuria's onscreen no-man's-land-like landscape reflected its ambiguous national status. Unlike Japan's formal colonies in Taiwan, Korea, or Karafuto, the appearance of Manchukuo as being wholly independent of Japan was as illusory as a movie set. Manchukuo was liminal; officially it lay outside Japan's boundaries since it was a separate country, ruled by puppet emperor Pu-yi, but remained within Japan's sphere of control. In August 1937, Japanese government officials decided that the national image of Manchukuo was too important to leave to the indigenous population, and so they established a semiofficial corporation called the Manchurian Motion Picture Corporation (commonly known as Manei).[48]

As the official film studio of Manchukuo, all film production and distribution in north and northeastern China effectively fell under Manei's control. An official brochure for the company printed in English proclaimed that its mission was to "control the exportation, importation and distribution of motion picture films and to carry on enterprises relating to the production of educational, cultural and entertainment films, with a view to contributing to the exaltation of the national spirit and to the promotion of national education."[49] Advertisements for Manei Studios told readers to "[l]earn about Manchukuo, the world's paradise, through the Manchuria Motion Picture Production and Distribution Co. (Manei) films."[50] Manei Studios became synonymous with state-of-the-art filmmaking in Asia. The company recruited film personnel from Japan to establish the most extensive film facilities in Asia—a rival to Hollywood in the heart of Manchukuo. Ironically, although the independence of Manchukuo the nation-state may have been a façade, Manei's independence from the Japanese film industry was very much a reality. Manei broke away from the sort of colonial management mentality that bogged down film production and exhibition in Taiwan and Korea, and the studio actively challenged the film industries of China, Europe, and even Japan.

Without doubt the reason that Manei was able to assert its independence from Japan was due to the strength and charisma of its managing director, Amakasu Masahiko. From the beginning Amakasu was adamant that Manei should not be subordinated to the Japanese film industry, and in a 1942 article entitled "Making Films for the Manchurians," he displayed an openly hostile attitude toward any Japanese interference in Manchukuo:

> There is not even the slightest reason why Manei should have to report on any of its activities to the Japanese film industry. Nor should it have been necessary for Manei to build a film school or similar facilities. If the Japanese film industry had bothered to build these in the first place, we never would have had to. But because Japan did not build these facilities, we were left with no alternative.[51]

Such straightforward criticism of Japan's film industry was rare in any part of the empire at that time. The fact that Amakasu had no experience in the film industry played to his advantage in that he had no allegiances to any film faction in Japan. Amakasu was a ferocious character who became infamous in Japan for

滿人のために映画を作る

株式會社滿洲映畫協會理事長

甘粕 正彦氏（談）

Amakasu Masahiko on "Making Films for the Manchurians" (1942).

orchestrating the 1923 murders of leading Japanese anarchists Osugi Sakai, his common-law wife Ito Noe, and six-year old nephew. From 1921 to 1923, Amakasu was a lieutenant in charge of a detachment of military police in Tokyo. Fearing that Osugi and other anarchists would seize upon the confusion following the Great Kanto Earthquake of 1923 to create civil unrest and overthrow the government, Amakasu and three other military police officers abducted Osugi, Ito, and their nephew on September 19, 1923. Amakasu took them to Military Police Headquarters where they were interrogated, tortured, and finally killed. When it was discovered that Amakasu's men had disposed of the bodies in an old well behind police headquarters, newspapers plastered the lurid details of what was now called the "Amakasu Incident" across the headlines.

The Amakasu Incident was one of several such "incidents" in which the military police either detained or murdered socialist activists and collectively would spark a public outcry. Public opinion forced the military to court martial Amakasu, but there were many voices within the military who thought that Amakasu had done his job well. After serving only three years of a ten-year prison sentence, Amakasu was released from prison, entered the Reserve Officer's Training, and spent three years studying in France, where all of his expenses were paid for by the Imperial Japanese Army. He returned to Japan briefly in 1930 before going to Manchukuo with the support of strong right-wing militarist ties. There, Amakasu was responsible for, among other things, protecting Emperor Pu-yi, and he played a role in the Manchurian Incident.[52]

In 1937 Amakasu replaced former Nikkatsu Tamagawa Studio Chief Negishi Kanichi as the head of Manei. [53] During his tenure as head of Manei, Amakasu was critical of what he perceived as Japanese arrogance toward Manchukuo and often warned visiting Japanese film personnel that "[j]ust because you were top-class in Japan does not automatically mean that you will be top-class in Manchuria. Lose your attitude and get to work making films that fit our conditions here in Manchuria."[54] Even Japanese journalists hesitated to publicly criticize Amakasu's sometimes ferocious attacks on the Japanese film industry; they often used indirect language to express their fear: "He was a little rude, but I really learned to like him. Maybe he can get a little personal."[55]

Amakasu ruled Manei with an iron hand but was unusually broadminded in his hiring of a staff from a variety of ideological and political backgrounds. Ironically, many left-wing filmmakers purged from the Japanese film industry after the anti-Communist crackdowns in the early 1930s not only found a home at Manei but by all accounts appeared to have a free hand in their work.[56] Manei created an unlikely space where former Communists produced films side-by-side with right-wing ultranationalists.[57] Thus, the film world of Manchukuo was a chimera that, like other motion picture production centers in Shanghai, Hollywood, New Babelsberg, Cinecittà, was more a "state of mind" than merely a geographic point on a map; it exceeded national boundaries. Manei was a dream factory that at its peak boasted a film culture rivaling its competition in Japan and Hollywood, although on a significantly smaller in scale. Manei had a well-established star system and a growing pool of international and domestic talent, published studio film magazines, and sold ancillary products. By partially subsidizing Manei, the Manchukuo government created one of the largest, state-of-the-art film facilities in Asia, and that included Japan.[58] Manei's true success came from its breadth of experienced film personnel, although it took Amakasu, an industry outsider, to create and run a studio that wisely avoided merely copying either Hollywood or Japan.

Amakasu's pursuit of self-sufficiency alienated him from the Japanese film world, but it may have aided him in production. After 1938 the Japanese government commandeered all film stock, claiming it was a necessary war resource. Cellulose nitrate, a primary element in raw film stock, was also used to make gunpowder. The colonial governments in Taiwan and Korea also seized control of their film industries by controlling access to film stock. Most of the raw film stock used in Japan before the war had been supplied by Eastman Kodak. After the attack on Pearl Harbor and the start of the Pacific War, Japan searched for a new supply. Japanese film processing companies like Fuji never produced enough film to supply the domestic demand for raw film stock and eventually Japan imported it from AGFA in Germany. Amakasu said that technicians at Manei had found a substitute source for creating film stock, and that this had enabled Manei to break the cycle of dependency on Japan: "Thankfully Manchuria is blessed with a bountiful soy crop and from this we happened to find a way to create film stock. Together with our successful experiments in producing gelatin, we are well on our way to being able to supply enough product for all of our needs by ourselves."[59] Whether or not Amakasu and company were actually able to create film stock from a soybean base is a matter of debate, but it was a powerful image—in Manchuria they grew their own film!

Manei's representation of self-sufficiency, relatively stable food supplies, and high salaries, tapped into the Taisho era fantasies of a romantic Manchuria that was a haven for film personnel seeking to escape widespread industry downsizing and massive food rationing in Japan. For many in the Japanese film industry, imperial film territories in general and Manchuria in particular offered hope of living and working in their chosen profession. Manei the dream factory popularized the image of Manchuria as the breadbasket of the Japanese empire, and its fables of plenty enabled it to siphon off the best filmmaking talent from Shanghai and Japan.[60] Manei's structure was based on Germany's Universum-Film AG (UFA), but its business practices perhaps more closely resembled Hollywood with its aggressive raiding of leading film industries for their best talent. Consequently, Manei became a melting pot of employees, and no evidence suggests that personnel previously considered "subversive" in Japan faced any stigma at Manei. Manei's film policy was aggressive, and the target was clear:

> All Manei must do is to make films that the Manchurians will enjoy. There is absolutely no need to make films that exoticize Manchukuo for Japan. Japan will probably make films that get it wrong anyhow, vulgarizing the unusual aspects of Manchuria. We must not forget that our focus is the Manchurians and, after we make headway, nothing should keep us from producing films for Japan.[61]

Amakasu increased the number of indigenous film crew members. He raised their salaries to levels more competitive with their Japanese counterparts, and by 1945 a significant number of films were being written, directed, and acted in by local Chinese.[62] Like studio heads in Germany, Italy, and the United States at that time, Amakasu realized the critical importance of entertainment per se and demonstrated a sharp understanding of the industry when he stated that "it is not impossible to insert propaganda into entertainment."[63] Japanese theaters rarely screened Manei films, and those that made it to the screen faced stern criticism.

Japanese critics routinely complained that Manei films had weak plots, poor acting, and low production values. Many believed that Manchurian-produced films
would never become a part of Japanese film exhibition. *Film Criticism* film critic
Mitsukichi Kaya wrote a particularly harsh review after watching a Manei film
in a "suffocatingly dirty and dusty" theater "filled with the distinctive stench of
Manchurians": "It was one of those Manei films where the director, cameraman,
etc. are supervised by Japanese, but the actors are Manchurians. The acting was
poor and the film insipid. But what was even more mystifying was how [the
Manchurians] roared out loud in belly-laughs at all of the most absurd parts of
the film. Of course, I never felt the slightest inclination to laugh."[64] Professing
to be at a complete loss as to what local audiences found so funny, Mitsukichi
noted, however, that the loud and "absurd" laughter was real and admitted that
it was clear the films were not made for Japanese audiences. Mitsukichi's tone
implies that the "low level" of these films reflects a larger deficiency within the
indigenous population and makes him pause to consider "whether or not such
films are really necessary for Manchurians."[65]

Mitsukichi epitomizes the type of Japanese film critic that Amakasu despised,
and it was directly at such critics that Amakasu hurled his strongest remarks. Making films for Manchurians was exactly what Amakasu had in mind, and in consciously catering to the domestic audience in Manchukuo, he had no compunc-
tion about snubbing the Japanese film industry in Japan. Manei was definitely
not an average Japanese film studio, and Amakasu was not a typical studio head.
The gap between films produced for audiences in the Japanese home islands
and those for Manchurian audiences showed up in the final product.[66] After 1937
Japanese film critics began to talk about Japanese overseas film enterprises differ-
ently. The rhetoric shifted from a semicolonial discourse into a Pan-Asianist vision that Japanese film ideologues called the "Greater East Asian Film Sphere."

The Greater East Asian Film Sphere

Japanese film critics, filmmakers, and film personnel first coined the term Greater
East Asian Film Sphere around 1941. The concept was an ideological offspring of
the Greater East Asian Co-Prosperity Sphere, officially proclaimed by Japanese
Foreign Minister Matsuoka Yosuke and Prime Minister Konoe Fumimaro in
August 1940. The Greater East Asian Co-Prosperity Sphere was part of a Japanese
Pan-Asianist movement that called on all Asians to break the shackles of Western imperialism. A concise definition of the Greater East Asian Film Sphere is
difficult to find—even its creators struggled with how to define it.[67] Essentially,
it called for a quarantine of the Asian film market against "corrosive Western
influences" through the establishment of a New (Order in East) Asia. Once this
separate sphere was created, the theory posited, Asian nations could collectively

produce Greater East Asian Films that best represented a pure and innate "Oriental Spirit."[68] Some Japanese film critics, filmmakers, and industry personnel specifically suggested that the Greater East Asian Film Sphere actually stood for the Japanese advance into Southeast Asia. Others defined the Greater East Asian Film Sphere as a literal declaration of war against the presence of Euro-American films in any Asian markets. Two broad generalizations can be made: the sphere was an imperial space to be managed by the Japanese by virtue of their technological and spiritual superiority, and conditions in the Japanese film industry had to be drastically overhauled to meet the challenge.[69]

Although the name Greater East Asian Film Sphere seems to imply an acknowledgment, or even the involvement, of the nations of East Asia, this was not the case, as the leading Japanese film critic of the day, Iijima Tadashi, wrote in 1943: "The East Asian Film Sphere consists of elements that are at once foreign and domestic and must not be considered independent. Japanese film should be distributed widely throughout the Greater East Asian Film Sphere, but only on the primary condition that it is 'Japanese' film."[70] Some Japanese critics and filmmakers, however, did not believe that Japanese film could fill the tremendous demand for films throughout Asia's markets. Among the serious problems facing Japanese filmmakers were the need to increase domestic film production, to link up with local filmmakers and encourage local film production throughout the Japanese empire, and to make films that represented East Asian "reality." Nonetheless, Iijima was one of the very few Japanese film critics or filmmakers who tried to define the concept, and he had the following to say about Japan's role in the Greater East Asian Film Sphere.

> Japanese film must project Japanese reality [and] Japanese reality cannot simply be understood domestically. It goes without saying that the Japanese reality is the Greater East Asian Co-Prosperity Sphere's reality. Communicating that reality through film is a domestic issue: one that specifically involves film production.[71]

Iijima wanted Japanese film to reflect Japanese reality, but he did not problematize the origin of the medium. Other critics, like Tsumura Hideo, clearly associated film technology, along with military, communication, and transportation technologies, with Western science. Tsumura suggested that Western technology and its techniques could still be useful if they were first infused with Japanese spirit.[72]

This new "reality" found its fullest expression in the construction film (*kensetsu eiga*) genre. *Vow in the Desert* (1940) and *The Green Earth* (*Midori no daichi*, 1942) are two examples that epitomize the spirit of the Greater East Asian Film Sphere in terms of their representation of the themes of modernization, construction, and patriotism. Both films are set in China and share a similar obsession with the technological modernization of China as a central part of the "civilizing" nature of Japanese empire-building. These films are instructive as neither was considered a classic (then or now), but each represents a typical release from the major Japanese film studios. *Vow in the Desert* is perhaps best known as the final installment of a trilogy of "goodwill films" (*shinzen eiga*) popularized by Yamaguchi Yoshiko (Ri Koran) and Hasegawa Kazuo. In the opening scene Japanese engineer Sugiyama Ichiro has been commissioned by the Colonial Construction Ministry to construct a road between Xian and Beijing. He and his Chinese coworker Yang stand atop the Great Wall of China debating the merits of tradition versus modernization.

> Sugiyama: "Whenever I think of the planning that went into this Great Wall, it makes me realize how extraordinary the power of man is!"
> Yang: "Hmm . . . perhaps. All in all, this is just a useless colossus."
> Sugiyama: "No it's not . . . It's the rugged power of man. Think of how much effort was poured into it brick by brick."
> Yang: "But you can't drive a truck over it."
> Sugiyama: "A truck? . . . (laughs) No, I guess you couldn't at that. Yang old man, why don't we build a Great Wall that you *could* drive a truck on? A modern Great Wall that could stand up to this one. . . .We'll build a new Great Wall at the foot of that mountain!"

The scene begins with a long pan revealing a caravan of camels crossing the exotic deserts of Xian that gradually disappears mirage-like in a slow dissolve to the Japanese engineers atop the Great Wall of China. Stylistically, the Japanese engineers on the Great Wall represent a regime shift in which modern Japan, the technological leader of Asia, has replaced the historical glory of China. The old technologies that built the Great Wall must give way to the new technologies (trucks, bridges, canals) that will characterize the new order in Asia. *Vow in the Desert* implies that Japan is capitalizing on potential that China has squandered. However, this scene is not simply critical of China; it melds Sugiyama's sense of awe for China's several-thousand-year history with his unshakable belief in the veracity and inevitability of the Japanese-led Asian Co-Prosperity Sphere. Sugiyama recognizes the disjuncture between his imagined China of the past and its contemporary reality, but he is able to perceive value in China's past. This recognition is what qualifies him to rescue China's history from the oblivion it would presumably suffer at the hands of the less appreciative Chinese like Yang. Sugiyama is the first to suggest building a new wall, because only his mastery of modern engineering can close the gap between historical China and the potential future of a united Greater East Asia. Throughout the film Sugiyama is a bridge both literally and figuratively. As a bearer of modern (that is, Western) technology, he demonstrates that he has the vision necessary to adapt new technology to modernize China (even to the extent of improving on the Great Wall). But Sugiyama is also able to understand and appreciate China's past in a way that Western colonists presumably never could precisely because he is an "East Asian."[73] Yang, on the other hand, appears unimpressed; he is not resistant to Japanese rule (in fact quite the opposite, he is an assimilated colonial elite presented as aspiring to Japanization). He is simply unable to see the same Chinese scene in the way Sugiyama does. Yang's inability to see anything but China's faults and the uselessness of its past are expressed in his sardonic attitude.

For the Japanese in this film the grandeur of historical China stands at odds with the problems of modern China. Many Chinese at the time felt similarly, such as the noted author Lu Xun. Lu was convinced after watching the beheading of a Chinese by a Japanese soldier in a newsreel that the "people of a weak and backward country, however strong and healthy they may be, can only serve to be made examples of . . . " He decided to quit studying medicine in Tokyo and become an author because "the most important thing was to change [the Chinese] spirit."[74] Throughout the 1930s and 1940s Japanese films often represented China's underdevelopment as a result of the backwardness of its people. Stereotypical representations of the Chinese took various forms, including uncleanliness and childish or superstitious behavior. Onscreen, Japanese characters talk about armed resistance by Communist "bandits" as an extreme form of misunderstanding. However, off-screen, Chinese armed resistance against Japanese imperialism was a reality that required all Japanese film crews to travel under the protection of the imperial Japanese army. In *Vow in the Desert*, Sugiyama and the other Japanese architects of the New East Asia also require a military escort as they survey the Chinese countryside. These Japanese are determined to fight Chinese "ignorance" with education, making their civilizing mission not unlike the "White Man's Burden" in Western colonial films. For example, Sugiyama tries to convince Mr. Li, an elderly Chinese man, to vacate his land for the construction of the new road:

> Sugiyama: "I would like to ask you for part of your land for the construction of a road. . . . Everyone working for the construction of a new East Asia is prepared to die for it. It is because of this great faith that we risk our lives to build this road for the benefit of the Chinese, for the benefit of a New East Asia! Think how the average people here suffer for the lack of proper roads! When it rains the paths turn to muddy swamps that neither carts nor mules can cross. Because of that transportation grinds to halt and no one can move their crops. All the crops everyone worked so hard to prepare must be sent back. The suffering of these farmers is great. Likewise, life for those in the ghettos worsens and their children waste away.

Think how convenient it would be if only you had finished roads? Road
construction brings light into a world of darkness."
Li: (in Chinese) "Light in a world of darkness?"
Sugiyama: "Did you understand? Thank you!"

The road represents both a literal and a metaphorical link between what is presented to us as a familiar split—technology versus backwardness, knowledge versus ignorance, and ultimately Japanese modernity versus Chinese traditionalism.
Sugiyama attempts to point out to Li the benefits of modernization as a necessary
part of a healthy agricultural economy presumably because Li himself cannot
recognize the issue. By making possible the flow of goods and communication
among the villagers, the road also becomes a symbol for social solidarity.

The theme of road construction is also used as a metaphor for Chinese solidarity in the Chinese leftist film, *The Big Road* (*Dalu*, 1933, dir. Sun Yu). We know
that many in the Japanese film industry saw Chinese leftist films while in Shanghai, and it is possible that Japanese filmmakers were on some level responding to
Chinese criticism of Japanese imperialism. Japanese filmmakers were well aware
of the tremendous popularity of Chinese leftist films in China and definitely
perceived them as a film threat.[75] In *The Big Road*, Chinese workers (essentially
indentured slaves) are building a road for the Chinese Nationalist Army to stop
the invading Japanese. When a wealthy Chinese landowner tries to slow construction to give the Japanese a military advantage, the workers revolt, but they
are soon imprisoned in the dungeon of the landowner's estate and ultimately
killed in a Japanese bombing raid.

By contrast, in the Japanese film *Vow in the Desert* mutual understanding between Sugiyama and Li is achieved through a type of nonverbal communication
strikingly similar to the Japanese concept of *ishin denshin* (literally, heart to heart).
This "heart to heart" communication between two people is immediate and tran-
scends words.[76] This makes sense, however, when we consider that in addition to
being a construction film, *Vow in the Desert* was also a continental "goodwill"
film with a standard melodramatic intercultural/interracial romantic subplot.[77]

Another Japanese film, *The Green Earth*, tells of a Japanese construction company in Qingdao that is planning to build a canal through the countryside. As
in *Vow in the Desert*, for the new project to proceed smoothly, it is necessary that
part of the old countryside be destroyed. In this case, construction of the canal
requires that an entire Chinese village as well as its graveyard must be cleared.
Here again, the film presents Chinese "ignorance" of progress, but this time it is
not shown as a gap between the Japanese and Chinese but rather as one between
two generations within a single Chinese family. Mr. Yang is a Japan-educated,
Japanese-speaking Chinese member of the board of directors of the Japanese

"China is revealed for the first time on film by the
Japanese." Caption on poster for *The Road to
Peace in the Orient* (1938).

engineering company sent to build the canal. Throughout the film he functions
as a mediator between Japanese management and their Chinese workers. He
is represented as the fundamental opposite of his son, Ko Min (played by Japanese heartthrob Ikebe Ryo), whom he describes variously as lazy, overeducated,
and a sort of artist. When Ko Min learns of the proposed canal and the necessary destruction of the graveyard, he accuses his father of collaborating with the
Japanese.

> Ko Min: "I never thought you would let yourself be seduced by the Japa-
> nese into approving the canal construction without at least knowing that
> [they're going to destroy a village]! Are you just going to let the Chinese
> people be sacrificed?"
> Father: "Is that the kind of man you think I am? I joined up with Japanese
> capital and technology *precisely because* I want China to prosper."

Ko Min: "You only say that now because business is good. But China's at
   war, its culture is weak and in turmoil."
Father: "If we cooperate with Japan, business will come back."

The message is clear. China's future prosperity lies with Japanese technology
and capital. When seen from a Japanese point of view, this may have seemed like
a logical, even attractive argument. Japan had only narrowly avoided Western
colonization and had risen to "first class" nation status precisely by linking up
with foreign capital and technology only decades before. Mr. Yang's enlightened,
almost visionary status is shown to result directly from his embracing Japanese
technology and ability to assimilate Japanese ways. He seems vaguely aware that
he is perceived as a Japanese collaborator, but his "vision" stems in part from his
ability to look beyond the stigma that other Chinese, including his own son, have
attached to his assimilation of and collaboration with the Japanese.

   Mr. Yang functions as a racist stereotype insofar as his character does not seem
to be motivated either by patriotism or conviction of purpose so much as a desire
to do "good business." In this film and others like it, there is a palpable assumption
that what motivates Chinese basically is personal economic profit. Yet rather than
condemn Yang's attitude as simply greedy, the film celebrates it. Yang's brand of
greed is good as long as it serves the needs of Greater East Asia. Further, linking
capital and technology between Japan and its imperial territories is presented as
an attractive business proposal, but one that also happens to extend the empire.

   Throughout the film the Japanese essentially challenge the Chinese to "do
more for China" than the Japanese have done. And throughout the 1930s, theoriz-
ing how best to modernize China was a topic of hot debate among Japanese propa-
gandists. Chinese intellectuals also debated the relative merits of modernization.
Films like *The Green Earth* make it clear that the topic of modernizing China
was not only a Japanese debate but a Chinese one as well. What is interesting in
the film is how the Japanese are, in effect, invoking a form of Chinese nationalism without presenting it as Japanese propaganda. By redefining collaboration as
Chinese patriotism, it follows that those who love China will naturally want to
help anyone who helps China. Conversely, by this logic, those who oppose Japan
helping China, or dare to resist, are pronounced "ignorant" and immediately la-
beled as an impediment to modern progress. Izawa Kozo, the Japanese secretary
to the executive of the board of directors of the construction company, berates a
coalition of local Chinese whose opposition essentially threatens construction of
the canal. He claims they are not doing enough for China.

   I know you're worried about rising prices and the scarcity of goods. But
   who do you think is responsible for that? I tell you it's those who oppose
   the construction of the canal. Who do you think has been trying to keep
   prices down? We have, the Canal Construction Committee! What the

devil can you say that *you've* done for China? Nothing! Except unproductive opposition![78]

Japanese film censorship regulations prevented filmmakers from showing what really happened to those who did not accept the benefits of Japanese technology. But Japanese construction film heroes assumed that if the Chinese thought they were being outperformed by the Japanese, shame should motivate them to do more. None of the primary sources available suggest that construction films were widely screened in Chinese theaters in China. However, Japanese filmmakers demonstrated a clear awareness of a need to explain Japan's motivations for imperial expansionism to an audience beyond that in the Japanese home islands.

Filmmakers realized that their audiences did not live in a vacuum, and they struggled to keep film relevant at a time when popular media across the empire were increasingly seen as luxuries. Competition with other consumer products and information services for the hearts and minds of imperial subjects was intense. Especially in the domestic Japanese market, producers and screenwriters turned to the aggressive marketing of films, stars, and ancillary products through strategic media tie-ups in the hopes of both targeting existing audiences and creating new ones that had traditionally fallen outside the realm of film exhibition. Companies recycled familiar themes and images of Asia and Asians from a variety of popular media that had demonstrated mass appeal with Japanese audiences since the late nineteenth and early twentieth centuries.

To engage broader audiences, film became integrated into a media network that included children's comics, popular music, and film magazines to disseminate an imperial worldview and at the same time link what had been disparate audiences together into a Greater East Asian audience. This very process of attracting and constructing audiences through film and film-related media was itself expansionist in nature, and the worldview it articulated made familiar assumptions of racial hierarchies that instructed a variety of Japanese audiences in the Japanese home islands how to interact with other Asian imperial subjects.

CHAPTER TWO

Media Empire

Creating Audiences

Throughout the 1930s cultural producers in Japan gradually became aware that their sphere of influence was expanding beyond the borders of the Japanese home islands. Japanese animated films were screened in Taiwan, Chinese-themed melodies like "China Tango" played in dance halls in Shanghai, and Japanese film magazines were sold in Manchuria. The Japanese were no longer the only ones in the audience. Bringing together the vastly different ethnicities and cultures of Asia into a single Greater East Asian audience required the cooperation of hitherto untapped audiences. Film and media companies now had to determine how to create and represent an attractive image of a Japan-led Asian empire to the domestic Japanese audience. I examine three media—comic books, popular music, and film magazines—to see how film culture engaged parallel forms of media to create imperial subjects.

The idea of a Greater East Asian audience is similar to the notion of "imagined communities" where "each communicant is well aware that the ceremony he performs is being replicated simultaneously by thousands (or millions) of others of whose existence he is confident, yet of whose identity he has not the slightest notion."[1] The concept of imagined community, however, is difficult to apply wholesale to imperial film culture because imperial Japanese subjects realized (some consciously, others unconsciously) that not everyone throughout the empire shared the same set of linguistic, ethnic, cultural, or historical traditions. This is one reason why imperial film culture focused so intently on the modernity of the Japanese empire as a new order that broke with the past. Examining how the domestic Japanese media came to terms with the concept of Asia underscores some fundamental paradoxes of Japan's imperial project. One of the biggest challenges producers of imperial film culture faced was how to overcome decades of deeply entrenched negative stereotypes of Asians that popular Japanese media had propagated and replace them with positive images of Pan-Asian co-prosperity.

"Boys, Be Ambitious"

Ever since the Meiji period (1867–1911) Japanese ideologues and cultural producers had recognized the importance of youth in the project of empire building.[2] The ways in which images of Asia represented in comic books (*manga*), illustrated novels, and animated films were used to transform young, predominately male audiences into obedient imperial subjects is crucial to understanding how attractive images of empire circulated. These young subjects learned through idealized tales about Japan's empire who ruled it, and how they, as imperial Japanese subjects, should interact with those who were ruled by it. From the late 1880s multipanel comic strips introduced new graphic conventions to a mass readership in magazines, illustrated novels, and newspapers. Comics were the "products of photography and of applied technologies that successfully wedded press and picture."[3] Comic strips were similar to film in that their narratives unfolded over a series of individual panels, much as those of the movies evolved over a series of individual shots or film frames.

Comic books grew out of the comic-strip format and provide a fascinating site for examining how popular/populist images of the Japanese empire proliferated. Like film, comics were a visual medium that required relatively little linguistic skill to communicate their basic message, even to those readers with the most meager of educations. Publishing companies like Kodansha proved particularly adept at tapping the tastes of an emerging mass audience of young men by churning out a steady stream of popular characters in illustrated magazines such as *Boys' Club (Shonen kurabu)* and *King*.[4] Kodansha kept magazines' prices within the reach of its readership through mass printing technology, industry rationalization, and economies of scale. This helped grant even the poorest children access to their magazines, thereby ensuring that the publications occupied an integral place in the lives of their readers. In 1934 Kodansha's founder, Noma Seiji, discussed his motivations for creating *Boys' Club* in his autobiography: "Above all, great emphasis was laid on what I called 'national culture.' If my long experience as a teacher had taught me anything, it was that our school education lacked this national culture. The history of primary and middle school education in Japan was taken from the West. This 'Japanese national culture' that had been neglected in our Primary Schools was what I proposed to promote through *Boys' Club*."[5]

Noma targeted boys from ages eleven to fifteen because he thought existing children's literature was "written in an academic stilted style, too difficult even for ordinary adults to read."[6] Noma believed that children's magazines should instead consist of interesting content that was "like the genial talk of favorite chums and big brothers," and in this sense his publications fit squarely within an international network of imperialist juvenile literature that included British magazines like *Chums* and *Boys' Friend*.[7] Noma also realized that literature served the nation best by educating, and he actively sought to include "instructive matter of an intellectual and moral character" in his publications. Blending entertainment with education, publishers of boys' literature in Japan saw it as their responsibility to prepare their young readers to become the next generation of imperial soldiers. Noma, however, could not and did not seek exclusively to mold the young minds of his readers. He understood that readers (or parents who purchased their books) expressed support for his publications through the act of consumption, and he therefore balanced his agenda to indoctrinate his readership with a clear understanding of the demands of the market. British media historian Jeffrey Richards describes a similar relationship between British publishers of imperial juvenile literature and the young readers of twentieth-century Great Britain:

> [Juvenile literature] both reflects popular attitudes, ideas and preconceptions and it generates support for selected views and opinions. So it can act— sometimes simultaneously—as a form of social control, directing the popular will towards certain viewpoints and attributes deemed desirable by those controlling the production of popular fiction, and as a mirror of widely held public views. There is a two-way reciprocal relationship between producers and consumers. The consumers, by what they buy, tell the producers what they want. The producers, aiming to maximize profit, seek to . . . dramatize what they perceive as the dominant ideas and headline topics of the day.[8]

The culture of the Japanese empire not only stressed education and camaraderie but represented its builders as beacons of rationality bringing order to a world of chaos. To be an empire-builder meant to be an adventurer, a hero, a selfless laborer for others who stood out in sharp contrast to the untamed, childlike denizens of Asia whom they ruled. It was this same kind of imagery that dominated the representations of Japan's imperial heroes in imperial film culture.

Imperial Heroes and Asian Others

In the 1930s, patriotic publishers like Noma responded to a sense of inner duty and market demand by publishing stories about heroes in exotic outposts of the Japanese empire. Imperial heroes came in all shapes and sizes. Some took the form of young Japanese boys, such as Dankichi in *Daring Dankichi* (*Boken Dankichi*), or stray dogs like *Blackie the Stray Pup* (*Norakuro*), or even robotic warriors like *Tank Tankuro*. These heroes shared in common a strong sense of duty and unwavering confidence in the imperial project. Imperial heroes protected the empire from enemies within and without. Contrary to the popular assumption that the Chinese were not explicitly represented as the enemy in Japanese popular culture, stereotypical Chinese characters appeared frequently in popular comic books of the 1930s. It was not uncommon to find stories of Japanese heroes battling sneaky Chinese or conquering dim-witted natives in the South Seas. While the number of negative images did decline with the rise of Pan-Asianist rhetoric in the 1940s, negative representations of East and Southeast Asians played a large role in shaping the assumptions of young Japanese about how non-Japanese looked, behaved, and spoke.

Blackie the Stray Pup introduced young readers to the empire through the comic misadventures of a lovable stray dog who enlists in the imperial Japanese army. The protocols of army life became part of the reader's daily lives as they read about Blackie being thrown into the guardhouse for some unintended infraction of duty. Blackie fights armies of uniformed monkeys and pigs on battlefields covered with Chinese castles and city streets strewn with Chinese billboards. The comic-book medium gave its creators the freedom to create fantastic situations that would have been too expensive or simply impossible to represent in a live-action film. *Blackie the Stray Pup* represented a comic version of the Japanese imperial hero, but one who successfully learns to become a competent soldier despite frequent blunders. Over the course of the serial, Blackie gradually moves up in rank in the imperial army until his creators felt that the character had advanced too far to relate to its original audience. In the final installment, Blackie says goodbye to his soldier friends and leaves on a new mission to an unnamed continent across the sea.[9]

Other comics, like *General Pokopen* (*Pokopen taisho*) by Yoshimoto Sanpei (1934), were unique in that the story is set entirely in China, and all of the main characters are soldiers in the Chinese Nationalist Army (KMT). Yoshimoto represented the Chinese soldiers as comic imbeciles, mocking their language, appearance, and behavior. In the first panel, a KMT soldier gives a left-handed salute to a general wearing a Fu Manchu-style moustache. The general turns to scold the solider and discovers that he is hiding a sweet-bean bun—which the general promptly confiscates and eats. In the following panel, the general bends down to pick up a coin on the street, and a passerby happens to see him. Embarrassed, the general covers his face but continues picking up the coin saying: "If cover face and pick up, it's okay!" The passerby, however, manages to snatch the coin out from under the general and runs off. Reluctantly, the general takes a coin from his own pocket and says: "Oh well, I drop my own coin. Then pick up, makes me feel okay."[10]

What is striking about this comic is how similar Japanese representations of racist Chinese stereotypes are to American stereotypes of Chinese in film and

comics of the same period. The general sense of the foreignness of Chinese soldiers is intensified most obviously in their speech. The general's ungrammatical
sentences, together with his illogical behavior, underscore his total incompetence,
thereby heightening, presumably, the overall comic effect for Japanese readers.
Yoshimoto's mockery of China's military system operates on two levels. First, it
assumes a complete lack of professionalism running throughout the Chinese
military—foot soldiers cannot execute proper salutes, and generals are greedy
thieves. His parody also points to an attitude that was common in Japanese film
discourse at the time, which tended to condemn Chinese society in general for
even allowing such slothfulness. Japanese censorship laws prevented Japanese
comic artists from treating their military figures as ridiculous, and due to its
extreme nature this sort of scenario could only have been conceivable set in a
context outside Japan.

Shabana Bontaro's comic strips contained graphically violent gags depicting
imperial Japanese soldiers in hand-to-hand combat with KMT soldiers. For example, the story entitled "Full-on Attack" (sokogeki) featured in the comic-book
series *Speedy Hei's Platoon at the Chinese Front* (*Hokushi sensen–kaisoku Heichan
butai*) begins with two Japanese soldiers bayoneting several KMT soldiers. While
a Japanese captain slices a KMT soldier in half with a military sword, Hei-chan,
a Japanese foot soldier and the hero of the series, bayonets another KMT soldier,
shouting: "*THIS* is how ya use a bayonet!" Unable to pull his bayonet from the
moaning KMT soldier, Hei-chan laughingly calls for help: "Oops! Hey! Somebody
gimme a hand here! I can't pull it out!" As the two Japanese soldiers leverage their
feet against the speared KMT soldier's body, they joke "Ugh, this thing's stuck in
there real good!" To this the KMT soldier cries out: "Oww-oww-oww, you please
pull quick!" Accidentally, the rifle discharges with a loud bang, sending everyone
sprawling and leaving two gaping holes in the KMT soldier's chest.[11]

The cartoonish artwork, light comic tone of the dialogue, and fantastic context
of the story make it clear that this is meant to be funny. Even though the KMT
soldier cries out, his facial expressions and body language all indicate that he
isn't really in pain, thus allowing young readers to suspend any belief that this
character is being tortured. Stylistically, the KMT soldiers are represented as distinctly nonhuman, making it less likely for Japanese readers to sympathize with
them. In *General Pokopen*, having all the KMT soldiers speak in broken Japanese
distances them from Japanese readers and makes them appear inept in their own
environment. In *Speedy Hei's Platoon at the Chinese Front*, representation of the
inferiority of the KMT soldiers is far more direct. The imperial Japanese soldiers
are clearly superior both physically and mentally. Obvious juxtapositions like this
made it easy for Japanese readers to identify with strong heroes who spoke natural Japanese, while the linguistically incomprehensible KMT soldiers appeared
nearly nonhuman by comparison.

Speedy Hei bayonets a Chinese KMT soldier in *Full-on Attack* (1937).

The most popular imperial heroes were not Japanese supersoldiers at all, but rather young boys such as the hero of *Daring Dankichi*, a popular Taisho era comic strip that was remade in the 1930s into a successful animated film series. Publishers directly appealed to their young male readership by making boys the heroes of these stories. Dankichi is a typical Japanese boy without superpowers or material wealth. Together with his rat-companion Kariko, they find themselves on an uncharted island in the South Seas after falling asleep while fishing off the shore of Japan. They awake on a tropical island inhabited by dark-skinned "savages" whom Dankichi tames with such blinding efficiency and speed that they unanimously decide to make him their new king. Dankichi is a classic imperial hero who resembles Robinson Crusoe. Like Crusoe, Dankichi enters an untamed wilderness by accident and immediately begins to modernize and educate the backward natives. When he first arrives on the island, Dankichi is dressed in Western-style shorts, a shirt, leather shoes, a wristwatch, and a Japanese schoolboy's cap. He quickly discards everything except his leather shoes and wristwatch, however, in favor of a grass skirt, and he paints his body black to conceal his whiteness, thereby avoiding detection by the natives. He eventually sweats off the black paint but retains the grass skirt, leather shoes, and wristwatch, even after he is proclaimed king.

Cultural historian Kawamura Minato reads Dankichi as an allegory of Japanese modernity juxtaposed against Southeast Asian underdevelopment. He argues that Dankichi's leather shoes and wristwatch clearly associate him with modern technology, and it is these symbols of modernity that in effect validate his position of superiority over the natives. Kawamura maintains that at the time this series was published (1933–1939), Japan was still asserting its modernity, having only just become a modern nation itself scant decades before. In this sense, Kawamura does not see Dankichi as representative of most real Japanese boys, for few of them would have had the means to own expensive items like wristwatches.[12]

It is not only Dankichi's accessories that establish his position of authority, he also embodies the virtues of physical health, mental agility, and vigor at a time when these virtues were particularly lauded for Japan's imperial project. Dankichi represents the ability to assimilate Western technology with the Japanese spirit— he literally embodies the Meiji era ideology of *wakon yosai* (Japanese spirit and Western knowledge). It is this fusion of intelligence, spirit, and physical health that qualifies him spiritually and materially to rule the island. Yet in spite of these skills, he is unable to identify his own imperial subjects, who have names like "Banana" and "Pineapple" and other items commonly found on the newly renamed Dankichi Island. The narrator explains: "Dankichi was speechless. There were darkies everywhere he looked and no way of telling who was Banana and who was Pineapple. Hold it," Dankichi exclaims: "I've got a plan to show who's who just by looking at them." Then he drains some white sap out of a rubber tree and begins to paint numbers on their coal-black chests. "1, 2, 3 . . . "

Dankichi numbers his subjects with rubber tree sap (1933).

Dankichi's inability to distinguish among his own subjects parallels the imprecise mixing by Shimada Keizo, the strip's creator, of the animals, plants, and customs on Dankichi Island. On this island the languages, cultures, and customs of many different ethnicities become interchangeable. Shimada wrote:

> I based the story on my own preconceptions of the tropical south as a place where wild birds and ferocious beasts traversed, and Negro headhunters lived. The animals of Africa, India, South America, and Borneo all came out jumbled together. As each chapter progressed, I began to wonder where on earth Dankichi Island could be. It got to the point where even I didn't know. As its popularity grew, so did the criticism. [There were times] I broke out in buckets of cold sweat, but after all I really can't take responsibility for it.[13]

If Shimada appears to have spent little thought on the accuracy of his stories, the same may also have been true of his young audience. Many young readers did not demand that stories be logical so long as they were entertaining. The stories were accepted uncritically as illustrations of how imperial subjects from "first-class" nations like Japan interacted with underdeveloped peoples. Shimada and other Japanese comic artists created heroes who represented Japan's civilizing presence in Asia as both natural and beneficial. *Daring Dankichi* legitimized the subjugation of native populations and naturalized the imperial project.

Labeling other Asians "savage" or "underdeveloped" was a crucial way of defining Japanese as "civilized" and "scientific."[14] In this context, these stories were didactic in their message that the Japanese helped Southeast Asians who were unwilling or unable to help themselves. Japanese stereotypes of southern cultures, as illustrated in *Dankichi* and other such comics, are still evident in modern Japan, which has led one contemporary Japanese historian to call this phenomenon Dankichi Syndrome.[15] This syndrome is marked by a strong colonial desire to bring order to chaos in the name of civilization. This is illustrated in the last installment of *Daring Dankichi*, when the narrator explains reflectively: "When Dankichi first came to this southern island, things were completely out of hand. Villages and tribes always fought each other and wild mountain beasts stalked all the life on the island. It was Dankichi's adventures and long-suffering work that finally made this a peaceful island."[16] Dankichi Syndrome displays an almost unshakable belief in the inevitable linear development of cultures. In this way, even the most horrible means of colonization and conquest can be overlooked if the ends are justified.

Animated Films

Animated films were far less free to represent certain subjects than comic books.[17] One reason for this disparity was that animated films were seen by much more diverse audiences in public theaters, and they were therefore subjected to greater scrutiny before being passed by the censors. After passage of the Japanese Film Law in 1939, Japanese animated films were part of an integrated program that consisted of the compulsory screening of newsreels, "culture" films (*bunka eiga*), short films, and full-length feature films.[18] Animated films were often shown between the short films and before the main feature, and they ran anywhere from one half to a full reel of film in length. This was generally shorter than Hollywood animated shorts, which by the 1930s had become standardized at one reel.[19]

Animated shorts enjoyed a worldwide boom in popularity due to a series of successful experimentations with color and sound, which eventually culminated in full-length features. American animated films dominated world film markets, and by the late 1930s most Japanese audiences were as acquainted with Betty Boop, Popeye, Mickey Mouse, and Felix the Cat as they were with *Blackie the Stray Pup* and *Daring Dankichi*. Animated films traveled across national borders with far greater ease than comic books. After the phenomenal worldwide success of

Snow White in 1937, most of the world's leading film industries rushed to produce their own full-length animated films. Government officials like Nazi Propaganda Minister Joseph Goebbels also spoke on animated films, and he considered it the government's responsibility to protect national film audiences from the harmful effects of "Americanization" that came with Hollywood films. Goebbels called on the German film industry to produce its own animated films both for domestic consumption and for export in order to de-Americanize the genre.[20]

In Japan, too, discourse on animated films became increasingly nationalized by the 1940s, when media critics like Imamura Taihei started taking serious notice of the genre. In 1941 Imamura wrote *A Theory of Animated Film*, the first book-length study of the subject to be published in Japan. In the book Imamura addressed the subject of Americanism: "What is Americanism? Animated films portray a distinct and particular lifestyle in the spirit of High Capitalism and are its most radical expressions. Concrete examples of this include an emphasis on mechanical technology and mechanical rationalism. Animated films are in fact modern myths that sing the praises of the greatness of mechanical power."[21] Imamura thought that Western, and especially American, animated films had a mythic quality to them and that their power lay in the ability to teach by metaphor. Imamura compared the power of Disney films to ancient Greek fables and held the genre in high esteem.

At the same time that Imamura was writing his book, Shochiku studios was producing the first feature-length Japanese animated film. The story was based on the Japanese folk tale of the mythic boy-hero Momotaro, the Peach Boy. *Momotaro* would not be the first full-length animated film produced in Asia, but it was the biggest.[22] Its budget was larger than any previous Japanese animated project. It spurred one sequel, *Momotaro: Divine Soldiers of the Sea* (*Momotaro: Umi no shinpei*,1945), cost over 4 billion yen, and took over three years to complete.[23] The animation style blends epic realism with broad caricature. The caricature is most evident in the representation of the animals, which have overaccentuated physical features such as eyes, ears, trunks, and tails. The epic realist style is used to represent military technologies, such as planes, and an impressive sequence retelling of the history of Western colonialism in the Pacific. The characters in this historical sequence are rendered almost entirely in a style reminiscent of German silhouette films of the 1920s and Balinese shadow plays.[24] The European history sequence eschews any representation of the Western colonist's facial expressions, thus making them appear sinister and larger than life. The colonizers express themselves only by their actions, which appear highly stylized, as in a silent film.

The use of music in this film is particularly significant in two scenes. The first instance occurs when the indigenous animals on the island attend Japanese language class. The teacher, a rabbit soldier from the Japanese mainland, drills his

Momotaro's fighting Sea Eagles bomb FDR, Bluto, Popeye,
and Betty Boop. The top caption reads, "Destroy American-
made animated films!" (1945).

students in pronunciation. It soon becomes apparent that they are only imitating
the teacher's sounds and do not understand their meaning. Pandemonium ensues
when the teacher asks the class questions, the indigenous animals squawk, fight,
and create disorder. A monkey soldier from the Japanese mainland plays a tune
on a harmonica, capturing the animals' attention and restoring harmony through
music. Significantly, the lyrics to this song are the Japanese vowels that the rabbit
was unable to teach the animals only moments before. Through the power of
music, the animals return to their seats, and Pan-Asian order is restored.[25] With
order restored, the animals naturally take their places, laundering, cooking, and
preparing weaponry for the impending attack, all in rhythm to the song. In this

instance, music functions as a common language, facilitating communication between different species of animals that do not naturally understand each other.

Buy the Record, See the Film

> I imagine nearly 80 percent of all the films people in the South [Pacific]
> watch are musicals. It's no exaggeration to say that true friendship between
> ethnicities begins with music. Even cultural types who have gone down
> there will tell you that music can communicate when words cannot. I think
> you'd do better to take some good musicals down South rather than a bunch
> of films full of difficult logic.[26]

Japanese actor/director Shima Koji gave this advice to Manchurian-born Japanese
singer/actress Ri Koran in a 1942 roundtable discussion entitled "Musical Films
have No National Borders" that appeared in the popular magazine *Film Friend*.
The participants generally sustained the popular notion that film and music were
universal languages, capable of mediating fundamental differences between cultures and ethnicities. The most outspoken advocates of the universal language
theory preached that art had the power to the end wars, achieve class equality
and racial harmony, and ultimately even create a united brotherhood of man.
However, contemporary Japanese music critic Hosokawa Shuhei reminds us that
"the ideology of artistic universality was born of and deeply tied to nineteenth
century colonialism." Hosokawa argues that the concept of a universal art powerful enough to extend beyond political economic borders was a Western invention
designed to balance the expansion of its political influence.[27]

This mix of universality versus specificity in film and music takes on a most
intriguing form in representations of Asia in Japanese film music during the 1930s
and 1940s. On the one hand, Japanese government ideologues implemented a
film music policy that counted on the supposed universal appeal of music and
films to take their message to non-Japanese-speaking peoples throughout the
empire. On the other hand, film music also fulfilled a need expressed by many
imperial Japanese subjects, who began going to movie theaters in droves both
to see *and* hear Japanese films. Film's popularity and ideological power literally
exploded in the 1930s because it was multimedia, a combination of visual and
aural effects. Like the other popular media discussed above, Japanese popular
songs (*ryukoka*) added an emotional dimension to the moviegoing experience
that exceeded mere visual narrative and at the same time reflected the political
realities of imperial Japan. The popularity of sing-along films in 1920s America
or the songs in 1930s Chinese leftist films bespeak a similar phenomenon where
the communal act of singing in a movie theater bound audiences together in
an "imagined community." Music, and film music in particular, became an

important conduit through which imperial Japanese subjects could define their imperial identities.

Popular Songs in Japanese Film

By the end of the Taisho era (1912–1926), Japanese musicians, critics, and consumers widely used the term *ryukoka* to refer to contemporary popular songs of both foreign and domestic origin.[28] Music was a vital element in the filmgoing experience even before the advent of sound, and silent films were nearly always shown with some sort of musical accompaniment, both to entice customers into the theater and advance the narrative.[29] Legendary American filmmaker King Vidor explained the importance of musical accompaniment to the silent film: "I would roughly say that [it accounted for] forty or fifty percent of the [total emotional] value for the person watching."[30]

Most histories of silent film presentation in Japan have been overshadowed by discussions of the *benshi*, or film narrators, yet equally important were the full orchestras of *gakushi*, or inhouse musicians, who accompanied first-run films in the larger theaters in major urban centers.[31] The big-budget foreign blockbusters, such as *Orphans of the Storm* (1922), *The Thief of Bagdad* (1923), or *The Gold Rush* (1925), usually arrived in Japan with an original score that was either used or discarded according to the discretion of the theater owner or musical director. Most Japanese films, however, did not have original scores composed for them and were accompanied by a mixture of traditional folk music, Western classical themes, and popular Japanese *ryukoka*.[32]

Early experiments in sound film both in Japan and abroad became common by the mid-to-late 1920s and Japanese filmmakers soon realized they could dramatically increase their profits by inserting popular songs, literally called "insert songs" (*sonyu-uta*), into their films. Insert songs were popular jazz-inspired songs that fell under the general heading of popular music. Singers who appeared in the film were hired to make personal appearances at movie theaters to sing their songs along with the audience when their scene appeared onscreen.[33] The burgeoning power of the crossover between music and film inspired record companies to press records of popular film songs as well as records of famous *benshi* performances, which not only boosted record sales but also movie ticket sales.[34]

Stylistically, popular songs drew from an eclectic mixture of musical styles both domestic, such as the *kouta* (literally, small songs) and *kayo* (songs), and such foreign styles as Argentinean tango, European cabaret music, and especially American jazz. This mixing of national and cultural musical styles provided a wealth of inspiration for Japanese filmmakers and gave them familiar stereotypes and images to draw from. An increasingly large number of songs were set in exotic locales and depicted exotic peoples within the Japanese empire.

Sheet music for "The Chieftain's Daughter" (1930).

One of the earliest of these songs, "The Chieftain's Daughter" ("Shucho no musume"), is situated in the Japanese-mandated Marshall Islands, and its lyrics describe the backward habits of a native island woman from the viewpoint of her Japanese *rabaa* (lover):

> My lover is the chieftain's daughter,
> She may be black, but in the South that's a beauty.
> Down below the equator in the Marshall Islands,
> She dances under the shade of a palm tree
> Dance, dance, drink raw sake,
> You're happy that tomorrow's the headhunting festival.
> Yesterday I saw her on the beach,
> today she's fast asleep under a banana tree.[35]

"The Chieftain's Daughter" was made into a film with the same title in 1929 (released in 1930), and the storyline appealed to a crossover audience of music fans and filmgoers. The story is set entirely within the specifically Japanese imperial space of the Marshall Islands. This is not an uncharted or foreign-controlled area "somewhere in the South Pacific," but an instantly recognizable part of the Japanese empire that was known by and, theoretically, accessible to all imperial Japanese subjects.[36]

The song evokes images of "islanders" that are reminiscent of those found in the comic-book series *Daring Dankichi*. The hodgepodge visual metaphors of Dankichi Island are rehashed here in a musical shorthand that offers listeners the shortest possible path to "understanding" these islanders. By drawing on a familiar set of stereotypical images, this musical shorthand, like visual ones, reduces everything to instantly recognizable parts—palm trees, bananas, and beaches. Even the chieftain's daughter, becomes part of this scenic map. She never speaks, and listeners know her only through descriptions of her actions— she sleeps, dances, and dreams of headhunts. Both she and the island represent a familiar colonial trope, the fecundity of empire as virgin territory waiting to be conquered both geographically and sexually.

"The Chieftain's Daughter" was one of many similar popular songs, such as "Banana Maiden" and "South Seas Maiden," that helped fuel Japanese male fantasies of sexual and imperial conquest. The colonial attitudes found in these songs do not appear uniquely Japanese when placed within the general context of international popular music at that time. Many Western filmmakers and songwriters held similar assumptions about Asians. Since the late 1920s, island songs were a staple in European and American popular music, with everyone from crooners like Ronnie Munroe ("Ukulele Dream Girl," 1926) to comedians such as Eddie Cantor ("On a Windy Day in Waikiki," 1924) singing about their "darkskinned mamas" somewhere in the South Pacific. Likewise, part-talking movies such as *White Shadows in the South Seas, Aloma of the South Seas,* and *The Pagan* all packed theaters due in large part to their catchy theme songs.[37]

Japanese songs and films throughout the 1930s and 1940s exhibited what might be called "commonsense colonialism," or an attitude that justifies the impulse to subjugate underdeveloped cultures because they, like the landscape they occupy, are thought to be waiting to be dominated. In the roundtable discussion with Ri Koran mentioned previously, director Shima Koji says that untamed climates produce untamed behavior, which is often manifest in primitive music. When asked if he knows whether there are folk songs in Malay, Shima replies: "I would certainly imagine there are. Any place that hot is bound to have an inordinate number of folk songs. If you don't sing and dance [in such a place], you're liable to go mad."[38] Shima's serious tone betrays his lack of regard for accurate representations of Asia and recall Shimada Keizo's description of Dankichi Island.

Hosokawa Shuhei points out that this stereotype was also applied to popular songs about China:

> Just as there were Manchurian Nyannyan Festivals, and *guniang* (Chinese "maidens") on the continent, the south was full of girls who loved to dance. Native women were the only women who made good songs. This is where we can see a deep relationship between colonial domination and male domination. Whether in a China dress or a grass skirt, exoticism and eroticism intersect turning the colony into a metaphor (*rabaa*) of unfulfilled desire on the part of the mainland.[39]

Popular songs with Chinese themes were known as continent songs (*tairiku uta*), and their popularity exploded on the Japanese popular music scene after the 1931 Manchurian Incident. Stylistically, they found expression in a variety of musical styles, including marches, military songs, jazz songs, ballads, comic songs, chansons, and even rumbas.[40] "Manchurian Lover," "Little Miss China," and "Manchurian Maiden" trivialized and infantilized Chinese women, just as "The Chieftain's Daughter" had South Pacific island women. It is interesting to note the English loanword lover (*rabaa*) is used in both "The Chieftain's Daughter" and "Manchurian Lover." Songs like "Manchurian Gypsy," "Little Miss China," "China Maiden," and "Manchurian Rumba" all illustrate a mixing of exotic, romantic themes from the West with similar references for China and Manchuria. Japanese composers such as Hattori Ryoichi skillfully utilized Western musical genres such as the fox-trot and tango while blending them together with themes that reflected an imperial context in songs such as the Korean "Arirang Blues" and "Hot China."[41]

The eclectic mixing of musical styles and exotic settings in popular songs found a parallel on movie screens as continent songs became a wellspring of inspiration for Japanese filmmakers. In 1932, a year after the Manchurian Incident, film companies produced dozens of "continent films" (*tairiku eiga*) based on these highly popular songs. As the Japanese military pushed deeper into Asia, continent songs advanced further into the heart of the Japanese imperialist imagination. As an incentive for music buyers, photos of film stars were inserted with the records and sheet music for popular films. Gradually, photos of the singers themselves, posed either with the film's stars or alone, were superimposed onto the record's label. Singers were hired to perform in films, and what had been fairly rigid lines separating the domains of singer and star had, by the mid-1930s, started to blur. The phenomenal film success of singers like Dick Mine, Watanabe Hamako, and Fujiyama Ichiro soon prompted film studios to have stars like Sano Shuji and Tanaka Kinuyo attempt to sing their own songs.[42] Music critic and government music censor Ogawa Chikagoro wrote the following in his 1941 book, *Popular Song and the Times*:

Popular singer Shoji Taro and film star Sano Shuji on the
record label of "On a Street in Shanghai" (1938).

Film and records have recently become deeply interrelated increasing the
number of hit theme songs. "Incident" songs have made the biggest hit
with the masses, especially those released by Columbia and tied in with
Shochiku films. If the level of entertainment films, which clearly have a
profound influence over the masses, does not improve, it will be impossible
to extract the vulgarity from these songs. Every company has a large number
of songs about Shanghai. They are full of sentimentalism and eroticism—
falling lilacs, the scent of horse chestnut trees (I doubt even whether there
are any such trees in Shanghai!), and the nearly obligatory appearance of a
guniang tearfully playing her lute by the window of a tea house. While you
might get away with this sort of thing in lyrical poetry, it has no *spirit*. [43]

What Ogawa found lacking in Japanese popular music lyrics, especially film
music, was the sort of spirit that would remind Japanese imperial subjects of why
their troops were fighting. He recognized the trivialization inherent in the popular continent songs but associated it with an ignorance of the duty to create a new
Asia. "With each victory we are expanding and occupying China's major cities.
After each victory come songs that portray the charm of a "Canton Flower Girl"
or the exoticism of a "South Sea Island Girl." Fine. But songs must also make us

feel the pulse of New China, they must beat with the trials and hopes of the con-struction of a New Asia."[44] For Ogawa, popular music and film were literal tools for the construction of a new culture in Asia and as such had to be completely removed from previous forms of art. Most of the blame for the vulgarity and the generally "low standard of popular entertainment," he argued, rested squarely on the shoulders of Japan's intellectuals and leaders and not on the masses, whom he generally regarded as mindless. The "gravely serious state" of Japanese popular music called for serious action, or what Ogawa called more hands-on government leadership over music production for the sake of Japan's future.

Japan historian Louise Young characterizes the popular music and films of this period as a part of an empire-wide sense of war fever. She vividly describes how the cultural production industries reused older themes of the empire in crisis, heroism in battle, and the glory of sacrifice—what she calls mythmaking—to stir up appreciation of these forms from a new generation. For Young, the selling of the Japanese empire is a sort of marketing fad similar to what we would now call media events. She focuses on the many songs commemorating the Three Human Bullets (*bakudan sanyushi*) to illustrate that the music and film indus-tries were out to make money on the war.[45] Continent songs and continent films were popular because they helped to divert the attention of imperial Japanese audiences from domestic anxieties about the failing Japanese economy, the war, and other problems.

The Japanese Musical Film

The Japanese music film (*ongaku eiga*) was also tied up with the phenomenal success of the European operetta, revue films, and American film musicals. Japa-nese film critics often compared domestic music films with such popular foreign films as *The Love Parade* (1929), *Under the Roofs of Paris* (1930), and *Maidens in Uniform* (1931), nearly always to the detriment of the local product. Japan's first all-talking film,[46] *The Neighbor's Wife and Mine* (*Madamu to nyobo*, 1931), was not considered to be a musical despite having several musical sequences. *A Tipsy Life* (*Hoyoroi jinsei*, 1933), which most critics agree was Japan's first musical, was more a showcase of the day's talented singers than a fully developed musical where the music propels the plot. One musical film historian described such early musicals as "lack[ing] any cinematic structure, style, purpose or direct[ion], other than to showcase a string of performers, their songs and their dancing. Such films clearly relied upon the spectacular at the expense of narrative."[47]

This assessment holds true in the Japanese case as well where the spectacle expressed in most contemporary musicals was not the music per se, but also the Japanese urban environment. At a time when over half of the Japanese popula-tion in the home islands lived in a rural environment, it is no wonder that, as literary critic Kobayashi Hideo has suggested, audiences may have found the Ginza district every bit as exotic as the deserts of Morocco.[48] Japan's urban spaces may or may not have appeared exotic to imperial Japanese subjects in the *naichi*, but representations of Japan's imperial possessions most definitely did.

By 1935 Japanese imperial audiences grew bored with elaborate musicals, and film studios countered by banking their fortunes on vehicles for stage performers who had star value. Photo Chemical Laboratories (P.C.L.), the forerunner of Toho, was one of the first film studios to invest heavily in the production of a series of films that adapted stage successes of headlining talents Enomoto Kenichi and Furukawa Roppa. Enoken (as Enomoto was affectionately known to his audience) and Roppa pictures were prestige pictures and required substantially greater capital to produce than other Toho films. The largest part of the budget for these films was allocated for the headlining musical performers' salaries, which for a typical Enoken picture could amount to nearly three times the cost of other Toho productions.[49] The fact that these films commanded a substantial portion of the studio's annual budget and that their success or failure held serious ramifications for the studio's survival is a key point. Studios like P.C.L. knew that period films were surefire moneymakers and decided to blend the musical together with the period film to attract a broader audience.

Yaji and Kita Sing! (*Utau Yaji Kita*, 1936) was a period (*jidaigeki*) musical ostensibly set in Japan's historical past. The film starred Furukawa Roppa as Yajirobei and Tokuyama Tamaki as Kitahachi, in a reworking of the famous Edo period comic work *Shanks' Mare* (*Hizakurige*).[50] The comic duo essentially reprised their stage roles, singing and laughing their way down the Tokaido. *Jidaigeki* musicals generally performed well at the box office throughout the late 1930s.[51] They illustrate an attempt to de-Westernize the musical genre by integrating native musical styles with foreign ones in order to create a new national musical genre. The Yaji/Kita films were particularly successful (called dollar boxes) and inspired several sequels, two of which were set in China: *Enoken Busts onto the Continent* (*Enoken tairiku tosshin*, 1938) and *Yaji and Kita on the Road to the Continent* (*Yaji Kita tairiku dochu*, 1939).

Because Toho's top comic talent (Enoken, Roppa) starred in these films, we can assume that Toho saw them as prestige pictures and therefore gave them large production budgets. The storyline was sufficiently attractive to the studio for them to approve of the production. Likewise, the plot device of placing mythic Japanese characters in a Chinese setting was timely (as were all of Enoken and Roppa's films) and could be expected to draw large audiences. Finally, because mainstream comedians such as Enoken and Roppa had chosen these themes, it is safe to assume that the cinematic appropriation of China as a space to be used by Japanese filmmakers had become an attractive part of the Japanese imagination of its own empire.[52]

The Japanese imagination of Asia found its fullest representation in the 1940 Enoken musical *The Monkey King* (*Songoku*), a big-budget musical extravaganza loosely based on the Chinese literary classic *Journey to the West*. *The Monkey King* resembles other Japanese *jidaigeki* musicals, such as Roppa's *Yaji and Kita Sing!*, in its using of fictional characters from an idealized (in this case Chinese) past while infusing them with modern (Japanese) sensibilities. Formally, it does this by blending Japanese visual and aural stereotypes of China with Western Orientalist fantasies of China, India, and the Middle East.

The establishment of the atmosphere of mythical China begins even before the opening credits, in an Orientalist musical prelude that employs gongs, marimbas, cymbals, and lutes—all of which were musical instruments that Japanese traditionally associated with China.[53] In the opening credits, the Orientalist atmosphere gives way to orchestrated film music, punctuated only occasionally with Orientalist musical phrases. Amid thundering taiko drums and crashing gongs, the film opens with a tight shot of a Chinese incense urn; the camera then gradually pulls back to reveal a virtual harem of women wearing pseudo-Chinese/Indian costumes and dancing to a Middle Eastern melody in Busby Berkeley-inspired geometric formations. A high overhead camera angle makes the association with American film musicals even more obvious while serving to emphasize the sheer spectacle of the scene. Flamboyant costumes, oversized sets with polished tile floors, Oriental props, and stylized choreography all combine to establish the setting as taking place sometime in China's mythical past.

The harem dancers (played by the Nichigeki Dancing Team) drop to their knees with the arrival of the Chinese emperor. The emperor sings a command to his high priest Sanzo to go to the land of Tenjiku and obtain a blessed scripture. Sanzo is warned of the dangers of this mission, but all verbal communication is completely subsumed within an operetta structure and the straight-on camera angle further emphasizes the stage-like atmosphere of the scene. As the chorus sings the last bars delineating his mission, Sanzo is escorted out of the palace by armed palace guards into what appears to be the Forbidden City, lined with hundreds of female subjects waving Sanzo farewell. The smooth blending of both Western and Eastern musical styles in this sequence, together with the various visual referents, all suggest the sort of hybridism that historian John Mackenzie identifies in his writing on Orientalism and Western music: "When exotic instruments and rhythmic and melodic figures are first introduced into a native tradition, they stand out as dramatically and intriguingly alien. If, however, they are fully assimilated . . . they cease to operate as an exotic intrusion and extend and enrich that musical tradition."[54] Visually and musically, *The Monkey King* actively revives certain Japanese stereotypes about Asia in general and China in particular, while at the same time creating new ones.

Much of Enoken's reputation as a musical stage performer was built on his

Enomoto Kenichi (second from the right) stars as *The Monkey King* (1940).

facility in popularizing Japanese "covers" of such Western jazz hits as "My Blue Heaven," "Dinah," and many others. Such musical grafting of Chinese melodies with Japanese lyrics was an important part of the professional image of many of his singer costars in *Songoku*, including Watanabe Hamako and Hattori Tomiko, both of whom had several hit continent songs and often appeared in Chinese costumes. Also appearing in *The Monkey King* is Ri Koran, who spoke and sang fluently in Chinese, and Chinese actress Wang Yang, who played the role of China Doll, the only ethnic Chinese performer to appear in this film. Intriguingly, the only cast members who masquerade as Chinese characters in this film are women. This conscious feminization of China is reinforced by the motif of Chinese women in distress—either trapped in palaces or locked in secluded bungalows.

In *The Monkey King* Japanese popular singer Hattori Tomiko plays Shuka, a young Chinese maiden held captive by the pig-monster, Tonhakkai (Zhu Bajie in the Chinese story) played by popular Japanese jazz singer/comedian Kishii Akira. Hattori built her career as a singer of "young maiden" songs (*musume mono*), including such popular tunes as "Manchurian Maiden" and "China Maiden," both of which would have been well known to the film's audiences. Shuka introduces the audience to the character of Tonhakkai but also extends the exotic image of

Chinese women that was established in the opening musical number. While Shuka embodies the passive, enslaved Chinese woman, other women characters in *Songoku*, particularly the sex-starved queen (played by Japanese singer Mimasu Aiko), represent female sexual power as a threat.

In the original story, Sanzo's quest to bring the Buddhist scriptures back took place in the lands along the Silk Road between China and India, where he was constantly beset by various goblins and ogres. Buddha (here replaced by a Chinese emperor) provided Sanzo with three companions—Songoku, Tonhakkai, and Sagojo—to protect him and atone for the sins they committed in their past lives. In the film, these four protagonists cross and are drugged by a group of Arabian dancing girls at a desert oasis where everyone except Songoku is taken to a hidden desert kingdom ruled by a carnal queen. After imprisoning the men in her desert palace, the queen attempts to force herself on Sanzo and orders that Tonhakkai and Sagojo be executed. Such subplots were familiar to Japanese readers of pulp fiction such as H. Rider Haggard's *She* or colonial films such as *Queen of Atlantis* (1921, *L'Atlantide*, France), all of which had been quite popular in Japan. These works also featured mysterious queens who lured men of action into their desert kingdoms to seduce, enslave, and ultimately discard them.[55] Just as those narratives had been set in a mishmash of exotic locales, so too was *The Monkey King* an intentionally vague and imprecise mixing of Chinese and Middle Eastern sets, costumes, and dancing. *The Monkey King* expresses a Japanese imperialist imagination that is strikingly similar in both form and content to that found in Western films.

While waiting to be executed, Tonhakkai flirts with the women in the harem, who blindfold him in a game of blind man's bluff. As Tonhakkai mugs his way through the scene, the "Woman of the Orient" (played by Ri Koran) sings a low-key blues song, appearing almost wraith-like. Tonhakkai removes his blindfold to find the Woman of the Orient coyly seducing him by removing her veil. He pursues her in a slow, playful chase—continually grasping for her, but never quite able to reach her—to the strains of Ri's signature tune, "China Night," on the soundtrack. The slowness of the chase further emphasizes the Woman of the Orient's ephemeral nature—she appears to be as elusive as a dream. Equally ambiguous is her nationality. Most Japanese audiences familiar with Ri Koran the actress would associate her with the Chinese continent—and the background music was meant to facilitate this identification—but her costume is reminiscent of a character from the Arabian Nights. Adding to the mix of visual and aural symbols is the fact that she sings a blues song (as opposed to her usual Chinese-themed songs) in perfect Japanese. In the context of the sequence, the Woman of the Orient is presumably Chinese, but she is dressed like an Arab, and sings the blues in Japanese. As with the inhabitants of Dankichi Island, we may wonder where is this Orient that she represents?

The only ethnically Chinese actress in this film, Wang Yang, does not appear until later in the story. At first it is not entirely clear whether or not she is human. Only when two palace guards place an imaginary key in her back and motion as if winding her up, do we understand she is a life-sized "China Doll" ordered to perform for the queen's guests. In contrast to the other musical numbers that mixed foreign melodies with Japanese lyrics, China Doll's song in Chinese is left entirely untranslated, as if the mere spectacle of a Chinese singer singing and dancing in exotic Chinese robes was sufficient. At the end of her number, her movements become more and more jerky until, finally, after singing the last note of the song, she slumps over, literally spent after performing for her Japanese owners. At this point, the same guards who brought her in unceremoniously take her out.

The link between music and film is a continuity of "commercial, ideological, and cultural practices" that are located within specific historical and social moments.[56] This seems especially applicable to the present discussion. While recognizing the distinctiveness of the music industry as a separate medium, it seems important also to recognize that the integration of popular music, popular singers, film, and Asia represented a continuation in the growth of the economy of empire. Popular singers such as Watanabe Hamako and Ri Koran, or variety performers such as Enoken and Roppa, brought their fans to the movie theaters in droves to see them sing in opulent Orientalist fantasies like *The Monkey King* that united spectators and music listeners in a mass media event. Each new "incident" on the Chinese continent churned out a new batch of films, songs, and ancillary products that loyal subjects consumed as though consumption itself were a form of patriotism. While singer-stars like Watanabe Hamako and Hattori Tomiko dressed in Chinese clothes and sang of Chinese *musume*, "Chinese" stars like Ri Koran and Wang Yang offered the promise that coexistence and goodwill were possible throughout the Greater East Asian Film Sphere. These were ambassadors of song, who stayed fresh in the minds of their imperial fans through their songs, their film appearances, and other media such as film magazines. For readers of film magazines were also incorporated into imperial Japanese film culture through their active consumption of film magazines.[57]

Reading All About It

Beginning with the first Japanese film magazine, published in 1909, the number of film publications grew rapidly. They experienced a substantial boom in the Taisho era until they finally peaked at around sixty-five titles in 1931, at the time of the Manchurian Incident. This may seem an insignificant number, especially when compared with the estimated 25,000 titles published by the Japanese magazine industry at its peak in 1937 after the China Incident.[58] But the jump in the number of movie-related publications corresponds to similar increases in both domestic Japanese film production and record sales, where each experienced a significant leap, following the military "incident" on the Chinese continent.[59] In fact, very little primary data exists on precisely how many film magazines there were, what their circulation was, or how large their print runs were, and this discrepancy suggests that even before the war, Japanese film magazines were not considered to be on par with serious literature.

Just as film studios were creating house styles and genre films to attract a wider audience, film magazine companies in the 1920s and into the early 1930s also sought ways to differentiate their product from that of their competitors in the huge mass magazine market. Japanese film magazines, like those of other imperial nations, were fairly representative of a variety of tastes. Magazines like *Film Technology* (*Eiga gijutsu*) featured technical articles on filmmaking for industry professionals and covered all the latest developments in the film technologies. *Scenario* (*Shinario*) and *Screenplay* (*Eiga kyakuhon*) were specialty magazines for screenwriters, and *Film Criticism* (*Eiga hyoron*) and *Film Era* (*Eiga jidai*), which often included translations of articles by famous foreign filmmakers, were aimed at a predominately intellectual audience. In addition, there were the standard fanzines full of photos and gossip, like *Star* (*Sutaa*) and *Cinema* (*Kinema*), studio magazines such as *Kamata* and *Toho*, as well as magazines that specialized in scenarios or novelizations of films like *The Moving Picture Club* (*Katsudo shashin kurabu*).

However, in 1940 the Planning Division of the Ministry of the Interior executed the first magazine consolidation under the rationale that nonessential industries like the magazine industry needed to be regulated, given the seriousness of the war, the severe shortages of paper, and so forth.[60] The government, however, made it clear that it did not want to appear to be the one pulling the switch. Film historian Imamura Miyoo described the government's approach toward individual publishing companies as follows: "The government will not take compulsory measures to close [you] down. However, we cannot let things remain as they are now. We would like the industry to discuss this matter among yourselves, come to a consensus, and present us with your results."[61]

Representatives from the thirteen leading film magazines met several times to determine how best to consolidate their industry, and, after much deliberation, it was decided that two companies would publish seven magazines under the governance of a coalition known as the Japanese Film Magazine Association (Nippon Eiga Zasshi Kyokai).[62] *Cinema Bi-weekly* (*Kinema junpo*) had to drop the foreign loanword "cinema" from its title and change its name to the more Japanese-sounding *Film Bi-weekly* (*Eiga junpo*). *New Film* (*Shin eiga*) continued publication after incorporating *Star* (*Sutaa*) magazine; *Culture Film* (*Bunka eiga*) absorbed two film journals, and *Film Friend* (*Eiga no tomo*) continued publication as before. *Film Criticism* (*Eiga hyoron*) absorbed *Film World* (*Eigakai*), *Film and Music* (*Eiga to ongaku*), and *Scenario Studies* (*Shinario kenkyu*) and the two magazines *Film and Technology* (*Eiga to gijutsu*) and *Film Projection Technology* (*Eisha gijutsu*) continued publication under the title of *Film Technology* (*Eiga gijutsu*). Another journal, *Japanese Film* (*Nihon eiga*) was originally published by Bungei Shunshusha, but it gradually became a state propaganda organ, and, despite subsequent massive consolidations, was allowed to continue publication without interruption through March of 1945. When conditions grew worse for Japan late in the war, and offices and printing factories were being bombed, and materials became even more scarce, events triggered a second consolidation that reduced the number of publications to three—*Japanese Film* (*Nihon eiga*), *Film Criticism* (*Eiga hyoron*), and *New Film* (*Shin eiga*).

Empire in Film Magazines

Nearly all of the major film magazines carried stories about film in Asia. In the 1940s, *Film Criticism*, for example, published story after story introducing various Asian cinemas to their Japanese readers. Most of these fanzines ran articles about popular stars in Korea or Manchuria in language that quantified them as star/products in a separate but familiar sphere. Technical magazines also responded to the changing realities of the Japanese empire by publishing articles that dealt with specific technical problems facing filmmakers throughout the Greater East Asian Film Sphere. It became fairly common to see stories with such specialized topics as how to handle film in the blistering tropical climates of Thailand or how to keep film and cameras from freezing in the subzero temperatures of Manchuria or the Aleutian Islands.[63] Writers in the journal *Film Technology* displayed an obsession with replacing the film technologies and equipment then currently in use in the Greater East Asian Film Sphere with Japanese-made machinery.[64]

Other film magazines such as *Film Friend* appealed in a completely different manner to its predominately mass readership. The magazine was popular and put phonetic readings beside the Chinese characters for the benefit of younger or undereducated readers. It also used full-page or even two-page, single-panel comic strips to reach out to its audiences, following patterns that by the 1940s had already been well established by successful youth magazine companies like Kodansha. Comic strips published in film magazines depicted Japanese coexistence with indigenous Asian cultures via film activity, and it did so with a visual veracity that would have made Japanese Pan-Asianist ideologues jealous.[65]

A two-page single panel comic entitled "The Studio Gets Southern Fever," for example, displays the goings-on in a make-believe film production company

"The Studio Gets Southern Fever" (1942).

named Tochiku Studios (a play on the names Toho and Shochiku) that has
entirely switched over to producing Southeast Asian theme films.[66] The make-
believe world of filmmaking offers an intriguing parallel to the Japanese-imagined
world of Japanese coexistence with other Asian races. The film lot functions as a
substitute for the Greater East Asian Film Sphere—an animated playground for
cartoon film people and, by extension, *Film Friend* readers "experience" what
living with other Southeast Asian cultures might be like. The cartoon format in
Film Friend draws on comic-book conventions such as those discussed above.
The full-page, one-panel omnibus style would have been readily familiar to regular readers of *Boys' Club* and suggests that there was audience crossover between
film and illustrated magazine readers.

    Representations of blackness are the source of several intended gags in this
panel strip. For example, the makeup room is full of light-skinned Japanese
"blacking up" for the day's shoot. One man, apparently out of makeup, has run
up to the roof to ask the chimney sweep to give him some ashes. In the studio
lagoon, a group of men in black body paint are swimming with alligators. One
of them has just come out of the lagoon, white from the chest down, dripping
black paint. His "native" friend tells him: "Hey, your ink came off!" Another actor
sitting half-darkened next to the studio lagoon wishes he would "hurry up and

tan!" Blackness, like any other prop on the lot, is meant to create a desired effect. It is interesting to note that, with only one possible exception, no one on the lot is actually from the South Seas. All of the Japanese there are merely "acting southern," either through their body paint or costumes. The punch line of these vignettes comes from a betrayal of the reader's expectations of or associations with notions of blackness. Consider the Japanese woman who remarks to a darker-skinned woman in native garb: "Goodness! Just what are you made up to be?" To which the other woman replies: "Why, a Filipina bride!" The overall playfulness of the tone only serves to strengthen the sense of Otherness from the Japanese. A hint of Japanese fear of, or at least discomfort with, blackness is hinted at in the comic figure in blackface and turban who gives a toothy smile to a passing Japanese woman, making her scream.[67]

Another critical undercurrent in this cartoon is the presentation of the constructed as real. Just as film studios around the world are often referred to as dream factories—places that can turn fantasy into reality—this studio is no exception. All over the lot, workers are busy building braces for limp studio palms, painting rugby balls to look like coconuts, and making set facades to look like Javanese temples. The effectiveness of the fantasy manifests itself by the actual responses to the lifelike representations of the unreal. A woman in native dress runs screaming from a man dressed in a tiger suit. In another part of the lot, a director looks at the facades of two Javanese huts and congratulates himself: "Hmm . . . not bad. Just like being in Java." There is even a muted sense of dissatisfaction with the unreal, as we see in the reaction of one director who has insisted that real banana plants and palm trees be planted on the lot for future use. He insists that "after all, there's nothing like the real thing."

Despite the fanciful tone of the piece, there are little reminders here and there of both the threat of war and the value of the South Seas beyond its usefulness as fodder for the dream factory. Below the cartoon running across both pages is another, narrow cartoon entitled, "An Introduction to the Resources of the South." The strip is divided into seven small panels, and a key displays the natural resources found on the islands of Mindanao, Celebes, Borneo, Java, Sumatra, and Malay. Oil, hemp, rubber, copra, and copper were what these dreams were made of, and although the style is light, the message is clear. Also, in a very small corner of the lot, a crew is shooting a picture on what appears to be a Manchurian set. The director has to remind the actors, who look longingly at the others on the lot having fun, not to be distracted by the South. Everyone on the lot has their work to do, including the extras who play soldiers. It is also a helpful reminder to the readers that the empire is not about one single area. Just below the hill where the Manchurian set is being shot, a small door to a cave is marked "air-raid shelter"— just another reminder that all is not fun and games in dreamland.

Opinion Polls and Readership Drives

One of the few resources for discovering how spectators felt about the movies are the opinion polls conducted by magazine staff members and printed in magazines such as *Film Bi-weekly* and *Film Friend*. Magazines conducted these polls in the form of written questionnaires that supposedly reached a variety of people in the readership demographics. In 1941 *Film Friend* began what would become a three-part public opinion poll on the impressions of "typical moviegoers" entitled "Here's What I Think." The preface to the first installment described in detail why the magazine was conducting the poll and what methods they were using:

> It's the critic's job to review the merits of a film, but the people who really like movies are more receptive than critics. Without their support, there wouldn't be any movies. So our magazine started this inquiry because we thought we should find out just how average moviegoers interact with movies on a daily basis. We collected 482 responses from 800 of our readers polled on the basis of age, profession, and locale in an effort to represent a fair cross section of all social levels and geographic areas. Between the fact that there was little time to tabulate the results and that some of the respondents did not correctly interpret the intent of our questions, we must acknowledge the possibility for a slight margin of error. Overall, we feel that our first public opinion poll was a worthwhile endeavor.[68]

Magazine editors took great pains to emphasize that while the responses had been condensed, they had not been falsified in any way and were "the true voice of the average people" and as such contained elements that could not be dismissed. While it is not clear how faithfully the respondents' remarks were recorded and tabulated in this article, they do offer an indication of how audience tastes in imperial Japan were *perceived*. This first poll predictably asked its readers: (1) for their favorite production company, (2) favorite stars, (3) which directors and performers had the most talent, (4) which recent films they liked and disliked, and (5) what sorts of films they would like to see made in the future. It is interesting to note that none of the films on the best-film list were set in countries other than Japan (with the exception of *Vow in the Desert*, at number 9). By contrast, the number 1 and number 2 worst films in the Toho category were *Vow in the Desert* and *The Monkey King*.[69]

By all accounts *Vow in the Desert* was a successful and popular film, yet by 1941 it was appearing both on the best and the worst lists. Among the various answers given to question 5, three respondents suggested that more films be made that were set in territories outside of the Japanese home islands. One person, identified only as a salesperson, said: "I can't stand the way they're always bragging about the New System, I mean it's fine to have continent-theme films, but Toho's films make a mockery of the holy war and really irritate me." An office worker hoped for more "films set in Japan/Manchuria/China that could be exported abroad." A typist wanted "many more films set in Nanyo to show us the importance of the southern advance." The masses' "true voice" seems to have suggested that, at least on some level, they were not simply waiting for policies to be shoved down their throats, but instead were actively pushing for films more compliant with national policy that went beyond what the industry required.

The second installment of "Here's What I Think" rehashed different versions of previous questions, yet what was significant was that a majority of readers expressed support of official film policy, while at the same time over 740 readers exposed their desire to see foreign pictures even if they were banned. Western films were still major box office draws, despite the inroads made by domestic and imperial film genres. But the popularity of films set in imperial locations such as China or Manchuria was still a subject of controversy. When asked what films they definitely would not like to see remade in the future, respondents resoundingly replied: *Aizen Katsura* (108 people), *China Nights* (76), *Hearts Don't Lie* (55), *Sing & It's Heaven* (42), *Vow in the Desert* (39), and *The Monkey King* (35).[70] Nearly half of these titles were either set in imperial possessions or represented the people from these areas, and all of them have been described in primary and secondary sources at various times as hits.

If films set in the imperial territories were indeed popular, why were they specifically targeted by readers as films they would not like to see remade? The disjunction here seems to have been a temporary one when we look at the third installment of "Here's What I Think." The final poll demonstrated a clear shift from general ambivalence toward a definite desire for more films set in Japanese imperial possessions. This is prominently revealed in the answers to the seventh question: "What sort of films would you like see made by each of the major studios?" The answers included:

Shochiku	*Southern Winds* (623), *Torii Kyouemon* (196), *Sumida River* (90)
Toho	*Mother's Map* (240), *The War at Sea from Hawaii to Malay* (204), *The Opium War* (105)
Daiei:	*New Snow* (213), *Malay War Document* (192), *Genghis Khan* (134)[71]

These three polls indicate that public tastes were clearly becoming more conscious of empire. *Southern Winds* has vital parts of its storyline set in Nanyo. *The War at Sea from Hawaii to Malay* deals with the Japan's victorious attack on Pearl Harbor and the subsequent drive into Asia that radically expanded the boundaries of the Japanese empire. *Malay War Document* is a semidocumentary about the Japanese military advance into Malaysia that liberated it from

Western colonialism. *The Opium War* is a period film that condemns Western (predominantly British) colonialism as well as Britain's use of opium to weaken the Chinese people while lining their own pockets with profits from the drug trade. *Genghis Khan* is a period film that valorizes resistance to foreign (non-Asian) aggressors and encourages cooperation among Asians to defeat Western interference. Through their conspicuous consumption, audiences demonstrated that not only were films with content pertinent to the Japanese empire popular, but also that many of the consolidations within the industry were met with initial support.[72]

For example, in 1942 all film distribution was divided into two lines—white and red. Prior to 1942 films were released to theaters according to the company affiliation of the theater. Vertical integration resulted when film studios purchased movie theater chains to ensure a venue for their films. In other words, Toho-owned theaters (or their direct affiliates) generally screened Toho films. The same was true with the other major studios such as Nikkatsu, Teikine and Shochiku. However, after 1942, all film distribution routes within Japan were consolidated into two lines regardless of ties between a theater and a production company. Japanese film critics writing in after the war regularly cite the consolidation of the film distribution system as an example of government manipulation and oppression of the Japanese film industry.[73] But a 1942 article in *Film Bi-weekly* entitled "Asking the Viewers" reveals that readers were generally supportive of the changes: "It's good the businessmen are no longer allowed to use film for their own stupid self-interest. That alone makes up for whatever might have been lost by closing such low-class dives as the Daito and the Shinko. I think they ought to torch every film Shochiku, Toho, and Daiei put out (and there's plenty of them) just like when the Nazis burnt books."[74]

Film magazines tapped into popular support of film policies by encouraging readers' direct participation through an endless cycle of drives for the submission of new script ideas, songs, and even proposals on how film should expand throughout the empire.[75] Such use of readership drives was not limited to the 1930s. Early Japanese film journals such as *Cinema Bi-weekly* (*Kinema junpo*) and *Motion Picture Illustrated* (*Katsudo shashin gaho*) regularly ran advertisements for reader contributions.[76] One of the most popular forms of participation in imperial Japanese film culture drives was also one of the most direct—the drive for the Japanese "movie song." A full-page advertisement in the April 1942 issue of *Film Bi-weekly* announced the winner and several runners-up, and furthermore it printed the music and lyrics to the Japanese "Film Song." The article stated the method and motivation behind the drive in the following preamble:

> By the application deadline last December tenth, we received an overwhelming 1,751 applications for our Japanese "Film Song" drive sponsored

by the Japanese Film Magazine Association with support from the Cabinet Information Bureau. We received applications from people in the *naichi* and even a few from our brave soldiers way off at the Chinese front. We are pleased to announce that Yamada Kosaku composed the music, and we are proud to offer our selection to everyone in the Japanese film industry and everyone who loves films![77]

The film magazine industry was clearly directed by the government, but its efforts were also in accord with the wishes of the film industry and shaped by the desires of its readership. Popular participation in imperial film culture was expressed in a variety of ways in film magazines, including readers' polls, comic strips, and drives for song submissions. The methods suggest that not only were film or magazine companies anxious to include popular input, but readers were equally anxious to offer it, as we have seen by their enthusiastic response to questionnaires, surveys, and drives for reader submissions.

Film magazines, popular music in films, and comic strips all interacted dynamically, both expanding the audience base for film while at the same inviting the viewers' and readers' vicarious participation in the imperial project through their consumption. While it is obvious that all of these media drew from each other for inspiration, they provided their audiences with more than escapism alone. Adventure heroes like Dankichi or Hei-chan educated consumer subjects by providing models for how people from a "first-rate nation" interacted with other Asian races. The interrelation between film and popular music demonstrated an awareness of audiences beyond the home islands of Japan as well as an assumption that exotic peoples and cultures in the Japanese empire held wide, if not universal, appeal.

CHAPTER THREE

Imperial Acts

Japan Performs Asia

Kozo: Do you think Yang genuinely likes [us] Japanese? I never know if *those people* truly mean what they say.

Mine: I really couldn't say, I've never associated with any.

Kozo: You mean you've been here all this time and you still can't speak Chinese?

Mine: Well then, let's see you speak Chinese with that waiter. Excuse me, Boy!

Kozo: No wait! . . . you know that I . . .

Mine: . . . can't speak? (laughs) *That's* why you don't know what they think . . . [1]

This sequence from the 1942 film *The Green Earth* hints that under the façade of the images of Japan as the leading nation of Asia idealized in its "goodwill" films was a palpable fear of interacting with the cultures and people it subjugated through rapid colonial expansion. That Japanese could effortlessly summon non-Japanese waiters without any knowledge of the local language or customs instructed viewers of the lack of any need to understand what the Chinese were saying.[2] Fictions like these were meant to reassure Japanese audiences that this was their empire and inspired one Japanese film critic to suggest that the value of these films lay in their "realistic depiction of Japanese living amid the fact [of empire], rather than in the depiction of those facts themselves."[3]

This chapter analyzes how mainstream Japanese feature films mediated that fact of Japanese empire with representations of the ethnic and cultural differences of Chinese, Koreans, and Southeast Asians. Japanese assumptions of Asian difference were first identified and then subsumed in order to construct a seamless onscreen image of an idealized Pan-Asian subject. This chapter focuses on shifting debates over elements of mise-en-scène, including acting styles, gestures, makeup, and language. Japanese filmmakers did not attempt to entirely erase Asian difference, but rather struggled to find an acceptable level of Asianess to represent to its audiences.

Japan's Many Chinas

The image of China stood as something of a paradox for many Japanese. It was impossible to deny China's immense influence on Japanese civilization, which had included the introduction of, among other things, the writing system, Buddhism, and the legal system. By the early twentieth century, most Japanese saw China as an ossified, backward nation so possessed by visions its own glorious imperial past as to render it unable to either modernize or defend itself. Imperial Japan was, as other historians have noted, anti-Western and anti-Chinese as circumstances demanded. In this sense, the Japanese empire was an attractive alternative to oppressive Western colonial regimes in Asia, and initially appeared to be a natural ally to many independence leaders.[4] China was an archive from which Japanese filmmakers drew inspiration to define Japan's own identity. Alternately associating with and distinguishing themselves from China, Japanese filmmakers recycled a range of Chinese stereotypes—from highly educated and assimilated Chinese to the ignorantly rebellious—all could be applied to almost any political configuration.[5]

While no official Japanese ideology was ever established to demonize China in the same way as it did the West after 1941, references to China as the enemy appeared frequently in Japanese mass culture throughout the 1930s.[6] After the China Incident of 1937, Japanese films like *Five Scouts* (*Gonin no sekkohei*, 1938) and *Mud and Soldiers* (*Tsuchi to heitai*, 1939) avoided any direct representations of the Chinese as enemy soldiers and referred to them only generally as Chinamen (*Shinajin*). By the 1940s Japanese ideologues and intellectuals became concerned over the quality of films depicting the Chinese and the topic of how to define Chinese became a hotbed of debate that spilled into the public sphere and included everyone from filmmakers to Chinese intellectuals.[7]

For the majority of Japanese who lived in the rural areas outside Japan's major cities there were limited chances to have intimate interactions with non-Japanese. These Japanese depended on films, newspapers, and to a lesser degree radio as their chief sources of information about China and the Chinese. Continent films owed much of their box-office success to their exotic representations of the empire that, through a variety of media convergence, satisfied (and later saturated) the curiosity of these audiences. One viewer stated in a 1940 interview in a leading Japanese film magazine that audiences went to the movies for a variety of reasons: "We can learn about history, economics, and culture from books, but it's very hard to learn about how [Chinese] people think and live, which is what we really want to know. That's why we are so delighted that we can find out a little more about them through the movies."[8]

Audiences in the Japanese home islands welcomed Japanese actors playing Chinese roles but were no more prepared to accept films about China from a Chinese perspective than white audiences in America were willing to patronize films with all-black casts. *The Road to Peace in the Orient* (*Toyo heiwa no michi*, 1938) is one example. This film was produced by the Japanese distribution company Towa Shoji as a follow-up to its 1936 Japanese/German coproduction *The New Earth* (*Atarashiki tsuchi*). *The Road to Peace in the Orient* told the story of a young Chinese farming couple in war-ravaged China who overcame their distrust of the Japanese after being helped by Japanese soldiers.[9] Towa Shoji President Kawakita Nagamasa explained that he produced the film with three specific goals in mind:

> Showing this film to the Japanese people teaches them about the land, feelings, and customs of their neighbors on the Chinese continent, helping them understand China. Showing this film to the Chinese people teaches them the truth of the [China] incident and shows them the way they must go in the future. Showing this film widely in other nations corrects mistaken assumptions about our true intentions in this incident, by (a) explaining the meaning behind the battle and (b) giving foreign countries a true picture of the Orient.[10]

Contrary to Kawakita's intentions, Japanese critics and audiences generally disliked the picture but split on the use of Chinese actors in the lead roles. While noting that some film critics praised the use of amateur actors, Kawakita worried about the audience's negative response: "The international phenomenon of Japanese/Chinese peace influences the public, not the films themselves. The facts are printed almost daily in newspaper. No matter how much you publicized it, [Japanese] audiences then just weren't interested in no-name Chinese actors."[11] Part of the problem was that Japanese audiences wanted to see familiar images of China onscreen, not realistic representations. But the times had changed as well. After 1937 Japanese audiences grew less interested in pacifist-themed films, and it was the combination of the two, together with the film's nonprofessional Chinese cast, that amounted to box-office poison. One contemporary film scholar suggests that the film failed due to the absence of any Japanese stars and because the great amount of Chinese dialogue resulted in an imposing number of subtitles.[12] Kawakita himself suggested that the lack of Chinese and Japanese star value was also a decisive factor in the film's poor reception, but the question of subtitles per se does not appear to have been an issue. Japanese audiences at this time demonstrated absolutely no aversion to reading subtitles, even lengthy ones, in the many European and American films Kawakita himself had introduced to the domestic Japanese film market. The larger issue for many Japanese was language. Those same audiences that would willingly read subtitles for Western films were uninterested, if not actually hostile, to doing so for a Chinese language film especially in light of the Japanese assimilation policies being conducted at that very time throughout the empire.

The Road to Peace in the Orient failed at the box office due to a combination of factors that included Kawakita's attempt to change the shape of Japanese film. Kawakita was part of the international film community and realized that all successful national cinemas produced films with multinational perspectives as an industry strategy to expand their prospective audiences. Unlike many of his contemporaries, Kawakita knew that to make Japanese film relevant both domestically and internationally, one had to engage the West and China. Just as publishers like Noma Seiji worked to make popular literature serve national agendas, so Kawakita also used a three-point strategy to actively search for new ways to enhance imperial Japan's image internationally through film.[13]

The international vision of Kawakita, however, was an anomaly, and many in the Japanese film industry were unwilling to risk alienating domestic audiences (and losing possible revenue) by gambling on cosmopolitan film policies. Filmmakers found it easier to create the familiar representations of China and Chinese that they assumed audiences wanted. No one in the Japanese film industry was willing to recruit Chinese directors to make "real" films about China, despite occasional complaints from Japanese novelists like Ueda Hiroshi who lamented that too few films represented China and those that did were inauthentic. Calling on the Japanese film industry to more accurately "depict the Chinaman!" Ueda claimed it was "vital to think about our soldiers on the battlefield. Only by understanding the real Chinaman will we be able to understand the true meaning of what the [China] Incident is about."[14] Ueda did not offer any clarification as to what constituted a real Chinaman, and two years later, in 1942, journeyman Japanese directors such as Shimazu Yasujiro still complained of a lack of accurate film representations of the Chinese. Shimazu claimed that "in order to make true continent films that will go straight to the Chinese people's hearts, we as filmmakers must stick our necks right into the lives of everyday Chinese, directly experiencing life on the continent for ourselves, first hand."[15]

Japanese film studios did not employ Chinese actors in films produced in Japan for a host of reasons. First and foremost, Japanese producers and directors were adamant that it was difficult, if not impossible, to find capable Chinese actors willing to work for the Japanese. Kawakita admitted to using nonprofessional actors partly out of necessity; more experienced Chinese actors refused to risk being stigmatized as Japanese collaborators. Chinese amateur actors also feared for their lives, which compelled Kawakita to guarantee their safety even after

English-language advertisement for *The Road to
Peace in the Orient* (1938).

filming was completed. The possibility of violence against Japanese collaborators was not an idle threat. China historian Murata Atsuro recalled that as early
as 1924, local anti-Japanese elements attacked a Chinese film studio for inviting
Japanese actress Okamoto Fumiko to appear in a Chinese film, forcing production to shut down.[16]

The lack of a common language further diminished chances for successful collaboration. Audiences had to understand what characters were saying for stories to
be both believable and ideologically viable. Even in Taiwan and Korea, where the
local colonial governments had implemented official Japanese language policies
for decades, the chances of finding bilingual, seasoned actors were exceedingly
slim. Japanese production studios found it far easier to use Japanese actors in
Asian roles. While Japanese audiences uncritically accepted Japanese actors playing Chinese characters and speaking Chinese, Chinese-speaking audiences were
far less forgiving. Most Japanese actors memorized foreign-language dialogue
phonetically, as Japanese actress Yamada Isuzu did for *Moon Over Shanghai*

(*Shanhai no tsuki*, 1941). In other cases, as when Japanese actress Hara Setsuko played the role of Meizhu in *Shanghai Landing Squad* (*Shanhai rikusentai*, 1938) her dialogue was dubbed into Chinese during postproduction. Both approaches produced reactions that ranged from laughable to disastrous. What Japanese audiences accepted as legitimate, Chinese audiences treated with derision. China-born Japanese actress Ri Koran (Yamaguchi Yoshiko) spoke out on Yamada's poor Chinese intonation in a 1942 roundtable discussion with Japanese film distributor Hazumi Tsuneo and actor Uehara Ken.

> Hazumi: Chinese is the biggest problem. Yamada Isuzu speaks it in *Shanghai Moon*, but could you understand what she was saying?
>
> Ri: No, I couldn't. I could catch simple words commonly used, but anything resembling dialogue that linked together more than a few words was incomprehensible . . . her pronunciation was good, but her intonation, which is crucial, was not.
>
> Uehara: I spoke [Chinese] in *Tank Commander Nishizumi*, I even had someone coach me, but thinking back on it now, they must have been just being nice when they praised me. They told me that they could understand me, and I believed them. But later, when I went to Peking and used some of the same phrases thinking they would be understood, no one knew what on earth I was talking about! Oh, I assume they got a general idea of what I said, but not the real the gist of it.
>
> Ri: That's exactly how Yamada's Chinese was.[17]

Born and raised in Manchuria, Ri was a native speaker of both Mandarin Chinese and Japanese. No single personality so perfectly exemplified the exoticism, mystery, and allure of a Japanified China as Ri Koran. Unlike the vast array of singers and actresses who performed in Chinese clothes, Ri Koran exuded authenticity, and although many of her fans throughout the Japanese empire were unaware of her Japanese identity before 1945, she nevertheless became an imperial icon.

Ri Koran, Icon of Empire

Ri Koran was born Yamaguchi Yoshiko in 1920 in the city of Fushun, Manchuria (modern-day Liaoning province). Her parents moved to Manchuria for her father's job at the semigovernmental company, the Southern Manchurian Railway, better known as Mantetsu. Yamaguchi learned Japanese at home with her family and at Japanese schools. She studied Chinese first with her father, who tutored other Mantetsu employees in Chinese, and later with her Chinese friends. Yamaguchi became so adept at Chinese that her father sent her to a girl's school in Beijing where she successfully "passed" as Chinese. Yamaguchi also demonstrated an aptitude for music and, after catching the attention of Japanese talent scouts in 1938, debuted that same year as a singer on a Manchurian radio program. Yamaguchi's reputation as a popular singer resulted in an invitation to audition at the Manchurian Film Company (Manei) as a singer for postproduction dubbing. Producers immediately noticed Yamguchi's stunning looks, bilingual ability, and excellent singing voice and put her under contract as an actress in Chinese-language musicals.[18]

Producers hid Yamaguchi's Japanese identity from the public and her own colleagues for the first three years of her career. When Manchurian audiences saw her in *Honeymoon Express* (*Mitsugetsu kaisha*, 1938) they assumed she was Chinese. The following year, when Toho Studios and Manei co-produced her first big crossover feature film, *Song of the White Orchid* (*Byakuran no uta*, 1939) Japanese audiences were similarly convinced that Ri Koran was Chinese. Japanese audiences were so mesmerized by her "exotic" looks, smooth singing voice, and exceptionally "fluent" Japanese, that one female fan gushed: "Beautiful, skillful at Japanese, why wouldn't fans love her?" Another male fan spoke of her exotic physical appeal: "Your bewitching continental looks and beautiful voice are just as popular now as when you debuted as a Manchurian actress. Your personality and looks perfectly suit Manchurian, Chinese, Korean, Japanese, or even Western clothes, depending on how one looks at you."[19]

Much of Ri Koran's charm lay in this ability to assume multiple identities simultaneously. Her spiritual predecessors were Hayakawa Sessue and Kamiyama Sojin, who decades earlier had gone to Hollywood, broken the color barrier, and become Japan's first truly international stars. Whereas those actors' careers effectively ended with the advent of sound films, Ri Koran's was built on linguistic mastery—she could transform into almost any nationality simply by changing her costumes and language. In addition to passing as Chinese, Manchurian, Korean, and Japanese, Ri Koran also played Mongolian and Russian roles. In a 1940 photo spread entitled "Ethnic Harmony—the Transformations of Ri Koran," published in the Manei Studio film magazine *Manchurian Film*, Ri appears in five pictures. In each she is wearing a different ethnic garb, so that she visually (and bluntly) depicts the Japanese ideological slogan "Harmony of the Five Races" (*gozoku kyowa*).[20] A caption appeared under each photo (Japanese, Korean, Chinese, Russian, Mongolian) just in case readers were unable or uninterested in making the connection between her costume and the message. In her many incarnations, Ri Koran was a powerful tool of propaganda that brought disturbing new life to Japanese Pan-Asianist slogans, for in no uncertain terms she promised the fulfillment of the catchphrase "Asia is one."[21]

Like all icons, Ri's smooth multiethnic image covered up serious gaps separating Japanese and Chinese, while at the same time emphasizing their similarities.

Looking at Ri, audiences could physically see and hear what a united Asia under the Japanese might actually look and sound like. For Japanese ideologues and filmmakers, Ri was a public relations dream that exceeded their wildest expectations. For audiences, Ri was like a movie screen onto which they could project their deepest imperial fantasies. Japanese audiences could go anywhere via the film exploits of Ri Koran—she appeared in local clothes, took on other customs, and spoke foreign languages, all with an ease that made mutual understanding seem like a very attractive and attainable goal. Most of the magazine articles written about her assumed she was Chinese, or at the very least an authentic voice on Chinese matters. The promise of Pan-Asian unity that Ri Koran embodied went a long way toward neutralizing the Japanese fear of communicating with alien races quoted at the beginning of this chapter. Manchurian Film Company executives knew that presented as a Japanese actress, Yamaguchi lacked any power to inspire Asians to willingly submit themselves to Japanese assimilation policies, but by presenting her as Chinese with a Japanese education, they correctly calculated that audiences would readily identify themselves with one of the two sides.[22]

Ambassadors of Goodwill

Ri Koran's onscreen presence reminded Japanese filmmakers and filmgoers that in addition to the Japanese many Chinese also spent their money to see her films, hear her records, and purchase the products that she endorsed. Japanese filmmakers quickly tapped this popularity, and, hedging their bets against the possibility of any financial loss, Toho Studios paired Ri Koran with popular Japanese leading man Hasegawa Kazuo to star in a trio of interracial love melodramas euphemistically called goodwill films (shinzen eiga). The formula was simple: strong Japanese male (Hasegawa) meets feisty Chinese woman (Ri), and the two ultimately fall in love despite cultural and political differences. Casting Ri as the resistant but ultimately obtainable Chinese partner for Japanese imperial adventurer Hasegawa maximized their collective box-office appeal in Japan and quickly established Ri as an Asian sex symbol.[23]

Misunderstandings between the romantic leads are the major source of character motivation and narrative conflict in most traditional melodramas. Whereas conventional melodramas turn on misunderstandings that are romantic or familial in nature, the goodwill film genre invariably revolved around ideological misunderstandings that ultimately were resolved romantically. Goodwill films resemble the Good Neighbor films produced in the United States at this time, such as Down Argentine Way (1940), Weekend in Havana (1941), and That Night in Rio (1941). Both shared the genre convention of males from the dominant culture conquering females of the subjugated culture as well as a general emphasis on music. Whereas Good Neighbor films almost invariably separated its principle couples into racially segregated sets, Japanese goodwill films curiously did not rule out racial miscegenation as a possible solution to intercultural conflict.[24]

More importantly for Japanese exhibitors, goodwill films translated into good box office sales by offering exotic stories and settings for mass consumption. The film *China Nights* (*Shina no yoru*, 1940) provides an especially lucid example of one distinct cultural gap between Japan and China. After losing her parents and her home in a Japanese bombing raid, Keiran (played by Ri) is reduced to begging on the streets of Shanghai. We see her in tattered clothes and a dirty face being slapped by a Japanese man who tells her to return the money she has borrowed from him. Hase (Hasegawa), a Japanese boat captain, and his friend Senkichi step in to break up the argument. Hase warns the Japanese man against hitting Chinese women for no reason in front of other Chinese because it might give them a bad opinion of "us Japanese" and promptly pays off Keiran's debt, then leaving her and the crowd behind.

Keiran replies in Mandarin, but her dialogue is not translated. She does not want to be indebted to any Japanese. Presumably non-Chinese-speaking Japanese audiences would have been able to understand her only through the roundabout translation provided by the character of Senkichi. Senkichi serves as the initial bridge between Hase and Keiran by facilitating communication when the two first meet on the street:

> Senkichi: How do you like that? We do her a favor and now she's givin' us a hard time. She says you can't just help her and then walk off like that, it's a problem.
> Hase: Well of all the . . . I suppose it's money she is after?
> Senkichi: No, she says he—'er, that'd be you—are her benefactor. You're out the money . . . she doesn't want to owe you . . . so she says she'll go to your place and clean, do laundry, *anything* to pay back the money.
> Hase: Well, tell her I can't be bothered and let's go.
> Senkichi: Boss, she won't listen. Now she's sayin' she doesn't want to be in debt to any Japanese.
> Hase: What? (pause) Doesn't like Japanese, eh?
> Senkichi: Yeah, looks like this one's a real Japanese hater.

By establishing Keiran as a "real Japanese hater," the film has prepared the audience for a major struggle between the two principals. This plot device helps to render Keiran's eventual transformation all the more dramatic. The transformation/enlightenment motif was evident in *The Road to Peace in the Orient*, and it became a standard motif in Japanese representations of Chinese throughout the 1940s. In Japanese films of this period, this sort of scene was nearly as predictable as the arrival of the cavalry in the last reel in a Hollywood Western.

The theme of gendered domestication of Chinese women in the goodwill film genre has led to inevitable comparisons with Shakespeare's *The Taming of the Shrew*.[25] While the process that Hase undertakes—including brusquely dragging her, kicking and screaming, to the bathroom—appears similar, the differences in motivation are intriguing. While Petrucio (and the Henry Higgins character in the 1939 film adaptation *Pygmalion*)[26] take on the civilizing project mainly for the sake of challenge and the promise of monetary gain, Japanese males in goodwill films are motivated by a larger ideological mission; to correct mistaken Chinese perceptions about Japan and the Japanese. Character conflicts in goodwill films do not originate from class differences, for we find that the subjugated woman character is almost always from an upper-class family that has fallen on hard times. In fact, the inevitable revelation that the Chinese woman is not from an inferior class obscures her racial difference, making her appear as an even more suitable mate for the Japanese man. This is one area where Japanese colonial discourse clearly differs from European models in which the motivation for civilizing was based on notions of racial superiority as articulated by the concept of the White Man's Burden. In goodwill films, the difference between China and Japan was neither insurmountable nor was it only ethnic or class-based—it represented a natural regime shift.

In *China Nights*, for example, it is Keiran's Chinese pride that blinds her to the kind intentions of the Japanese around her. When Keiran returns to the Yamato Hotel soaked from a heavy rain, the Japanese women residents welcome her and offer her warm food. Keiran is convinced that all Japanese are devious and knocks the food back into their faces. Hase, no longer able to contain himself, springs to his feet, grabs Keiran by the collar and slaps her across the face, knocking her into a wall. This act of physical violence appears to produce a cathartic change in Keiran, who slowly, gratefully looks at Hase:

> Hase: Well, Keiran, I finally hit you. I guess I lose. That's my punishment for trusting too much in my own ability [to change you]. I was an arrogant fool. Forgive me . . . you are free to go wherever you wish.
> Keiran: Hase-san. Don't make me leave. Forgive me! (crying) It didn't hurt. It didn't hurt at all to be hit by you. I was happy, happy! I'll be better, just watch. Please don't give up on me. Forgive me, Forgive me!

In her 1986 autobiography Yamaguchi wrote that there were two reasons why she would never forget this scene. The first reason was that when filming the scene, Hasegawa got carried away and actually hit Yamaguchi across the jaw full strength, sending her sprawling to the floor. She said the studio decided to use the scene but cut away after she fell down. The second reason is that this scene was part of the evidence used against her by the Chinese government after the war, when she was arrested and charged as a Chinese citizen for treason against

China. The prosecution showed this scene in court to convict her of collaborating with the Japanese. Only after she was able to prove that she was in fact not Chinese, but rather was a Japanese citizen, were the charges reluctantly dropped, and she was able to repatriate to Japan.

Yamaguchi wrote that the slap scene is a classic example of a cultural difference between the Japanese and Chinese. She maintains that if a Japanese man hit a Japanese woman, that woman would recognize this as an expression of love and return his feelings with affection. Yamaguchi continued: "But that was an expression that only was understood among Japanese. Had Hasegawa hit a Japanese character, there would have been no problem, but the fact that the scene showed the Japanese Hasegawa hitting the Chinese Ri Koran caused a serious problem. Average Chinese regarded women who fell in love with men who hit them as doubly shameful. Far from arousing any respect for or understanding of the sincerity of Japanese emotions, seeing this type of behavior enshrined on-screen served only to inspire Chinese hatred, causing them to strike back against the daily injustices they incurred under the Japanese.[27] Keiran's first step in understanding Japanese goodwill started with a hard slap.

The irony of the *goodwill film* genre is that the non-Japanese characters were able to arrive at an understanding of the sincerity of Japan's intentions only through similar acts of physical violence. For example, in *Soshu Nights* (*Soshu no yoru*, 1942) Ri Koran plays Koran, a young Chinese woman working in an orphanage. She is vehemently anti-Japanese until she meets Kano, a Japanese doctor who comes to examine the children. Koran initially opposes Kano's presence as an unwanted interference until he physically shoves her out of the room. After writing a prescription for a little girl, Kano leaves the room in a leisurely fashion, completely ignoring Koran, who now looks stunned and tamed.[28]

Japanese audiences found this scene and others like it a realistic reflection of actual colonial power relations. It illustrated how subjects from first-class nations like Japan interacted with subjugated people like Koran. Yet even in the Japanese film press there were those who denounced such negative film representations of Chinese as derogatory. One unlikely voice was that of Ri Koran herself, who spoke out about the Chinese reaction to these goodwill films in a 1942 roundtable discussion:

> Hazumi: Have you heard any good things from Chinese about *China Nights* or *Moon Over Shanghai*?
> Ri: The Chinese see it very much the same as we do—it's not very pleasant.
> Hazumi: Not a very good feeling?
> Ri: Of course not. I went with a Manchurian actress who became very upset. She said Japan only made themselves look good and showed absolutely no understanding of the good side of China and its people.[29]

These representations not only offended "Manchurian" actresses but also Chinese intellectuals, who were critical, and at times openly hostile, to such representations of the Chinese. In an unusual article the Japanese film journal *Film Bi-weekly* translated some of these opinions, which were initially published in the Chinese media, into Japanese, perhaps to refute claims that the Chinese generally ignored Japanese films as well as to illustrate that Japanese films were indeed being taken seriously.[30] In 1942 a Chinese intellectual, identified only as Xing, criticized Japanese attempts to dress and speak like the Chinese: "Japanese are certain that all they have to do is put on a Chinese long-sleeved gown, and immediately they are transformed into Chinese. Yet the gowns that they choose are not at all Chinese-like, and they only make the Japanese look badly out of place." In this same selection of essays, another Chinese, identified as Shang, commented on Japanese actors' general lack of linguistic ability. "I probably should not say so, but the Chinese spoken by Japanese actors is not good. The audience cannot understand what they are saying most of the time. I imagine it is the equivalent of Wang Yang's Japanese."[31] Wang Yang was a Chinese actress who began her career in Shanghai before working with the Japanese in a series of goodwill films. She learned her Japanese dialogue phonetically, and her poor pronunciation stood out in stark contrast to that of her co-star Ri Koran's smooth Japanese. These Chinese critics added that from what they could see in these films, the Japanese appeared to know precious little about China and cared even less. Not much had changed in the years since Japanese film critics praised their actors who passed as Chinese. For the Chinese, Japanese imitations of Chinese characters amounted to little more than a slapdash combination of ostentatious costumes and exaggerated stereotypical gestures.

Japanese filmmakers wanted desperately for Chinese audiences to accept Japanese films and reject Hollywood films, and Japanese producers employed a variety of technological innovations to create a Chinese audience for their films. Japanese films were dubbed, subtitled, and in more remote areas mobile projection units used slides with Chinese translations of the Japanese dialogue projected onto the screen. All of these approaches met with unsatisfactory results; Japanese attempts to create and reach "authentic" Chinese audiences were plagued by their misinterpretations of what China was.[32]

With Japanese filmmakers and producers so divided over how to represent China, it may come as no surprise that no single definitive image of China ever emerged. A semidocumentary like *The Road to Peace in the Orient* existed alongside stereotypes from earlier eras, such as Japanese actor Kamiyama Sojin's stage revival of his portrayal of the *Mongol Prince* (*Moko no oji*) in the American film *The Thief of Bagdad* (1924). The image of China Kamiyama created in his role must have appeared anachronistic, however, within the context of rising Japanese Pan-Asianism. Ironically, the closest that the Japanese film industry would ever approach to Chinese authenticity was the Japanese actress Ri Koran. Ri Koran symbolized a Japanese recognition of the tremendous gulf separating Japan from China as well as a desire to overcome that gap. However, Ri Koran was not the only example, nor was China the only site, of Japanese fear of ethnic difference in imperial Japanese film culture. Korean filmmaker Hae Young presents yet another side of the complex and transnational nature of imperial film culture.

Kimchee and *Takuan*

We would never be so insensitive as to tell Koreans that they must like *takuan* [Japanese-style pickled radishes] in order to be imperial subjects. If Koreans took a liking to them on their own . . . that's another matter . . . but for now, *kimchee* is fine. Mouths accustomed to *kimchee* can speak Japanese without problem, and there is no reason for them not to grasp the proper spirit of an imperial subject. It may sound odd to say so, but Korean films are made of the smell and taste of *kimchee.* No matter how strange that might seem to other races, *kimchee* is more important to them than *cheese, butter,* or even *takuan.* Japanese film companies may appear able to produce Korean films . . . but the result would be no more than Korean-made *takuan*; similar to but different than *kimchee.*[33]

Contemporary historians note that because Japanese respect for Korean culture was distinctly less than it was for Chinese culture, the assimilation program in Korea was much stronger than elsewhere in the empire.[34] If we understand Japanese filmmakers and audiences to have imagined China to be in a perpetual state of becoming Japanese, then Korea was represented as actually being Japanese. Representations of Koreans were complex; the people were projected as the Japanese wanted to see them: obedient, manageable, and thoroughly loyal. But despite representations of Koreans as tame or obedient subjects, many suspected that *kimchee* and *takuan* were ultimately two separate things.[35]

Conflict in films about Korea—those films produced in Korea either wholly or in part by Japanese talent and/or capital—often originated outside Korea, such as the marauding Communist bandits in *Suicide Troops of the Watchtower (Boro no kesshitai,* 1943). With the exception of this film, no other film about Korea approached China's picturesquely lawless frontiers. In 1941, when Korean resistance to colonial Japanese rule was at its peak and manifested itself in all the arts, the rationale for presenting Korea as a paragon of order and control seemed to make sound ideological sense.[36] Creating an image of Korea as safe and secure may have served the needs of colonial management within Korea, but it effectively ruined the Japanese audience's desire for the wild and exotic. Korea was indeed different, but at the same time it was familiar and ultimately knowable.[37]

Japanese audiences in Japan had almost no exposure to films made by Koreans, and what little they did know was generally not positive. With very few exceptions, Japanese held Korean films in very low esteem. Only rarely did Japanese film critics offer any explanation for this apathy toward Korean films, except to say that Korean films, like most Korean things in general, suffered from poor quality and a lack of resources.[38] Feature films like *You and I* (*Kimi to boku*, 1941) and *Suicide Troops of the Watchtower* tapped into Korea's exotic proximity to Manchuria, attempting to present it to audiences in the Japanese home islands as an attractive frontier outpost of the empire. Both films were produced with the support of the Korean Colonial Government as part of an effort to implement cultural politics (*bunka seiji*) that promoted the ideological concept of "Japan and Korea as one body" (*naisen ittai*). The films represent different responses of Japanese apathy toward Korea, a situation that was diametrically opposed to Japan's idealization of China and its eroticization of the South Seas.[39]

You and I Are One

In 1941, the Korean Military Information Division coproduced *You and I* with Shochiku Studios, to become one of the most successful Japanese/Korean coproductions of the colonial era. Japanese film critic Iijima Tadashi cowrote the film with Korean director/screenwriter Hae Young. *You and I* championed two colonial cultural policies—the Military Volunteer Program (*shiganhei seido*) and the Interracial Marriage Policy between Japanese and Koreans (*naisen kekkon*). The Emergency Measures Survey Committee within the Korean Colonial Government instituted the Interracial Marriage Policy in August 1938 in order to "create appropriate measures to encourage the marriage of Koreans [outside their race]."[40] The Korean Colonial Government established the Military Volunteer Program to entice young Korean males to join the imperial Japanese army, and initially it appears to have been a voluntary program. After Pearl Harbor, however, when the need for Japanese soldiers dramatically increased, many young Korean men were rounded up from their homes and forcibly conscripted into the Japanese army; others were sent throughout the empire to work as forced labor. After 1937 the Japanese military and Korean colonial police similarly abducted Korean women, sending them to the various battlefronts to work as sex slaves for Japanese soldiers.[41]

You and I offered Korean audiences a short precis on how to become a model imperial subject whom the Japanese would admire. The film tells the story of Kaneko Eisuke, a Korean imperial subject who dreams of being a soldier and ultimately joins the imperial Japanese army as a volunteer soldier (*shiganhei*).[42] There were an unusually large number of Japanese industry officials working on the film in a variety of capacities, ranging from gaffers to cameramen, and soundmen to screenwriters. The film provides a glimpse into the Korean Colonial Government's various assimilationist "imperialization" (*kominka*) policies, which attempted to eradicate Korean ethnic and cultural difference.[43] Contemporary anthropologist Jennifer Robertson suggests that the process of imperialization involved becoming an imperial Japanese subject rather than, strictly speaking, becoming Japanese. The focus was on changing the subject's attitude so that he or she would desire the goals of assimilation—changing the content of the subject so that the "form would follow suit."[44]

In the script for *You and I*, Kaneko and his friend Kinoshita—we only know their Japanese names—volunteer for military training. While in training, Kinoshita receives word from a friend that his baby son has died. He is perplexed as to why his wife did not tell him even when his (Japanese) squad leader knew. It is revealed that everyone in the barracks were told to keep quiet about it out of respect for his wife, who did not wish to disturb Kinoshita's "important training." The squad leader praises her for being a fine example of a "peninsula wife" and proceeds to read Kinoshita her letter. To this, Kinoshita replies: "Forgive me for seeming weak, but when I heard that my child died, any parent, anyone human, would be sad. I felt faint for a moment and thought I might collapse but collected myself saying 'is this all it takes to make me forget my martial spirit?' Crying isn't an option for an imperial soldier . . . but my tears weren't just for my dead child. You see my child was Japanese, and I was heartsick to think we had lost a Japanese boy."[45]

Not only is Kinoshita denied his real name, wife, and child, but he is even forbidden the right to mourn. Likewise, the screenwriter has coded Kinoshita's emotional reactions to the loss of his son as feminine. This is an example of gender politics as "a zero-sum game, where . . . power is coded 'masculine' and powerlessness 'feminine.' "[46] The idea that a mother or a father would not mourn their child lessens the film's credibility and pushes the characterization nearly to the point of caricature. As another example, when Kaneko graduates from boot camp, he goes to his parents' place to pay his respects before leaving for the front. Their conversation is conducted entirely in Japanese, making the scene feel as if it might have occurred in the Japanese home islands.

> Father: I've prepared for this day for quite a while now. Now that you are a soldier, you naturally want to go to the front.
> Kaneko: Thank you father. I'm sorry that I couldn't do anything for you and mother.
> Father: What do you mean? Don't worry about honoring your parents, serve the Emperor! It's what we want you to do.[47]

His parents chide him for shedding tears of happiness at hearing of their support for his decision to go. Later in the film, while making their farewells, Eisuke and the Japanese girl Mitsue reveal their feelings for each other. As Eisuke and Kinoshita prepare to leave for the front, the village turns out to see them off, and just as their bus pulls away from the station, the film ends with their friend shouting: "Don't worry about the home front! Japanese/Korean unity is solid!"[48]

Veteran filmmaker Tasaka Tomotaka is famous for having directed a trio of "humanistic" war films at Nikkatsu's Tamagawa Studios in the late 1930s. Tasaka originally agreed to direct *You and I* but quit before production started, citing personal reasons. Tasaka never explained why he quit, but he left a letter for Japanese critic/screenwriter Oguro Toyojiro that said: "Whether this film will contribute to the development of Korean film as a whole depends entirely on your passion. I'm sure you will have more than your share of dissatisfaction with the production conditions here [in Korea]. You will have to endure unpleasant things at all times. But you must keep your eye on the greater goal far off in the distance."[49]

Whatever doubts Tasaka may have had about the film, his replacement and the government/military officials in charge were definitely banking on its success. Hoping to avoid the dismal box-office reception of *The Road to Peace in the Orient*, which had used only native Chinese actors, the producers took special care to recruit the best talent from both Japan and Korea to ensure that *You and I* would become a Pan-Asian hit. Top Japanese stars Ohinata Den, Kosugi Isamu, and Asagiri Kyoko shared billing with Korea's top box-office stars Moon Ye-bong and Yi Hyang-ran.[50]

Contemporary Korean film scholarship characterizes the colonial period only in terms of resistance or collaboration. Much as many French postwar histories of the Nazi Occupation of France portray "every Frenchman as a member of the resistance," nationalist Korean historians also deemphasize Korean collaboration with Japan in favor of narratives of anti-Japanese resistance.[51] Korean collaboration with the Japanese was something that often could not be avoided, and in some cases Koreans actively sought to work with the Japanese rather than needing to be coerced. For upwardly mobile Korean colonial youths such as *You and I* screenwriter Hae Young, there were few alternatives outside of collaborating with the Japanese if one wanted to work in the film industry. Hae Young actively threw himself into imperial Japanese film culture, working as a director and screenwriter on projects in Japan, Korea, and Indonesia.[52]

Three Faces of Empire

Hae Young was as much the result of Japanese imperialization policies in Korea as the fictional character Eisuke he created for the film *You and I*. Both were born and raised in Korea into conditions where learning Japanese ways was a path to social advancement, and both wound up marrying Japanese women. Hae Young traveled to Japan in 1925 in hopes of studying film under the legendary "father of

Japanese film"—Makino Shozo. After arriving in Japan, Hae worked under the name Hinatsu Eitaro at the Makino Studios in Kyoto until financial problems forced the studio to close. Hinatsu then found employment with Shochiku, where he worked under many of the top directors of the day. Hinatsu excelled as an assistant director until one day in the spring of 1937 when he was rigging an explosion in front of Himeiji castle for a scene in the Japanese feature film *Summer Siege of Osaka Castle* (*Osaka natsu no jin*, 1937). Hinatsu miscalculated the amount of gunpowder and wound up slightly injuring himself and destroying a piece of the castle, which was considered a national treasure. Japanese police arrived on the scene and took Hinatsu to the police station where he was thoroughly interrogated. Only then did anyone discover that he was actually Korean.[53]

Several months passed until Hinatsu managed to find another job this time with Shinko Kinema in Kyoto. He worked on several major productions at Shinko, until he decided to return to Korea to produce a dramatization based on the life of Yi In-suk, a Korean volunteer soldier who was martyred in the line of duty defending the Japanese empire. It was then that Hinatsu was approached to work on *You and I*. Tanabe Masatomo was head of the Education Division of the Korean Colonial Government and Hinatsu's friend. Tanabe introduced Hinatsu to Japanese film director Tasaka Tomotaka. Tasaka first harbored deep reservations about the film but wholeheartedly supported the idea of building up the Korean film industry in general. Most of the Japanese and Korean staff who worked on this film seemed to have feelings similar to those of Tasaka.[54]

Postwar Korean and Japanese sources differ over the reception of *You and I*. Japanese film histories claim the film was a smashing success, while Korean film histories decry it as a miserable propagandist flop. In either case, both sides generally agree that *You and I* was the catalyst that motivated Hinatsu to leave Korea for Japanese-occupied Indonesia in 1942. Hinatsu arrived in Java in the spring of 1942 as part of a detachment of Japanese cultural experts working for the Japanese propaganda corps.[55] Hinatsu was attached to the theater group, but while he was there he directed a documentary film entitled *Calling Australia* (*Goshu no yobigoe*, 1944) for the imperial Japanese army that used real prisoners of war as actors.[56] Little information is available on the reception of this film at the time of its release, but the story behind the production of *Calling Australia* is fascinating. The film was commissioned by the imperial Japanese army and upon completion, prints were to be dropped by parachute over Australia. It was hoped the film would weaken the resolve of Australian soldiers and induce them to surrender to the Japanese. *Calling Australia* attempted to counter negative images of Japanese concentration camps by shooting on location and presenting conditions there as being similar to a country club. This film was never intended to be screened in regular theaters, and therefore no names or dates or other production data appear in any of the existing prints.

Hinatsu Eitaro (right) and Tasaka Tomotaka (middle) on the set of *You and I* (1941).

In 1945 the Netherlands Indies Film Unit produced *Nippon Presents*, which told the story of some of the prisoners of war who had been used in *Calling Australia*. *Nippon Presents* emphasizes that these people should not be stigmatized as collaborators, and in a mixture of interviews and clips from the film attempted to prove that all who participated were in fact making subtle resistance. In 1987 Australian documentary director Graham Shirley again assembled the surviving Australian prisoners of war who had been in both of the previous films to appear in his documentary, entitled *Prisoners of Propaganda*, which examined the production of the film as well as questioning the multiple exploitations of the prisoners. Parts of *Calling Australia* were screened during the 1945 Tokyo War Crimes Tribunal as evidence against the Japanese military leaders. After *Calling Australia*, Hinatsu turned his attention away from film to theater and worked with Indonesian theater people in Java.[57]

After the Japanese defeat in 1945, Hinatsu told a close friend: "You [Koreans] all came here [to Indonesia] in a group to work for the Japanese military. But I on my own initiative persuaded the Korean Colonial Government to make *You and I* with the support of the Colonial Military Forces. Everyone knows about *You and I*. Everyone knows that Hae Young and Hinatsu Eitaro are one and the same. And in addition to that, my Korean isn't even that good. I'm a Korean who knows almost nothing about Korean history other than what little I studied about in Tokyo. . . . If I returned to Japan now there wouldn't be any jobs for me and if I returned to Korea, I'd most likely be branded a Japanese collaborator."[58] Hinatsu changed his name again, this time to Dr. Huyung, married an Indonesian woman, and began making films for the fledgling Indonesian film industry. Dr. Huyung was responsible for shooting some of the earliest postliberation footage, which came out around the same time as Joris Ivens's *Indonesia Calling* (1946). He also filmed the first commercially successful Indonesian film, *Frieda* (1951). Although his life was not as well documented as Ri Koran's, Dr. Huyung serves as another example of the long-term impact that Japanese assimilation policies had on non-Japanese imperial Japanese subjects. Dr. Huyung died in Indonesia without ever returning to either Korea or Japan.[59]

Almost Japanese

Not all films set in the empire contained social or psychological themes. *Suicide Troops of the Watchtower*, for example, was a big-budget action thriller coproduced by Toho Studios and the Korean Colonial Government and supervised by the Korean colonial police. The film depicted the daily lives and struggles of a group of Japanese colonial police in a distant outpost on the Manchuria/Korean border who were locked in a battle with Communist Chinese bandits. The story was based on several factual incidents that were woven together into a fictional narrative. In 1986 director Imai Tadashi admitted that *Watchtower* owed its existence to the American film *Beau Geste*.[60] These films share much in common. Both are set in colonial hinterlands at near-deserted outposts, and they involve international, multiracial military forces fighting insurgent native groups that are portrayed as being as wild and unstoppable as the harsh climates where the stories take place. *Beau Geste's* barren North African deserts find their equivalence in the similarly barren but snowy hinterlands of the northern Korean/Manchurian borderlands in *Suicide Troops of the Watchtower*.

Colonial adventure stories set in exotic locales like *The Lost Patrol* (1934), *Lives of a Bengal Lancer* (1935), and *Gunga Din* (1939), as well as countless similar films turned on a fear of native revolt. They had tremendous box-office appeal both in Japan and the West. One striking difference between the two traditions is that the colonial heroes in the West often appeared introspective, filled with self-doubt, and they agonized over their duty. More often than not—and especially in Foreign Legion films—the hero had to leave his native country due to some shameful event in his past or as a result of a flaw in his character. Japanese filmmakers could never allow such nuance in their imperial heroes, and the characters of *Suicide Troops of the Watchtower* are no exception.[61]

Watchtower presents viewers with ideal Korean imperial subjects whose intense loyalty to the Japanese emperor comes before anything else, including their own lives and those of their families. Korean subjects are true and faithful servants who earn the respect and admiration of the Japanese around them through loyalty. Onscreen, these idealized Korean imperial subjects happily work together with their Japanese masters, willingly sacrificing themselves if need be to protect the Japanese empire. Colonial relationships like these revolve around the notion that the colonized is dependent on the colonizer, and such narrative tropes are well known in Western colonial cinema. Alexander Korda's colonial trilogy—*Sanders of the River* (1935) set in West Africa; *The Drum* (1938) set in India; and *The Four Feathers* (1939) set in the Sudan—presents similarly loyal indigenous imperial subjects serving in the British army, ready to lay down their lives to prove their loyalty and devotion to the British empire. The racial difference between indigenous imperial subjects like Gunga Din or Toomai, the elephant boy, and their white, Christian masters is usually mediated only through sacrifice. In *Suicide Troops of the Watchtower* there is no equivalent to the racial implications of Britain's White Man's Burden, for the Koreans were physically and culturally much closer to the Japanese than Indians were to the British. Therefore, in *Watchtower* Korean imperial subjects did not have to die to become Japanese, they became like Japanese in spirit through the "natural" process of Japanese assimilation.[62]

Suicide Troops of the Watchtower represents Koreans as loyal retainers from the first scenes. Women dressed in *chimachogori* (traditional Korean clothing) serve Japanese and Korean workers who are clearing a small village road. The image of Japanese and Koreans engaging in manual labor together provides a striking contrast to Hollywood or British colonial films, where assumptions about the "proper place" among races results in sharp divisions of labor that separates the colonizers from the colonized. In the context of Japanese colonialism, elite Koreans—that is, those who spoke Japanese or who had assimilated—rose in the ranks to the position of border police and were granted the authority to carry weapons. In *Watchtower* Korean guards Kim and Rin work together with the Japanese border police. In an early sequence, Kim and Rin attend a dinner in honor of a Japanese policeman newly arrived from Japan. As the dinner progresses, the Japanese encourage Kim to sing a Japanese folk song, which he does.

As Kim sings, Rin, carried away by the rhythm, stands up from his seat, and begins to dance around the table. Smiling a distant smile, with his eyes tightly closed shut, Rin dances slowly and rhythmically as if in a trance. Kim stands up and, looking directly into Rin's face, dances with him. The audience sees several shots of the Japanese police listening and watching appreciatively, but compared with the Koreans, the Japanese show no outward signs of being engulfed by the music. They remain in control of their bodies and emotions, and simply observe the Koreans dancing for them. As the song ends, Kim and Rin use the natural momentum of their dancing bodies to spin gracefully back to their seats. Impressed, the new Japanese police recruit offers Kim sake:

New recruit: Kim, if I hadn't seen you dance just now, I would have sworn you were Japanese.

Kim: (smiling) Maybe I am. What do you think Rin?

Rin: I think if I changed the pronunciation of my name to Hayashi, you'd never know the difference. And see my wife? Just look at how she's taken to Japanese clothes!

The attempts to represent Korea in terms of its geographic, ethnic, and cultural proximity to Japan only served to underscore the fact that in actuality imperialization policies could not entirely erase racial and cultural differences between Japanese and Koreans. Rin's comment about the pronunciation of his surname refers to the Name Law (1940), another Japanese cultural policy that attempted to eradicate Korean difference and replace it. Other differences, however, hovered just under the surface and manifested themselves in ways other than skin or hair color.[63]

Slight differences in speech patterns or pronunciation could immediately distinguish Korean speakers of Japanese from native Japanese in this film and others like it. Late in the film a Korean schoolteacher is teaching a group of Korean children the Japanese language. The schoolroom setting is peripheral to the plot, but important for the overall ambience of the film by showing audiences the process by which Korean subjects such as Kim and Rin became proficient in Japanese. The school also serves as a metaphor for order and colonial stability. Despite the somber mood of the school, this scene is played with a distinctly light, humorous touch. In the schoolhouse, a young Korean boy is standing beside his desk reciting a story in Japanese about the life of the Japanese scholar Ninomiya Kinjiro:

Child: . . . taking over for his father [Ninomiya] became quite poor [*pimbo* (*sic*)] . . .

Teacher: Wait, that's *bimbo*, not *pimpo*.

Child: (stretching his neck out, sputtering) . . . *Bimbo*![64]

Native Korean speakers commonly experience difficulty distinguishing between "b" and "p" sounds in Japanese. This very short scene emphasizes several important points, the first of which is the importance of correct education. Japanese language education was seen by many Koreans as their only avenue for promotion and advancement under harsh colonial conditions. Education was not available to every Korean, but those who had access to it, like Hinatsu Eitaro, used it to advance themselves within the colonial system.[65] The Japanese encouraged Koreans to gain an education in order to advance up the social ladder. At the same time, many urbanized Japanese looked admiringly on the "simplicity" of their Korean brothers and sisters, as if to remind themselves of a preindustrial Japan whose traditions were all but extinct.

Suicide Troops of the Watchtower reminded modern Japanese audiences of the value of old traditions in much the same way as Japanese travel guides to Korea encouraged readers in Japan to "take up . . . daily practices of the peninsula" and lauded Korean families for maintaining their values "as the people of the interior of Japan lose their glorious familial customs."[66] In *Watchtower*, the subplot of Ryu promising his dying friend Kim that he will look after Kim's sister Eishuku is an example of Koreans maintaining strict values of loyalty. When Eishuku drops out of medical school after her brother is killed, Ryu proves that he is not only a loyal imperial subject, but also a loyal friend. Ryu even approaches Takatsu, the Japanese garrison commander, to enlist his aid in helping to keep Eishuku in college: "Takatsu-san, the more I think about it, the more I realize that there's no avoiding it—I've decided to sell my farmland. I'll use the money to pay for Kim Eishuku's tuition. . . . It was Kim's dying wish that I look out for her and if she quits school, his wish will be in vain. But even if I sell my land to pay for her school fees, she will probably refuse the money. Will you tell Sugi to tell her that she [Sugi] will pay for her tuition?"[67] Ryu's selfless virtue is reflected to some degree in all the loyal Korean subjects, including Kim, Eishuku, and Rin. Japanese audiences watching *Suicide Troops of the Watchtower* could rest assured that they need not "worry about the home front because Japanese/Korean solidarity was indeed solid!"[68]

The Japanization of Koreans did not stem from any humanistic motives but was mainly an "excuse to expand Japan's sphere of influence."[69] The inherent futility of trying to make Korean *kimchee* into Japanese *takuan* was ultimately symbolic of this impossibility, and the tensions that accompanied the attempt underscore representations of Korea in imperial Japanese film culture. Themes of interracial marriage, forced acquisition of Japanese surnames, "volunteer" military service, and others set the Korean experience apart from other areas of the Japanese empire. For Hae Young, the Korean director who directed films in Japan and Indonesia, Japanese assimilation—or imperialization—policies were not simply empty political slogans or film industry trends; they fundamentally altered his life and that of millions of other Koreans. These policies forced him to constantly redefine himself against the changing circumstances of Japanese empire before, during, and after Japan's colonial era.

Stranger than Paradise

Micronesia, the Philippines, French Indochina, Thailand, Burma, India, Malaysia, Indonesia, Sumatra, Java, Borneo, Celebes, New Guinea, and thousands of small islands made up what was loosely referred to in prewar Japan as the South Seas (Nanyo) or what was sometimes called the Southern Territories (Nanpo). The former term refers primarily to what used to be called the Marshall Islands and are now known as Micronesia. Japan received the official mandate to rule them in 1914, during the First World War, when it joined the war against Germany, which had annexed the islands in 1886.[70] Official rule notwithstanding, many Japanese explorers, settlers, and prostitutes had already actively worked in the area since the late 1880s. There is no clear agreement on when the first films of the South Seas were shown in Japan, but in all likelihood they were newsreels dating from around 1914.[71]

Interest in the South Seas was stimulated throughout the Taisho era, partly by popular songs such as "The Chieftain's Daughter," which portrayed a native woman lover (rabaa) on an island in the Marshalls. Japanese educational films made no attempt to distinguish any of the islands or peoples from each other, but instead created films with titles such as A South Seas Native Tours Tokyo (Nanyo dojin no Tokyo kenbutsu, 1915, Nikkatsu) and The State of South Sea Islands (Nanyo gunto no genkyo, 1926, Nanyocho).The individual islands and cultures that comprised Japan's South Seas ran together, spilling over into each other and creating an indistinguishable mass of white beaches, black-skinned natives, and palm trees in the Japanese imperialist imagination.[72] The hodgepodge of animals and natives that made up the comic book world of Dankichi Island discussed in Chapter Two reflected to some extent Japanese anxiety and ambiguity over the sheer geographic scope and cultural diversity of the South Seas. Most Japanese feature films set in the area never attempted to distinguish the individual countries or people within the region to any extent. The term South Seas itself suggests that it was far easier to use a kind of linguistic shorthand for a complex, multilayered area. More often than not, the South Seas were represented as erotic, dangerous, or sometimes merely absurd.

Karayuki-san

Karayuki-san[73] is just a word regularly used on the Shimabara peninsula. Kara is from Karatensho and signifies French Indochina, the Malaysian peninsula, Borneo, Sumatra, and Celebes. Yuki means "to go," and san is a suffix that we would use at the end of a title like doctor or soldier. Middle-school students naturally shorten it to Karayuki. Broadly speaking, it refers to women who went down south—women who went there to make money—it means prostitute.[74]

Japanese prostitutes made up part of the economic fabric of Southeast Asia since the late 1800s. The term karayuki or karagaeri referred to Japanese women, mainly from the Amakusa and Shimabara regions of Kyushu Island in Japan, who were either sold to brothels by their parents or chose to go to Southeast Asia to make money selling sex. These women returned to Japan from the southern islands deeply changed by their experiences abroad—some positively, most negatively. Japanese films such as Karayuki-san, the Making of a Prostitute (Karayukisan,

1975) and *Whoremonger* (*Zegen*, 1987) all take a look back at the brutal realities of the Japanese sex trade in Southeast Asia in the early twentieth century. At the same time, censorship laws barred filmmakers from explicitly representing sex or prostitution other than in the most vague terms.[75]

Karayuki-san (1937) was the first Japanese feature film to deal with the highly controversial issues of Japanese prejudice against returning prostitutes and children of miscegenetic relationships. The film recounts the story of Yuki, who after twelve years of living in Singapore as a prostitute returns to Shimabara with Anton, her mixed-blood son. Anton's father was an Englishman who went to Singapore to study geology but died before returning to England. Other than a brief reference, he is never mentioned again in the film. The relationship among Yuki, Anton, and the father is clearly a thorny subject—in one version of the script Yuki is only a guardian, who takes care of Anton at the request of his dying father. All of the film reviews, however, clearly understood that the boy is meant to be of mixed blood and that Yuki is his mother. One Japanese film reviewer wrote that Anton's father was a Dutchman named Kessman, which suggests that perhaps more than one version of this film was screened.[76]

In the film Yuki, Anton, and the other prostitutes are forced to live on the outskirts of town because of the intense envy and prejudice they encounter from the villagers. The South Seas returnees build a village on a hill outside of town, where they all live together in peace. Anton attends a local school and is regularly bullied by the other children. However, not once in the film do the other children tease Anton about his name, appearance, or behavior—they simply call him a prostitute from the South Seas. Anton becomes a stand-in victim for his mother. The school principal, unlike the children, discriminates against Anton for his race by denying his application for admission to the junior high school despite Anton's having excellent grades. Yuki and the others are hated and discriminated against for being prostitutes. Yuki hopes that by donating her money to build a town hall for the villagers, they will realize that she and her friends are still members of a community. She decides to treat the villagers to her home movies of the South Seas on the day of the town hall's dedication. However, when the mayor presents Anton with an honorary plaque of achievement, the villagers grow angry. In a move to avoid a conflict, the mayor orders that the film be shown.

Images of the South Seas cause a commotion in the audience. Native scenery and houses flash onscreen. A drunk yells, "Bet there's lotsa *karayuki* there!" (laughter) An animal chases a native up a palm tree. A drunk shouts, "Look, Oyuki's palace!" Anton nearly cries. (laughter) Two Malaysians haul fish tied to a log. A drunk shouts, "Okiku and Osugi's boyfriends!" A house on stilts. Someone shouts, "That's Okoto and Otama's 'v-i-l-l-a'!" (laughter) The light from the screen makes their faces look more menacing. More shouts. "Hey Anton! Wanna go back there?" "Yeah, go build a town hall for them South Sea niggers!" "An' get yerself a nigger plaque while yer at it!"[77]

The extreme racism and violence of this scene is unusual in Japanese cinema. Representations of the South Seas are indeed a threat to the villagers when they perceive that these different lifestyles are closer to them than they realize. The difference between a native's skin color and that of a Japanese is frequently invoked to suggest that the Japanese did not see Southeast Asians as racially similar to themselves as they had Koreans or Chinese. Likewise, those women or children who were associated with miscegenation and prostitution were certainly not to be celebrated, but rather scorned. As one Japanese character comments early in the film, prostitutes bear "the stench of long-necked foreigners!"[78] In 1937, when the film was released, Japanese film critic Ueda Ichiro praised *Karayuki-san* for its hard-hitting message, something he said Japan was not generally known for: "*Karayuki-san* is a film that brings a number of problems for the Japanese film industry. It goes without saying that Japanese films are very narrow in their scope . . . but recently these films have gradually been let in. It is an encouraging trend."[79]

Other critics agreed that the film was a step in the right direction for more realistic depictions of the social problems that accompanied the expansion of the Japanese empire, but they did not give the film high marks. One of the major criticisms dealt with the appearance of the leading star (and producer), Irie Takako. Almost every critic mentioned that her makeup was too perfect and that she was too beautiful to play a character who should have looked more "leathery," like she had suffered much more. In off-handed jabs aimed at both the star and the studio system, the reviewers suggested that unless the present system changed, Japanese film would always suffer from a lack of realism (presumably, just like Hollywood).[80]

Southern Winds II (*Zoku minami no kaze*, 1942) shows us that not all representations of the Karayuki or the South Seas were negative. In a very brief sequence from *Southern Winds II*, a prostitute named Otama is presented as a very stylish but lonely woman living by herself in a large Western-style house. Otama dresses in the latest foreign fashions and drinks imported tea from Hanoi. While the film never identifies the nature of Otama's work, one man calls her "Singapore Otama with red sleeve garters," a vague reference to the attire of servant girls in Japanese-style inns. Like Yuki in *Karayuki-san*, Otama was married to an elderly French man in Indochina. She explains that she married him only out of pity because he was dying and because she had no other way of supporting her aging mother. Otama has returned to Amakusa (in Kyushu) after her husband dies (we never learn his name) and leads a solitary life with her memories of Southeast Asia. She seems to have limited interaction with people in the village, yet there is nothing either in the narrative or the setting to indicate that she is the object of prejudice. Her life in the South Seas and since that time are presented as positive experiences to the viewer.

Flowering Port (*Hanasaku minato*, 1943) juxtaposes two very different representations of prostitutes. The first is Okano, the successful proprietor of a popular inn in a small town. The other is Setsuyo, an unemployed prostitute who is constantly berated by her father. The villagers judge these two women according to the material wealth, or lack of it, that the women have been able to accumulate and bring back from the South Seas. Early in the film Okano is presented as a local hero and a success story. The local policeman even tells her: "You are one of the most successful prostitutes on this island," an indirect reference to the fact that there are others in the community. Okano describes her situation as being the result of hard work and saving her money. We are never told exactly how Okano earned so much money, but the assumption is that she earned it working in an inn much like the one she now owns. Her success is clearly associated with the production of capital, something that she was capable of acquiring only in the South Seas. For Setsuyo, the other prostitute, the South Seas has produced a considerably different career path. She has nothing to show for her stay there and now spends her time on the beach, looking out to sea and wishing she could return. Her father, Kesaji, constantly scolds Setsuyo for being lazy and compares her to Okano:

> Setsuyo: I wanted to stay longer and bring back as much money as I could, but the Nihonjin-kai [Japanese organization] told me that all unemployed or unnecessary people had to return to the *Japanese home islands* . . . aah, I wish I could go back again!
>
> Keisaji: What would a fool like you do in the South Seas? Just look at the difference between you and Okano! You're both prostitutes, but you come back a good-for-nothing disgrace—I can't stand to look at you![81]

As in *Southern Winds II*, the characters are peripheral to the plot. They exist only as colorful landscape in the Japanese empire. The erotic nature of their work was not a subject that could be represented, and it would be years after the Pacific War ended before filmmakers produced films that dealt with the issues of sex and imperialist expansionism.

Tropical Intrigues

> Under the burning southern sun, thundering waves beat upon the white coastline. Through palm fronds rustling in the ocean breeze, the entire city of Kotabar comes into view. . . . A Chinese Communist in dark sunglasses hurries across the street. His menacing eyes glint behind his glasses. He

moves as if he were trailing someone. One by one, henchmen join him.
They move together in tandem. He stops on the corner and calmly smokes
a cigarette, never once taking his eyes off the Chinese store across the street
. . . they were dealing with the Japanese . . .[82]

The beautiful tropical scenery and lazy pace that epitomized the South Seas in
the Japanese imperialist imagination also had an ugly, dangerous side lurking
just beneath the surface. *Tiger of Malay* (*Marai no tora*, 1943) represented the
South Seas as a nest of gangsters, spies, and overseas Chinese Communists, a
place more notable for its menace than opportunity. The celluloid communists
of *Tiger of Malay* look and sound more like gangsters in a Hollywood B-movie
than Chinese Communists. The henchmen—all played by Japanese actors—
wear black fedoras draped rakishly over one eye and long Chinese robes. Their
boss wears either garish Chinese clothes or white Western-style suits with small
round-lens sunglasses. In this film, the villains are recognizably evil as much by
how they look as by what they do.

Throughout the film the thugs extort, beat, and kill innocent Japanese and
native victims all in the name of Western (British) colonialism. The British colonial authorities are the ones orchestrating the Chinese actions in an attempt
to "exterminate all the Japanese." Not only do the British machinations result
in the death of many Japanese, but when the Japanese try to file a formal com-
plaint, they are openly discriminated against. Finally, the murders of his sister
and other Japanese killed on the orders of the (white) colonial authorities incite
an otherwise "normal" Japanese, Tani Yutaka (Harimao), into committing the
hideous murder of a colonial official. Now a fugitive from the law, and bound
to the villains he seeks revenge on by the act of murder, Tani transforms himself
into Harimao, the Tiger of Malay.[83]

The story was first serialized as a novel in the 1940s in the popular magazine
Boys' Club, and the cartoonish representations of Chinese Communists in the
film betray the story's pulp origins. In contrast to the strong, pure image of the
Japanese hero (Harimao) and the entirely evil villains (the Communist Chinese),
Harimao's band of Malaysians (all played by Japanese actors in "brownface") are
complicated. In a scene reminiscent of *Suicide Troops of the Watchtower*, Harimao's men also are given to spontaneous dancing and singing. But nevertheless,
they are highly organized and their hideout becomes an impregnable fortress that
the colonial police can not even find.

Oyama Takashi, a film critic writing in 1943, immediately drew the connection
between Japan's South Seas and the Algerian Casbah in *Pepe le Moko*. "Nanyo's
unique customs and the massive crowd scenes in this picture are unlike anything
that has ever been done in Japanese film. In fact, there are few examples even in
foreign film. The closest that comes to mind would be the 'Casbah' in *Pepe le*

Ad proclaims the *Tiger of Malay* to be "Japan's first jungle action film!" (1943)

Moko. Compared with the French film, *Tiger of Malay* has more people, more action, and much more impact."[84] Oyama contends that the film's greatest appeal is in its "harmonious" blending of entertainment and propaganda. Postwar cultural historian Yamamoto Akira, remembering his impressions of seeing *Tiger of Malay* as a child, disagreed. "I saw it, but it didn't leave much of an impression. Singapore was beautiful, and I'd heard about the plight of Malaysian workers, but I was disappointed by the jungles, which weren't as good as those [I'd read about in] Nanyo Ichiro's books. This film was cheap compared with *Stanley and Livingstone* (1939) and *Swiss Family Robinson* (1940), which I saw in the summer of 1940. It was a hit only with children in the countryside who didn't have many chances to see foreign films."[85]

Tiger of Malay was a successful film. Produced by Daiei (the third largest production studio in Japan), it supported a large budget, was shot both on location in Singapore and on a large set on the Daiei back lot in Tokyo, and employed hundreds of extras. The reviews were not stellar, but industry records show that it made a profit.[86] *Tiger of Malay*, and other films like it, held an appeal for Japanese audiences that similar fare from the West did not—they addressed topics of specific concern to imperial Japanese audiences. Their stories took place entirely within the Japanese-controlled space of the South Seas. Critics like Yamamoto would claim that other films were perhaps better produced but not as enjoyable to watch.

The film's producers presented the process of Japanese empire-building in Southeast Asia in their own way, as the opening title cards for *Tiger of Malay* indicate: "Autumn 1932, the city of Kotabar, British Malay. Disrupted by the Manchurian Incident, overseas Chinese Communists and their henchmen are manipulated by the British Colonial Government's strategy to boycott Japanese goods. They are extorting good overseas Chinese and instigating riots throughout the land."[87] Japan's expansion into the South Seas is recounted through a combination of newsreel footage and title cards—the withdrawal from the League of Nations, the China Incident, the Tripartite Treaty, and the beginning of the Pacific War. The violently anti-Western, anti-imperialist overtones in these films share much in common with Nazi Kolonialfilms and Italian films under fascism.

Japanese filmmakers presented the presence of their imperial navy in the South Seas as a stabilizing force there to protect "good and loyal Japanese subjects" from the various villains (communists and colonist thugs included). This underscored the Japanese notion that people of the South Seas were childlike and needed assistance to be liberated. *Fire on that Flag!* (*Ano hata o ute*, 1944) was a Japanese feature film produced jointly by Japanese and Philippine film personnel and shot entirely in the Philippines. The story begins with the fall of the American defense and the start of the Japanese occupation of Manila. The film emphasizes the American retreat from the Philippines as evidence of America's insincerity and natural cowardice—a broken promise to the Filipinos.

One of the most fascinating elements in this film is that much of the dialogue is in English, considered by Japanese at that time to be the language of the enemy. This was a fairly daring move at a time, when it was not uncommon in the Japanese film press to find articles decrying even the sound of English as offensive to the ears. English loanwords were being purged from Japanese advertising, popular music, sports, and even private use, such as personal names. In the official life of the Philippines and other former colonies of English-speaking nations, the fact that the common language of communication was not Japanese was a vexing daily reality and only served to highlight the extreme vagaries of the South Seas.

Thugs looting local businesses and evil Western imperialists lining their pockets with the people's money exemplify the lawlessness that the imperial Japanese army first targets in the film. One night soon after the arrival of the Japanese occupation army, two Filipino thieves attempt to rob an old woman. She screams, and almost immediately afterward Japanese soldiers catch the two thieves. A little boy who witnesses the event tells his friends about how heroic the Japanese soldiers were: "You should have seen it! The Japanese were real fast and brave, too! The robbers took off and got pretty far. One of them was really big. But he wasn't any match for those Japanese soldiers! The bad guys ran like the wind but wound up getting caught on the corner. [A Japanese] held his rifle like this (pretends to thrust a rifle) and the robbers surrendered!" The first boy runs over to Sergeant Ikejima and works up enough courage to extend his hand and ask for a handshake. Ikejima complies, and then all of the children want to meet him and shake his hand. Ikejima goes over and explains the previous night's events to the group of Filipino children who anxiously hang on his every word:

> Boy: . . . we were afraid of [Japanese] soldiers before, but not now.
> Ikejima: If you are good boys and good girls, you need not be afraid. You *are* good boys and girls, aren't you?
> Children: Yes sir!
> Ikejima: . . . that's good.

Ikejima is clearly portrayed as a big-brother figure, and his admonishments are not harsh but firm in tone. While talking with the children in the square, Ikejima notices a young boy, Tony, who is crippled, watching the others from his porch. We have learned in an earlier scene that Tony's injury was caused by the cowardly, unjust Americans. When the villagers were lining up to send off the retreating American forces, Tony noticed a Japanese propaganda leaflet caught in a tree. As it fell, he reached out to snatch it and was hit by a speeding American-made sedan that did not even slow down. The Americans, in other words, are responsible for turning Tony's healthy body into a useless appendage. Although this scene is more subdued than those in *Tiger of Malay*, the plot line recalls the cold-blooded killing of Tani's younger sister at the hands of the overseas Chinese Communists. Ikejima and the children approach Tony, and Ikejima explains why the American soldiers acted as they did: "They were bad men and deserved to be punished. You see Tony, all bad men, no matter how clever they are, are caught in the end. You pity them, but you don't have to be afraid of them because they're weaklings and haven't the moral support. In short, they have no guts. That's why they're afraid of hard work and they chose the easiest way. But the easiest way isn't the easiest way at all. It turns out to be the hardest way in the end, see?" The dialogue focuses on reason and logic, calling to mind many of the American propaganda leaflets dropped on Japan in the 1940s that encouraged their readers to "rethink" their actions before it was too late. Teaching young children to admire and respect the occupying Japanese forces headed off any possibility of future criminal behavior and served as a stern reminder of the price to be paid for rebellious behavior.

For filmmaker Abe Yutaka, who worked for several years in Hollywood under the name Jack Abe, filming in a predominantly English environment was almost a homecoming.[88] Abe's participation in the Japanese occupation of the Philippines provided him with the chance to rediscover his Hollywood film roots because Abe gained access there to nearly 3,000 confiscated Hollywood films. It is possible that Abe's exposure to these films was one influence on *Fire on That*

Flag!, especially *How Green Was My Valley*, which introduced him to pan-focus and supplied the subplot of the little boy Tony who was crippled by fleeing American soldiers.[89]

Funny Foreigners

For most Japanese, the South Seas represented the polar opposite of Japanese reality. From its people and customs, to its climate and topography, the South Seas appeared so different that it often was the butt of Japanese jokes. Essentially, Japanese audiences assumed a backwardness there that was fundamentally different from the backwardness they felt characterized China. At least with the Chinese and Koreans of East Asia, Japan could claim a shared race and culture. When it came to the various races of Southeast Asia, however, many Japanese thought the population was as foreign, perhaps even more so than that of the West. Films encouraged caution when dealing with these lesser people, because one never knew when they might turn violent.

Southeast Asian difference was and continues to be a source of great humor for the Japanese. The film *Southern Winds II* is an excellent example—it tells the story of two Japanese who will do anything for money, but who wind up being swindled out of astronomical sums by two shifty Cambodians in a phony religious scam. Kaseda, a Japanese adventurer, becomes friends with a Cambodian named Shen Chip (played by the comic Japanese character actor Saito Tatsuo), who tells him about a secret river of gold in the jungles of Cambodia. The two set out for the river and once they find it, Kaseda fills his pockets with gold sifted out of the river bed just before he contracts malaria and forgets everything. But Kaseda is lured by more than just the prospect of gold. He is led to believe that the leader of the local cult to which Shen Chip belongs and which is also connected to the gold, is in fact the illegitimate son of the famous Meiji era Japanese general, Saigo Takamori. This is why Kaseda and Munekata bring the two to Tokyo and initially treat them with such deference. In terms of genre, *South Winds II* is not strictly a comedy per se, but its representation of non-Japanese characters depends on Japanese assumptions about the people and cultures of the South Seas as being comic, odd, and irretrievably foreign.[90]

Shen agrees to tell Kaseda where the river is on condition that Kaseda take Shen and Nekku Soi (played by Japanese actor Kawamura Reikichi), the cult's leader, to Tokyo and establish a branch there. Kaseda lets his friend Munekata in on the deal, and Munekata invests his wealthy family's estate in the church. Once in Japan, the Japanese immigration office and the police detain Nekku Soi and Shen Chip on suspicion of having dangerous beliefs, and they soon uncover that Nekku Soi is too young to be related to Saigo in any way. Things finally come to a head in the following scene, when Kaseda explains the scam to Munekata, with Shen and Nekku, now in custody, in the room.

K: This guy [Shen] doesn't even know what's true and what's an illusion! He really believes his own lies! I can't figure him out!

S: But I figure myself out well. I am messenger of god.

K: Messenger? Why did you make up all those stories about Saigo? What was that?

S: I deen't do that! I be tricked by Nekku Soi. This man *bad*! Just look! (Nekku Soi grinds a finger into his nostril, absently looking at the ceiling, checks it, and continues.)

M: Didn't you know he's too young to be Saigo's son?

K: How was I supposed to know? I can't tell how old people with skin that black are! Even the police got a laugh at that! (to Shen) You'd better remember your promise.

S: Promise . . . ah . . . hmm . . . what that?

K: The mining rights to Kongkamenam River! What do you think?

S: Ah, fine, fine. I can give you ANY-time. (puzzled) But . . . why?

K: Wh-? To mine for gold, what else? How do you think we'll get his money back?

S: Gold? Oh no, none of that there.

K: Wh-what d'ya mean 'none of that?' You and I found some, didn't we!

S: Illusion! Only illusion. (wags finger) tsk, tsk, tsk . . . you same like me . . . illusion, true . . . you make same!

K: Whaaat illusion? Look, we went on a tough journey didn't we?

S: True! We go Laos from Daso into mountains: true! You stay at chief's house, we go Kongkamenam River: true!

K: Well, then, all of it's true!

S: You . . . me . . . scoop river water: true! But only sand . . .

K: Wait a minute, I really *did* find gold. I remember . . . chunks this big . . .

S: Illusion! Only illusion. You get malaria, *very* bad. Sometimes in sleep at chief's house you say such things. But then pass out . . . big fever . . . barf everywhere. I think maybe you die . . . very pity . . . Malaria bring such big fever.

K: T-Then you took advantage of me! You tricked me! And I trusted you!

S: (angrily) I deen't trick! *You* out of you mind!

K: Out of my . . . ? Why you little son of a— (Kaseda grabs Shen violently)

S: No angry, No angry! All for god, all for Hong Tai Kyo. (Praying) Tonrong Saya . . .

The comic timing in this scene is reminiscent of traditional comic narratives such as *rakugo* and *manzai*. Stylistically, *manzai* stands out for its rapid-fire exchange of dialogue between the two principals—the *boke* (straight man) and the *tsukomi* (comic foil)—each feed the other their lines to bring the brisk conversation around to a predictable punch line. The punch line usually depends on puns, wordplay, and physical slapstick to sell the joke. As in traditional *manzai*, this scene has a *boke* (Kaseda) and a *tsukomi* (Shen), and the humor is fueled to a large degree on mimicry and imitation. Few films of this period blend the concept of the foreign/er so naturally into the comic rhythm of the narrative. Shen Chip successfully takes advantage of two Japanese who should know better. The fact that he successfully makes off with a bundle in cash sets this storyline apart from the typical fare.[91]

Saito Tatsuo's performance in brownface,[92] buck teeth, native clothes, excessive gestures and linguistic foibles identify him as an instantly recognizable southern type. Film magazine readers were aware of the fact that Saito had actually lived in Singapore for many years from the time he was a teenager, a fact that contributes to his believability as a non-Japanese. Saito plays the part for laughs; by this time he was already an experienced character actor who had starred in dozens of comedies, often playing characters of different ethnicities. An article in the wartime film magazine *Film* stated that Saito was careful to "bring complete authenticity to his role." The article continued its praise of Saito, raving that even his incantations and prayers were spoken in actual Malaysian.[93] The fact that Saito's character is supposed to be Cambodian seems to have escaped the notice of both the reviewer and Saito. Saito told the author he had remade his false buck teeth twice so that they were "just right," and his skirt was a gift from his father, who had purchased it while in the South Seas. Even his hat (which hardly appears in the film) was a treasured possession from those years. All of this illustrates that he did not simply ad-lib his performance but crafted a carefully thought-out representation.[94]

The performances of Shen Chip and Nekku Soi highlight the duality in Japanese representations of the South Seas and its people, as both funny and weird. When Shen Chip and Nekku Soi return to Munekata's house from the police station, the maid, seeing Shen Chip's face, screams and drops her tray. After the scene is over, Munekata calls the maid to show them to their rooms, but a different maid appears. When Munekata asks where the first maid went, he is told: "Oh, she's right here." Munekata sees her obvious aversion at Shen Chip's appearance and says: "So you brought a bodyguard, did you?" As Shen Chip passes her, he gives a lecherous laugh that sends the young maid screaming down the hall. As these sequences were not in the original script, we can only assume they were added sometime during the shooting. They intriguingly illustrate representations of the foreign, especially the South Seas, in the Japanese imperialist imagination.[95]

Returning to Munekata and Kaseda, it is interesting to note that as late as 1942 these hucksters could still find a place onscreen. Fleecing people of their money is not something that a proper imperial Japanese subject would do, which may explain why the perpetrators in this film had to be foreign. Still, after the scam is revealed, Munekata and Kaseda are depicted as being sadder but wiser, and slightly more suspect of foreign hucksters. But rather than stay in Japan and work to pay back the money, the two decide to return to Cambodia. Again, the imperial space of the South Seas is represented as both haven and place of last resort. For it is here that the two can go to forget, rather than remember, the Japanese home islands: "Let's find ourselves a better place. Let's go south . . . down to the Nanyo. We'll let the southern blood flowing through our veins go wild. I tell you, if we stick around here, we're finished. C'mon, let's make our dreams come true. They say if life knocks you down seven times, get up eight."[96]

Japanese films represented the South Seas as being as geographically distant from the Japanese home islands as it was topographically different. Symbolized by descriptions of torrid heat, unusual (to Japanese) plants, and sickness, the South Seas was at once the Southern paradise that Munekata seeks in *Southern Winds II* as well as the torrid inferno infested with con men and malaria that Kaseda experienced. The landscape of the South Seas was an imperial hinterland whose film representations found parallels in Japanese literature that also emphasized the region's blistering heat and native corporeality.[97]

CHAPTER FOUR

Competing Empires in
Transnational Asia

Japanese ideologues and filmmakers realized that ethnic and cultural divisions within Japan's empire were not the only challenges facing its campaign for cultural hegemony in Asia; competition with the United States, Germany, France, and other nations with long-held ambitions in Asia were a constant source of concern. Japan gained and maintained its Asian empire vis-à-vis two different Western colonial forces. On the one side, Japan clashed with Hollywood for market domination of Asia, and the ascendancy of Japanese imperial power in Asia threatened American film dominance there, leading to a film war. Japan initially restricted access to Asian markets under its control by censoring or banning American films and finally placed a comprehensive embargo on all Hollywood films. These actions eventually led to a clandestine meeting between representatives of the Japanese film industry, Hollywood, and the U.S. Department of Commerce to discuss the opening of Japan's imperial markets to American films.

At the same time Japan attempted to maintain its Asian hegemony through legislation, distribution, and exhibition during its alliance with Nazi Germany and Fascist Italy in the early 1940s. Film scholarship often neglects such areas as distribution and exhibition, but examining how audience tastes were both perceived and shaped on the local level reveals what a tremendous impact they had on imperial Japanese film culture. Even before Pearl Harbor and the embargo of American films, Japanese distributors and exhibitors were importing colonial-themed films from Italy, Germany, and France, suggesting that the notion of empire sold films. At a time when imperial Japanese rhetoric was growing increasingly anti-Western, the popularity of foreign colonial films in Japan should shock us. What this illustrates, however, is that imperial Japanese film culture did not exist in isolation but was part of an international fraternity of film imperialists. Even if the Japanese government officially supported the importation of Axis films in a show of solidarity, distributors still had to select which films the market would support. That they chose colonial-themed films over other genres was a business decision that suggests the distributors considered more than official policy; they knew there was an audience for films about empire.

Empire-Building: Hollywood vs. Imperial Japan

Imperial Japan's eventual domination of Asia's film markets was never a foregone conclusion. From the 1910s, Hollywood film studios in Asia were actively displacing French film companies such as Lumière and Pathé to establish their own vast distribution network, which covered every major Asian territory from Japan to India. Asia's markets were much smaller than those of Great Britain, Europe, or Canada, but Asian markets were not insignificant, and Hollywood maintained its presence there because throughout the 1920s Hollywood grew ever more dependant on the revenue from overseas receipts. By the late 1920s most of the world's leading nations recognized the importance of film in communicating political and ideological power. With the coming of sound, nations across the globe increasingly saw films as potent expressions of ideological *and* literal power.

The maxim that "film followed the flag" expressed the interdependency of film and government. Hollywood had the "structural, entrepreneurial, and financial advantages of U.S. firms, combined with the experience gained from catering to a diverse domestic audience."[1] For many in the American film industry, the marriage of government and industry seemed not only divine but foreordained. As early as 1918 American film trades were talking about the inevitability of America dominating world film:

> We shall have to work for some sort of cooperative scheme by which each nation will supply the world the things which it is best suited to produce. Just as America is called upon to feed the world because of our abundance of all sorts of foodstuffs, so it will naturally fall to our lot to supply the bulk of the motion pictures as this is one of our national specialties.[2]

When *The Moving Picture World* published this blurb, few Americans probably saw their film industry as an empire. The unshakable belief that U.S. expansion into and domination of the world's film markets was an inalienable American right was, however, exactly what empire was all about. As the Japanese empire steadily expanded militarily into most of East Asia, Hollywood aggressively occupied Asia's film markets. With the exception of the Japanese domestic market, Hollywood films accounted for 50 to 90 percent of all the films screened in Asia through the 1930s.[3] It is no wonder, then, that the leading American film companies referred to themselves as film empires possessing film colonies in smaller markets. Media critics have noted that even the spinning globe logos used by film companies throughout the world indicate evidence of the expansionist aspirations of film studios.[4]

United Artists (UA), one of America's largest film distribution companies, is perhaps exemplary; after initially setting up a branch office in Tokyo, UA soon spread to Shanghai, Calcutta, Singapore, the Philippines, and Jakarta.[5] United Artists executives wanted to keep in close contact with the markets in Asia and chose Tokyo for two reasons—first, it was the most lucrative film market in Asia, and second, it had the worst film piracy record in all of Asia.[6]

America's domestic market virtually assured its film industry of recouping production costs, thereby relieving it of dependence on income from overseas markets initially. This tremendous advantage enabled Hollywood to undersell competitors in such Asian markets as the Dutch East Indies, Ceylon, or the Philippines. In this way, America managed to consolidate its share of local markets by dumping its films at rental rates far below those in other territories.[7]

By 1931 it became clear for two reasons that imperial Japan and Hollywood were on a collision course. The Manchurian Incident brought Hollywood face to face with the possible loss of lucrative film markets in Asia (including the domestic Japanese market) due to Japan's expanding military presence. And the coming of American talking movies to Japan forced many in the film industry and government there to pay attention to what Hollywood was saying. Both sides viewed the other as a potentially hostile force in what each considered their own market. While American film companies acted as if expansion into the world's film market was their right, leaders in imperial Japan increasingly saw this sort of expansionism as a threat that posed potentially lethal industrial and ideological problems. Thus any move on the part of the Japanese film industry to displace Hollywood from the markets of Asia—either independently or in cooperation with the government—was couched in nationalistic language that justified its actions as necessary to protect or liberate Asia from Western domination. After the China Incident of 1937, Japanese film journals decried the ideological threat that American films posed in such articles as "The Influence of American Films in Asia." Japanese filmmakers grew increasingly worried that Hollywood might have already won the hearts and minds of its Asian brothers and sisters.[8] Their first response was to underplay the influence of the Americans on local Asian audiences.

In 1940 Tsuji Hisaichi, Shanghai Communications Division attaché with the Imperial Japanese Army, cautioned Japanese readers not to overestimate the influence of American film in China:

> The distance between Western films and the average people is immense. The first problem is that we can't understand the language. Even with Chinese subtitles, the illiterate are left on their own. Of course far more

Shanghai Chinese speak English than we Japanese . . . and many more people in China understand English and see Western films. But their influence is exceedingly superficial . . . and on that point the Chinese people most stubbornly protect their own ethnic character. Western films merely float around the top far from the [cultural] base.[9]

Tsuji and other Japanese film critics thought that Chinese audiences wanted only meaningless entertainment films, the type Hollywood was known for, and thought they resisted films that required deeper thought. Japanese critics were puzzled why Asian audiences would prefer films with Caucasian actors to ones with Japanese. Initially, Japanese critics became self-critical. Tsuji even went so far as to say that Japanese films contained "nothing you could remotely call influence" on the Chinese, and that they lacked "any appeal whatsoever" for the Chinese. But Japanese critics soon reasoned that Asian audiences could differentiate among Japanese films by recognizing their educational value. Japanese filmmakers produced films to educate the Chinese on how to understand, hence appreciate, Japanese culture, thinking that this would beat Hollywood without resorting to making the same low-brow entertainment films the Americans were.[10]

Understanding each other's culture was a key concept to the initial construction of Japan's new film order. Tsuji concluded that the Chinese lacked interest in Japanese films because the Japanese in turn refused to watch Chinese films, calling them "worthless."[11] Even if Tsuji's position is an overstatement, it establishes the fact that regardless of their supposed lack of popularity, at least some Chinese audiences were watching Japanese films. Japanese distributors working with government officials took the position that it was crucial to expose the Chinese populace to as many Japanese films as possible. To that end Japanese traveling projection units spread across the Chinese interior, Shanghai, and Hong Kong, screening Japanese films. By the 1940s more Japanese films were shown in China than films from any other nation. Although the target audience for these films was primarily Japanese, Chinese did attend screenings, and their presence cannot be entirely ascribed to simple coercion.[12]

Each Japanese military victory in Asia significantly diminished the U.S. film presence in that area, which spurred worries in the U.S. government about what adverse ideological effects Japan's increased film activities might have on their Chinese allies. After the fall of Hong Kong in 1941, the Japanese immediately began screening Japanese films to Chinese audiences. A 1943 U.S. consular report took very seriously the effect of such Japanese films, warning:

We need not be gifted with very active imaginations to form a fair idea of the extent of the impact of such pictures on the mind of a half-illiterate dockyard worker or shop-runner for whom an infrequent visit to a "garden of the electric shadows" is an important adventure in an otherwise very restricted life. And for the Chinese of education and sensitivity, who had put so much faith in his Western learning and his Western friends, the total effect of the constantly repeated shock could only have been just that much more profound.[13]

The situation in China was not that different from other markets such as Singapore, Thailand, and the Philippines, where U.S. films dominated until the early 1940s.[14] Japan had protected its domestic film market against foreign domination through strict import and censorship restrictions starting in the late teens, which partially explains why American films never enjoyed the same percentage of market penetration in Japan as they did elsewhere in Asia. The Japanese government also actively banned American films and lodged formal complaints with the American government to forbid the exhibition of Hollywood films deemed offensive to Japanese national pride.

Japanese were not alone in their fear of a Hollywood takeover. Chinese film critics like Hong Sheng also wrote about the American film threat: "Shall we wait until American capital has completely taken over the Chinese film industry? Will imperialism not try to maintain its position by attempting to crush the rebellious spirit of those who are oppressed? Will we even remember how to make anti-imperialist films, or films about social revolution, or even patriotic films? Should this happen, we will have sealed our own fate and delivered the fatal weapon into another's hands. Each theater will be a site where slaves are raised, and one meekly defers to their domination and oppression."[15]

Government and film industry leaders in Japan recognized a link between Hollywood's presence in Asia—especially China—and its Orientalist representations of Asia onscreen. By the 1930s Hollywood took an increasingly paternal, expansionist interest in China as illustrated by such films as *Oil for the Lamps of China* (1935), *The Good Earth* (1937), and *The Dragon Seed* (1944).[16] *Oil for the Lamps of China* is especially intriguing because it illustrates how easily narratives about American business expanding into China blended with Hollywood's own sense of Manifest Destiny to rule the world's film markets. Based on the best-selling 1934 novel by Alice Tisdale Hobart, *Oil for the Lamps* is set almost entirely in China and tells the story of a large American oil conglomerate that demands absolute loyalty from its employees. In the opening scene a group of American oil salesmen are completing their training in New York. Their instructor gives them some final advice before being sending them to China, concisely explaining the purpose of their mission: "The company is sending you out to China to dispel the darkness of centuries with the light of a new era; oil for the lamps of China, gentlemen—American oil. Helping to build a great corporation . . . extend the frontier of civilization is a great ideal. You will have hardships, you will encounter dangers and you will be thwarted time and time again by foreign traditions and the logic of the Orient. Your ideals must remain progressive, American. But you must learn to think like a Chinese."[17]

Here we see how close the language of Japan's and Hollywood's competing imperialisms in Asia truly was. Japanese construction films like *Vow in the Desert* (1940) use exactly the same metaphors of light and darkness to explain the imperial landscape. *Oil for the Lamps of China* associates progress with modernity and casts (Chinese) tradition as either mysterious or regressive. In the film, American oil salesmen are backed by a company that functions as a substitute for the nation. The company code becomes a mantra repeated throughout this film: "the company takes care of its own." But in actuality, the company proves to be heartless. It betrays the protagonist's trust on several occasions despite the fact that he sacrifices his wife's health and even his child's life for the company. Whereas the book offers a scathing indictment of the oil industry, the film reduces its social criticism to one man's struggle against adversity (in China as well as within American corporate culture).

Film Threats into Film War

Friction between Japan and Hollywood came to a head in 1937 when Japan levied import restrictions on American films both in the domestic Japanese market and all of its imperial possessions. In one year the number of American films imported into Japan dropped by half, from 295 films in 1937 to 144 films in 1938.[18] This move angered both the Motion Picture Producers and Distributors Association (MPPDA) and the U.S. government. American consular records reveal meetings among several representatives from MPPDA, a United States consul general, and several Japanese government officials in an undisclosed location in Tokyo. The Americans asked the Japanese whether they felt a "sense of danger" over what might happen to them should they continue to ban American film products from Asia. The Americans handed the Japanese authorities an ultimatum that might have been taken straight from any Hollywood gangster film.

> Almost every plot must have a villain, and American producers find it difficult to discover a suitable nationality for such villains, encountering violent opposition which sometimes results in the exclusion or boycott of films with consequent financial losses . . . so that for the present a disproportionately large percentage of movie villains and characters arousing feelings of resentment are American. Should the producing companies decide that some one country is determined to rule them out entirely so that resentment as to villains from that particular country would not diminish the financial returns of their films, they might consider it an opportunity.[19]

In what amounted to little more than thinly veiled film blackmail, the Americans threatened to flood the world film markets with negative representations of Japan if they did not concede and reopen their markets to American films. This was no small threat. The Japanese fully realized the great power American film had to create and sway public opinion both domestically and internationally. One only had to remember the devastating worldwide effect that Hollywood's cycle of anti-Hun films produced during World War I had had on Germany for decades after the war ended.[20]

In 1939, one year and a half after the ban, Japanese distributors ran out of their stockpile of unreleased foreign films, and domestic Japanese film production had dwindled to the point that it could not produce enough to meet the growing audience demand throughout the empire. This paucity resulted in a temporary lifting of the film ban that allowed seventy American films into Japan. Japan also increased its imports from Germany and Manchuria (Manei) to help offset its dependence on Hollywood and placed strict import quotas on American films that would remain in place until the bombing of Pearl Harbor. The Japanese military's well-organized attack on December 7th was followed by sweeping victories throughout Asia. Japanese authorities, flush with victory, promptly banned the screening of American films in nearly all of the territories under their control.[21]

American reaction was equally swift. Making good on their threat four years earlier, Hollywood produced film after film that cast Japanese as the villains. Adding insult to injury, Japanese and Japanese-American actors were bypassed for playing these Japanese roles in favor of ethnic Chinese, Korean, and even Latino actors. Hollywood reissued older films that were often recut to reflect the current wartime mood.[22] One prominent example occurred in 1942 when Columbia decided to re-release Frank Capra's film adaptation of the popular James Hilton novel *Lost Horizon*. In 1937, when the film was originally released, the opening titles had read: "Our story starts in the wartorn Chinese city of Baskul, where Robert Conway has been sent to evacuate ninety white people before they are butchered in a local revolution . . . Baskul—the night of March 10, 1935." When Columbia re-released the film in 1942, producers changed the film's title to *The Lost Horizon of Shangri La*, a reference to a statement by Franklin D. Roosevelt who had claimed that the Doolittle bombing raids on Tokyo had originated from this fictitious Asian location. Further, the opening titles were rewritten entirely changing the film's historical setting and the antagonists: "The story starts in the wartorn Chinese city of Baskul, beset by the invaders from Japan, where Robert Conway has been sent to evacuate ninety white people before they are butchered by the Japanese hordes . . . Baskul—the night of July 7, 1937."[23] Not only did the producers change the ethnicity of the antagonists from Chinese revolutionaries to Japanese "hordes," but they also matched the date to coincide with the Japanese attack at the Marco Polo Bridge, or what is commonly known as the China

Incident. In this fascinating instance we can see a clear example of the ideological weight that film as a weapon can wield.[24]

If the war effort in either country was successful, it was due in part to the ability of that nation to read into the larger war many smaller personal wars in which individuals and industries had a personal investment. Hollywood supported America's war effort precisely because patriotism dovetailed with personal interest. Declining revenues from the spectacular losses of Hollywood's world markets in Europe, Asia, and South America prompted Hollywood to "go to war" making anti-Nazi films two years before the U.S. government actually declared war. Hollywood was a reciprocal structure that, much like imperial Japanese film culture, depended on and received participation from all levels of the industry. People working in the industry knew this and made jokes about their ambivalent political attitudes.

> It is stories, roles, dramatic artifices, which tyrannize Hollywood's attention, not goods or crops or machines. And this preoccupation with the fanciful must tend to blur perceptions of the real. When Mussolini's legions marched into Ethiopia . . . a producer was asked by a breathless friend, "Have you heard any late news?" To which that child of Hollywood replied hotly, "Yeah, Italy just banned *Marie Antoinette!*"[25]

Regardless of whether its collective motivations were private or national, Hollywood's reactions to the loss of its markets in Europe and Asia was as serious as a declaration of war. "Film war" became a catchphrase that seized the imagination of critics and filmmakers on both sides of the Pacific. Film people routinely compared the coming war to the process of filmmaking itself. This film-as-war metaphor is still common today. Actor Charlton Heston remarked: "Directing a picture, especially a large picture with physical dimensions of some size, is like landing a division on a hostile beach. It requires the same attention to communications, preparation, transportation, alternate choices, weather, and luck."[26] Some of America's leading directors, including William Wyler, John Ford, John Huston, and Frank Capra, flourished in the military, where they applied their extensive experience in handling large groups of people to achieve military goals.

Many filmmakers in Japan and America firmly believed that each new technological development was a breakthrough that could possibly turn the tide of the war. French cultural critic Paul Virilio cites an increase in the use of color films during World War II, citing their development in Germany the direct result of acts of "logistical piracy." Nazi Propaganda Minister Joseph Goebbels deeply involved himself in the German film industry. He banned the showing of the first German film in Agfacolor, entitled *Women are Better Diplomats (Frauen sind doch bessere diplomaten,* 1941), on the grounds that the color was depressing and of wretched quality. The vibrant Technicolor found in such American films

as *Gone with the Wind* (1939) also wielded a tremendous impact on Nazi administrators and eventually led to drastic improvements in Germany's domestic
color-process Agfacolor.[27] Even from these few examples, it is clear that political
and military leaders were concerned not only with film narratives but also film
style. Leaders such as Goebbels were aware that the look of a film was a reflection
of the nation's might.

Filmmakers in Japan and America watched the other side's films whenever they
managed to capture them.[28] Director Ozu Yasujiro and longtime cameraman Atsuta Hiroshi recalled watching *Gone with the Wind*, *Rebecca* (1940), *Northwest
Passage* (1940), *How Green was My Valley* (1941), and *The Little Foxes* (1941) while
stationed with the army in Singapore. In a 1947 interview, Ozu claimed that
the high production values of those films was a barometer of America's national
might: "Some of the films I enjoyed most were William Wyler's *The Westerner*,
Wuthering Heights, John Ford's *Grapes of Wrath*, and *Tobacco Road*. Those directors hadn't lost their touch even in wartime. Perhaps that's only natural, but it
made quite an impression on us. Even their national policy [propaganda] films
were better. Watching *Fantasia*, I became worried, thinking to myself, 'This is
bad.' It was then that I realized what a terribly awesome foe we were fighting."[29]

On the other side of the Pacific, the U.S. government recruited Frank Capra
to produce a series of films for military personnel to clarify America's war goals
and educate soldiers as to the causes of the war. In preparation, Capra watched
hours of captured Japanese films, and he incorporated footage from them into his
documentary series *Why We Fight*. One of these was the Japanese feature film
Chocolate and Soldiers (*Chokoretto to heitai*, 1939), which tells the story of a father
who is sent to fight at the Chinese front and collects discarded chocolate wrappers
to mail to his son in Japan. Near the end of the film, the Japanese father is shot
by an unseen [Chinese] sniper while reaching for a chocolate wrapper for his
son. The effect is reminiscent of the final scene in *All Quiet on the Western Front*
(1930), but after seeing this film Capra said: "We can't beat this kind of thing.
We make a film like that maybe once in a decade. We haven't got the actors."[30]
Ironically, it was precisely the sort of film that Hollywood studios were known for
that had informed this style of Japanese filmmaking. Japanese filmmakers had
learned to know their enemy quite well.

While Japanese ideologues found it comparatively easy to demonize the An-
glo-American enemies in their propaganda campaigns, it was much harder to
explain official collaboration with Nazi Germany and Fascist Italy. Cutting Hollywood out of Asia did not result in the complete disappearance of Western faces
on Asian screens. European films began to replace American ones as imperial
Japan turned to its Axis allies to supplement domestic film production and as a
possible source of new markets.

Axis Film Culture in Imperial Japan

Muto Tomio, a former high-ranking Japanese civil servant in the Manchukuo government, was an economic delegate in attendance at a meeting in Rome in 1936 between future Manchurian Motion Picture Company Studio Chief Amakasu Masahiko and Fascist Italian dictator Benito Mussolini. "Amakasu [speaking about the Italians] said, *'What a miserable race this is. If we don't make our move now, then we'll have to suffer through three weeks of sightseeing in Italy. Let's put them in their place here and now.'* Amakasu, who was only five feet three inches tall walked right up to the giant six-foot one-inch Mussolini and stopped abruptly in front of him. For an instant, the two glared at each other. Amakasu faced Mussolini as if to say, *'Don't fuck with us! Manchuria doesn't just belong to a bunch of Chinamen.'* Mussolini smiled a wordless reply as if to say, *'My apologies.'*"[31]

Muto's musings on this event twenty years after the fact raises more questions than it answers. Not the least of these touches on the motivations and justifications that the Axis nations used to explain their alliance to their home populations. If Axis solidarity was based, as historians suggest, mainly on political, economic, or military needs, then what, if any, room existed for possible cultural exchange and interaction that was not simply superficial or negligible?[32] What common ideologies could be employed as a basis for cultural exchange? Fundamental ethnic differences and the downright racism clearly present in the above anecdote question the very possibility for meaningful cultural exchange among imperial Japan and its Axis allies. They support assumptions that such divisions made Hitler's regime "embarrassed by their alliance with one of the *Untermenschen* (literally sub-humans)" and led the Japanese to either ignore or express contempt for their German and Italian allies."[33]

However strained interactions among the Axis nations may have been, nevertheless they were more than just empty ceremonies. They underscored the common need among allies to recognize one another's national sovereignty, thereby legitimizing their prestige as both regimes and empires. Increasingly from the 1930s onward, Axis nations exhibited an almost absolute faith in the ideological power of film, which, like stockpiled weapons, had "no other reason for existence than to be brandished and quantified in public [as] active elements of ideological conquest."[34] Axis film cultures shared ideological tendencies, including an obsession with the discourse of racial purity, imperialist expansionism, and a belief in the ability of film to create (or destroy) national prestige on a mass level.[35] The interactions among Axis film cultures were imperfect and sometimes failed, but they help us understand the attempt to create an Axis film culture.

Imperial Japan's participation in Axis film on the governmental, industrial, and commercial levels illuminates the comprehensive cultural interaction among the Axis powers across a variety of sociopolitical spheres. Imperial Japan proactively cooperated with Fascist Italy and Nazi Germany as an active member of the Axis, with widespread official and unofficial interaction on nearly every level. While such interactions did not lead to the successful formation of a collective "fascist" identity, they suggest that Japan needed global partners and feared isolation, but was never fully comfortable with its allies.[36] Axis interaction included film legislation and censorship, distribution and exhibition practices, and production and critical reception.

The first type of interaction, on the government level, was evident in the imperial Japanese government's study of German and Italian film legislation, which formed the basis of Japan's first comprehensive film law in 1939. Early attempts to define a collective Axis identity were also manifest in the creation of anti-Anglo-American film blocs that censored or banned films offensive to Axis nations in response to economic and ideological threats from the United States and Great Britain.

The distribution and marketing of Axis films fostered a second type of interaction in which the programming and exhibition of Axis films at specialized venues such as the Venice International Film Festival attempted to create new distribution routes and markets in order to compensate for those that Hollywood denied them. Amidst the rising anti-Western/Pan-Asian rhetoric of the period between the world wars, distributors in imperial Japan had to find a way for audiences to distinguish between friendly Western Axis nations and "dangerous" Western nations such as Britain and the United States. Paradoxically, they chose to emphasize Japan's shared colonial identity with its Axis allies.

The third type of interaction can be seen by examining the short, troubled history of the production and reception of the Japanese/German coproduction *The New Earth* (1936). This reveals not only the common ideologies and basic fissures between Japan and Germany, but also the backlash expressed by Japanese film journalists against German director Arnold Fanck's misrepresentation of their culture. The critical failure of this film brought to the surface culturally exclusive attitudes, with each side criticizing the other. However, these attitudes were not the result of any East/West split, as critics then argued, but rather they indicated the broader impossibility of mediating ideological differences within the Axis, to which the failed Italian/German coproduction *Condottieri* attests.

Legislating Solidarity

Japan's 1939 Film Law placed nearly every aspect of film production under the scrutiny of the Japanese government. It has been well documented that the law was partly inspired by Nazi film legislation, but the impetus for it can be traced back years before either the Japan/Germany Cultural Pact (1938) or even the Tripartite Pact (1940).[37] Factions within the Japanese government and the Japanese film industry studied official film policies in Great Britain, France, Fascist Italy, and particularly Nazi Germany for ways to consolidate and modernize Japan's film industry into an export-driven international enterprise.[38] The earliest studies of national film legislation in Japan reveal that Japanese policymakers were chiefly concerned with two issues: the possible adverse effects that representations of foreign customs might have on the Japanese populace (especially women and children), and the possibility of "incorrect" interpretations of Japan in foreign films that might damage the national dignity of the Japanese empire.[39]

In 1933 the 64th House Assembly in Japan introduced the "Proposal Concerning a National Policy for Films" to enable greater government control of the Japanese film industry and remove "various obstacles that interfere with its development."[40] Passed within one week after its introduction, this proposal became the impetus for the creation the following year of the Cabinet Film Regulatory Council, chaired by Minister of Home Affairs Yamamoto Tatsuo. The council was formed just two weeks after Nazi Germany implemented the Lichtspielgesetz, or Film Law, the mission of which was to "regulate film and legislate other important issues relating to film."[41] Concerned that Japan would be left behind other industrial nations like Germany, council members and politicians intently scrutinized the German film legislation in order to enact a series of film-related laws that would eventually become incorporated into Japan's Film Law.

Although Japanese lawmakers drafted the Film Law using an international perspective, it was much broader in scope than its German counterpart. The implementation of strict rules over the import and export of films, measures for pre- and postproduction censorship, and the compulsory registration of all film industry personnel reveals the extent to which the Japanese government was aware of film's power to articulate a domestic national identity as well as the need to officially regulate these representations. The Japanese film law required that all film personnel pass mandatory examinations in order to be licensed to work in the industry. Some examination questions had little or nothing to do with the applicant's technical expertise but were designed to gauge their ideological leanings. Applicants were evaluated in the following five areas: knowledge of standard Japanese, knowledge of national history, level of "national common sense" (kokumin joshiki), general knowledge of film, and personality. Anyone who failed to answer any question satisfactorily was denied a license and effectively shut out of the industry.[42]

The Japanese Film Law shared in common with the German film law the wholesale importation of Nazi anti-Semitic ideology and the notion of a "Jewish problem." It may seem odd to find a discussion of a "Jewish problem" in a nation with no domestic Jewish population, but this rhetoric, in combination with the

examination system component of the Japanese Film Law, clearly functioned as
a useful mechanism by which the government could—and did—effectively ex-
clude any elements deemed undesirable from the film industry. Postwar Japanese
film critics have argued that government and film industry leaders had to adapt
the notion of a "Jewish problem" to apply to what were called "ideological Jews"
within the culture industry. These people were considered a threat to the nation
and thus targeted for re-education or eradication.[43]

Japanese lawmakers also looked to Italian film laws for guidance in drafting
their domestic film law. The Italian law was established in 1934, the same year
that Germany passed its film law and Japan created the Cabinet Film Regulatory
Council. Italy's law was a comprehensive cultural law that regulated every form
of Italian media, including publishing, theatre, and film. Film critic Yamada
Eikichi wrote in 1940: "The Italian Fascists treat film as a vital organ by which
national policy is achieved and there is much that we can learn from the solid
results that they have been accumulating."[44] Particularly appealing to Yamada
was the model of a state-run film industry like Italy's LUCE, which he saw as a
successful symbiosis between the needs of the state and private industry. LUCE's
structure resembled a combination of Hollywood-style vertical integration with
Japanese national policy corporations like the Japanese-run Manchurian Motion
Picture Studios (Manei).

A common feature of all the film laws under discussion here is the strong
desire to legislate the government's right to censor or ban any films deemed injuri-
ous to the national dignity. This was extended to include protection against asper-
sions by one's ideological allies and those under their control. Censorship policies
proliferated after the advent of sound film, but it is important to recall that silent
film also was a source of great concern to the world's film-producing nations that
often generated diplomatic protests that could result in the altering or shelving
of problematic films.[45] Such exchanges were not isolated. Nations used whatever
political clout they possessed to attempt to control the reception of their national
image abroad. Hollywood, as the largest producer and distributor of films internationally, wielded great influence over which races would be portrayed as villains
to its global audience. America's adversaries formed loose alliances or film blocs
partially in response to the threat of being demonized as villains in American
films as well as to prevent being shut out of potentially lucrative markets. Such
alliances were the start of what I call cooperative film censorship, which were
developed in order to counteract the totalizing influence of Hollywood.[46]

American consular and trade reports of the time indicate that Japan actively
offered and received support from other Axis nations censoring films that negatively represented their respective national images. At a time when the national
borders of the Axis nations were rapidly expanding, political alliances shifted with

startling fluidity and sometimes resulted in diplomatically awkward situations. One year before the Nazi occupation of France, in early 1939, the French Embassy in Japan requested that the Japanese government ban a German film titled *The Accursed Ship*. Japan replied that it would "exercise great caution" in censoring the film but stopped short of an all-out ban so as to avoid offending their Nazi allies. The Japanese government granted the request only out of "consideration for the French action in cutting anti-Japanese propaganda out of Chinese films shown in France."[47]

After official promotion of intra-Axis cultural ties commenced in 1937, with the Japan-German Cultural Film Exchange Agreement, Japanese officials found even more reason to honor requests from their Axis allies to censor or ban negative film representations.[48] A string of such requests was immediately submitted by the Nazis to the Japanese government, which led to the prohibition of *Grand Illusion* (*La Grande Illusion*, 1937, France), *Confessions of a Nazi Spy* (1939, U.S.), and *The Great Dictator* (1940, U.S.).[49] Nor were feature films the only target of cooperative censorship requests. Newsreels were a primary target: William Randolph Hearst's *March of Time* series appears the most frequently in Japanese film censorship records. The following is a partial list of official actions taken by Japanese film censors with regard to various installments of *March of Time* from 1936 to 1937:

> March of Time, No. 16 (RKO-Radio). Total rejection. Part deals with assassination of a Japanese minister, and Japanese censor objects to anything dealing with political assassination or murder.
>
> March of Time, No. 21 (RKO-Radio). Relating to students at Princeton claiming bonus [as Veterans of Future Wars]. Delete subtitle "Cannon fodder"; delete word "nuts"—Rewritten title to read: "At Princeton University three undergraduates generate an idea."
>
> March of Time, No. 23 (RKO-Radio). All scenes of Mussolini and Ramsay MacDonald deleted.[50]

These records clearly indicate that Japanese censors consciously excised scenes or entirely banned problematic representations of imperial Japan as well as those of Fascist Italy. The extent of Japanese zealousness in preserving its imperial image is further evidenced by its requests for similar consideration from even small nations such as Lithuania and the Philippines. Lithuania appeared anxious to oblige Japan by promptly banning the Soviet-produced *The Days of Volotsayew* (*Volochayevskiye dni*, 1937), which represented the Japanese presence in Asia as aggression.[51] Apparently most offensive to the Japanese were nonauthorized representations of Japan's war in China. Perhaps out of deference to the substantial local Japanese population, film censors in the Philippines aggressively removed scenes of Japanese soldiers cruelly shooting Chinese civilians in the back from the feature films *Thunder in the Orient* (1939) and *Fight for Peace* (1939), five full years before the Japanese military occupied their islands.[52]

Imperial Japan's requests were respected by industrialized and developing nations alike and its power to influence the production and dissemination of cultural products worldwide should not be underestimated. As a leading industrialized film-producing empire and an Axis member nation, Japan could not be entirely ignored, even by Hollywood. Producers in Hollywood were less afraid of diplomatic pressure than the possible loss of lucrative foreign markets. In September 1937 their worst nightmares were realized when Japan placed a comprehensive embargo on all U.S. feature films and froze all U.S. assets throughout its empire.[53] This was a serious blow to Hollywood's hegemony in Asia, and American film journalists at the time were swift to place Japan's action within the larger context of the Axis alliance: "Up to the outbreak of the Sino-Japanese War, some 35 percent of the films shown in Japan were from Hollywood. However, Hollywood began to lose ground with the enactment of the German-Italian-Japanese "cultural" and economic pact, and eventually all Hollywood imports were barred. Control of the motion picture in Japan now completes control by and in the tri-cornered German-Italian-Japanese Alliance. The Nazis effected control several years ago, and Italy established a Government film monopoly on January 1st."[54]

Exhibition Markets

Shut out of many of the largest film markets, government and film industry leaders in the Axis nations proactively searched for new markets and new venues in which to sell their films while promoting their ideologies. The idea of exploiting nascent colonial film markets appealed in principle to government ideologues, but in reality those markets often lacked the necessary infrastructure and offered only minimal financial return. Axis-sponsored film festivals, which included the Venice International Film Festival from 1934 to 1944, promised greater visibility for high-profile films and possible new film markets.

Since at least the 1910s, Japanese filmmakers were enamored by the idea of Japan becoming a nation that exported film, and they believed this was a necessary step to raise the level of the Japanese film industry, as well as that of the nation, to an international standard. Kawakita Nagamasa, president of Towa Film and a major distributor of European films in Japan, was one of the most vocal exponents of such internationalization policies. Kawakita was one of very few Japanese with a practical working knowledge of the European film industry. The Axis alliance facilitated opportunities to use his extensive connections in the German film industry to help Japan break into the international market.

Kawakita initially intended to make his mark in production through a series of coproductions based on several successful European multilanguage-version films that were produced in the early 1930s in Europe. The international success of German producer Erich Pommer encouraged Kawakita to develop a Japanese/German coproduction entitled *The New Earth* (*Atarashiki tsuchi*, 1936).[55] *The New Earth* was meant to publicize Japan's New Order in Asia to the world at a time when few outside the Axis formally recognized it. Ultimately the film's failure to pioneer an international market or to start a new genre of Japanese export films led Kawakita to search for other strategies, such as the nascent international film festival circuit.[56]

In 1932 General Secretary Luciano De Feo of Italy's Educational Cinema Institute established the Venice International Film Festival for three purposes: to introduce Italians to world film, promote Italian film internationally, and spur the tourism industry. At its inception, the festival organizers wanted to remain politically and artistically independent of the government and consciously programmed artistically important films regardless of their national origin. Just two years later, in 1934, with the implementation of the Italian Film and Theater Law (Il cinematographo e il teatro nella legislazione fascsita), the state took control of the festival and required festival organizers to select films according to their political ideology rather than artistic merit. Eventually, this naturally led to the preferential treatment of films produced in Axis nations (especially Hitler's Germany and Franco's Spain). Such treatment, however, did not necessary translate into winning the festival's highest honors.

At the 1937 festival, Kawakita entered two Japanese feature films in the competition: *Children of the Storm* (*Kaze no naka no kodomo*, 1937) and *Moon Over the Ruins* (*Kojo no tsuki*, 1937).[57] Although the Japanese entries received unprecedented international critical acclaim, Japan's status as an Axis nation was not, by itself, enough to ensure victory; both films lost to Julien Duvivier's *Dance Program* (*Un Carnet du Bal*, 1937). Undaunted, Kawakita returned the next year and entered *Five Scouts* (*Gonin no sekkohei*, 1938), a war film set in China that glorified the Japanese military presence there. Contrary to all expectations, *Five Scouts* won the Popular Culture Prize, becoming the first Japanese film to win a major award at a prestigious international film festival—a full thirteen years before journalists would make the very same claim for Kurosawa Akira's *Rashomon*.[58]

This success, however, did not necessarily lead to greater Axis cultural interaction. Despite the fact that all the Japanese film entries were favorably reviewed in the Italian film press, there is no record of whether they were ever sold or exhibited outside Italy's main urban centers.[59] However, that same year the German film *Olympia* (1938) and the Italian film *Luciano Serra, Pilot* (*Luciano Serra pilota*, 1938), jointly won the Mussolini Prize and were widely released in Japan to great commercial and critical success. Japanese film critics particularly praised *Olympia* for its outstanding camerawork and rhythmic editing. The film's enthusiastic reception in Japan can be explained in part by its being feted at Venice as well as by its having been produced by Leni Riefenstahl, whose *Triumph of the Will* (*Triumph des Willens*, 1934) was also well received in Japan.

Certainly, the fact that Benito Mussolini's son Vittorio directed *Luciano Serra, Pilot* was an important draw to Japanese audiences, but equally so was the Futurist-influenced man-as-machine imagery associated with the film. Mechanical/technological themes also resonated more generally in a similar obsession with Japan's own empire-building activities in Asia. Moreover, Italy's Ethiopia was an exotic colonial setting that appealed to many imperial Japanese subjects.[60] Italian imperial epics were familiar to older Japanese filmgoers, who remembered early epics like *Quo Vadis?* (1912) and *Cabiria* (1914), both of which espoused imperialist rhetoric in their idealization of the Roman empire. Those films laid the foundation for the box-office success of 1930s Italian colonial epics like *Condottieri* (1936, Italy/Germany), *Scipio the African* (*Scipione L'Africano*, 1938), and *Cardinal Messias* (*Abuna Messias*, 1939), which revisited the myth of empire at the same time that contemporary films like *Luciano Serra, Pilot* rearticulated the notion of *impero*, or a hereditary birthright to imperial expansionism, in a modern context.[61] Italy's colonial films did not represent the same sort of grand imperial adventures as Alexander Korda's British colonial epics did; rather, they revealed what one historian has called the natural expression of Italy's "imperialistic nature," an attitude grounded in traditions inexorably linked to the Roman empire.[62]

The colonial film genre thus represented another link among Axis film cultures that assumed that in the New Order certain nations were rulers by birthright and others were to be ruled. Japanese distributors chose to market Italian colonial films in the Japanese film market because they were aware of a pre-existing audience taste for exotic settings and characters that had been in great demand since the silent era. Colonial films produced in Axis nations also shared narrative and stylistic links with the Foreign Legion film (or desert film) genre that presented the world from the viewpoint of the colonizer. Japanese film critics of the 1930s were keenly aware of the differences among colonial regimes, and they often compared and contrasted colonial worldviews represented in such films as *Beau Geste* (1926, U.S.), *Morocco* (1930, U.S.), or *Le grande jeu* (1934, France) with those of imperial Japan. Such comparisons led film critics like Shibata Yoshio to the uncomfortable conclusion that despite its moral superiority, the Japanese empire failed to seduce the imaginations of a generation of Japanese youths as effectively and completely as foreign colonial films had.

> Japanese often debate whether or not Foreign Legion films, marked by Feyder's human experiments or Duvivier's excessive atmosphere, are dreams or reality. When you think of it, urban Japanese know more about the Foreign

Legion in Morocco than they do about their own border patrol guards in Manchuria. Japanese urbanites are a sad lot. Imperialist capitalist expansionists may scoff at Manchuria's Royal Road, but how do those nations justify their Foreign Legions terrorizing local people at gunpoint?[63]

Naturalizing or legitimating the expansion into and seizure of foreign lands was an essential part of any imperial project and Japanese film distributors marketed the common experience of empire-building as a trope of modernity to which most urban Japanese could relate.[64] It may come as no surprise, then, that in the wake of the embargo of Hollywood films and within the context of mutually exclusive Axis doctrines of racial and cultural purity, Japanese distributors were left with little to exploit from Axis films other than the shared experience of empire.

One way that Japanese film distributors manufactured a resonance between Japanese audiences and imported Axis films was through the creation of film titles that could universalize, naturalize, and ultimately popularize the concept of expansion. The Japanese release title for *Luciano Serra, Pilot* was *Sora yukaba* or "If we should go to the skies," a direct reference to the popular early twentieth-century war song "Umi yukaba" or "If we should go to sea."[65] Japanese distributors marketed this film about Fascist Italian pilots fighting a colonial war in Africa by aesthetically linking Italian fascism and the Japanese martial spirit. This provided domestic audiences with a readily understandable metaphor that did not destabilize Japanese ideology.[66] The careful selection of film titles was not just an ideological ploy but made good business sense as well.

The appeal of the colonial modern was so thorough that even in the 1940s, when Japanese Pan-Asianist rhetoric was almost entirely articulated as an anti-Western anticolonial denunciation, audiences for imported colonial films never entirely disappeared. The enduring appeal of the colonial film genre may lie in the ambivalence inherent in its narratives, which could be reappropriated across cultures and political regimes for entirely different purposes.[67]

One purpose included instructing Japanese film audiences about their Axis allies. Japanese film critic Tsumura Hideo found the film style and narrative of Italian colonial films inferior to those of Germany, France, or even America. Nevertheless, he argued: "They let those of us in a corner of East Asia, far from southern Europe, imagine what the conditions in the film culture of our Axis Allies were like."[68] And they also provided viewers with insights into Italian politics and social conditions. Tsumura thought that in these films one could measure the pulse of a nation—even if the films were not accurate reflections of that nation. Tsumura also found in these imperfect films a model that domestic production of nationalistic (*kokka shugiteki*) documentary films could productively adapt for the representation of Japan's "development" of the neocolonial space of Manchuria.[69]

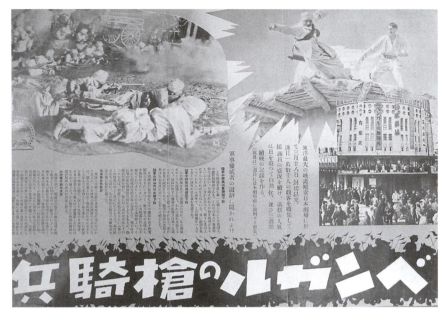

Ad campaign for *Lives of a Bengal Lancer* (1938) emphasized the film's popularity
with Japanese audiences (inset, right) and its support by military officials.

Like Italian colonial films, Nazi colonial films such as *La Habanera* (1937),
Uncle Krüger (*Ohm Krüger*, 1941), and *Carl Peters* (1941) were also imported into
Japan, but they were marketed in a significantly different manner than Italian
films. [70] One illustrative example can be found in the Japanese marketing of
Uncle Krüger. *Uncle Krüger*, coscripted by Nazi Propaganda Minister Joseph
Goebbels, was to have been the definitive German exposé of "British/Jewish imperialism" in South Africa. The film stylishly retells the history of the Boer War
(1899–1902) through a mixture of historical fact, fiction, and highly anti-British
caricature. Veteran film and stage actor Emil Jannings played an idealized version of "Uncle" Paulus Krüger, president of the Transvaal and leader of the Boers
during the Boer War, as a solitary hero who stands up to the British and the Jews.
In contradisctinction to the film's representation of Cecil Rhodes, Krüger appears
as the ideal melding of "Boer, citizen, and patriarch." By emphasizing Krüger's
opposition to British colonial rule, his usefulness as a model for wartime Nazi
Germans becomes even more potent. The Afrikaner State under Krüger appears
as a precursor to the order and efficiency of the Nazi regime. Krüger's defeat and
loss of power is highlighted in the film as a noble and lamentable failure in the
face of insurmountable odds.

Japanese distributors advertised the film as a warning of the horrors of British
imperialism, using a tag line that could have been written for the Greater East

Asian Co-Prosperity Sphere: "THIS!! is the real British Empire that hides behind a mask of chivalry. Judge for yourselves this page in the history of British imperial aggression painted red with the blood of women and children slaughtered in the name of Queen Victoria in a corner of South Africa!!" Film stills accompanying this advertisement show prison camps encircled with barbed wire, filled with Boer refugees, and looking eerily similar to Nazi concentration camps. The film's themes of anticapitalism and anti-Semitism are driven home by projecting onto the British enemy precisely the sort of ethnic prejudices behind Nazi violence against the Jews in Germany.[71]

Japanese film critics discussed *Uncle Krüger* less for its intrinsic value as entertainment than for its ideological merit. Ozuka Kyoichi suggested that Japanese filmmakers and, by extension, Japanese audiences should watch the film in order to learn valuable lessons from the Nazis. In a 1944 article published in the leading Japanese film journal, *Film Criticism*, entitled "What I Expect from Films That Encourage Hate for the Enemy," Ozuka praised *Uncle Krüger* for setting the standard for future anti-Western Japanese films:

> *Uncle Krüger's* crude tone and extremely obvious mode of expression has a certain kind of appeal, a filmic beauty, as a German anti-enemy film, which I believe is one of its strengths. There is more to its filmic expressiveness than simply the richness of the actors. While I do not advocate that every Japanese film encourage hatred for the enemy in that way, it does seem only natural that explicit anti-enemy films should overflow with raw energy.[72]

Many of the same critics who only a few years earlier had lavished praise on Jannings's performances in *Varieté* (1925, E. W. DuPont), *Faust* (1926, F. W. Murnau), *The Blue Angel* (*Der blaue angel*, 1930, Josef von Sternberg), and *The Last Command* (1928, Josef von Sternberg) were now cool to his work in *Ohm Krüger*, some even calling his acting "overblown." [73] What becomes clear was a realization that simply tailoring foreign films to suit the tastes of Japanese audiences was not enough. Producers like Kawakita Nagamasa and Nagata Masaichi concluded that true multilateral understanding and cooperation had to be created through international coproductions. Kawakita was the first to move into this area with a big-budget, high-profile German-Japanese coproduction on Japanese agricultural colonies in Manchuria.

Coproductions and Co-Prosperity

Even before ratification of the Anti-Comintern Pact in 1936, imperial Japan, Nazi Germany, and Fascist Italy were anxious to publicly demonstrate that their impending alliance was based on real solidarity and not merely military, political, and economic expediency. A flurry of high-profile official and unofficial cultural exchanges resulted in some particularly intriguing film projects. In Germany, Leni Riefenstahl directed and edited the film coverage of the 1936 Olympics, which prominently featured the participation of the German, Italian, and Japanese athletic teams and would become a highly acclaimed international success when it was released two years later. In Italy, in 1936, film director Giacomo Gentilomo and German director Luis Trenker gathered together a German and Italian crew to shoot the superproduction *Condottieri* on location with a cast of thousands. *Condottieri* told the story of the rebellion of Giovanni di Medici's knights against Cesare Borgia during Borgia's bid to unify Renaissance Italy. The problems surrounding the production of *Condottieri* and the disagreements between the film's directors led to two separate releases of Italian and German versions of the film and foreshadowed the fate of similar coproductions. *Condottieri* was pulled from German theaters only one week after its release, when censors lodged formal complaints regarding the film's representation of religion.

The same year, in Japan, producer Kawakita Nagamasa invited German filmmaker Arnold Fanck and his cameraman Richard Angst to Tokyo to begin production on *The New Earth*. Fanck, who had achieved international fame for directing a series of critically acclaimed *berg* or mountain films and for his discovery of a young actress-turned-director named Leni Riefenstahl, began writing the script for what he claimed would be the first film to "capture the true essence" of Japan. Kawakita explained in an interview with Japan's largest film journal that the title of the film referred to more than Manchuria: "We have named this film *The New Earth* and it certainly is new earth both for ourselves and for the Japanese film industry. We pray that this new earth will be fertile soil that gives rise to many different forms of plants and will eventually bear magnificent fruit."[74] Fanck said that he wanted to make a film that would satisfy the expectations of Western audiences, an approach that seemed entirely consistent with Kawakita's desire to create a new type of Japanese export film for international distribution.

The New Earth tells the story of a young Japanese university student, Teruo, who returns to Japan after spending several years, supported financially by his wealthy Japanese stepfather, studying modern agriculture in Germany. In Germany, Teruo falls in love with Gelda, whom he brings back to Japan in order to convince his stepfather (played by Hayakawa Sessue) to release him from his betrothal to his stepsister Mitsuko. Aboard a steamship headed home, claustrophobically decorated with Nazi and Japanese flags, cherry blossom branches, and Japanese lanterns, Teruo truly seems reluctant to marry his stepsister Mitsuko. But Teruo's desire for Gelda after arriving in Tokyo is never represented as much more than a flirtation with the West. In a conversation with Gelda, he gradually discovers that what he really wants is to farm his own land in Manchuria. During this sequence in the film, Teruo and Gelda are framed on opposite sides of a globe as they discuss the creation of Japan's new empire:

Gelda and Teruo are literally a world away from each other in *The New Earth* (1937).

Teruo: I'm Japanese and want to live for Japan. Manchuria is twice the size of Germany and Japan, with an abundance of land more than enough to support a large population . . . that is, if it is properly cultivated. But first we must bring order and peace to the land. That is Japan's intention. Japan must construct a nation on this land. And we believe that the construction of a nation not only requires real men, but also real women. We don't need any who have been raised as spoiled dolls.

As this scene suggests, Japan's new earth of Manchuria will be settled by a new breed of imperial subject—an ideal hybridization of rural and urban—epitomized by Teruo. Teruo's return to Japan is presented as a dilemma, expressed by his seeming reluctance to make a decisive choice between the traditional (Mitsuko) and the modern (Gelda). Initially, his temptation comes less from an infatuation with the West, as his ambiguous feelings for Gelda may indicate, than from a general desire for urban, modern life itself. Teruo's confusion is visualized most dramatically in a sequence set in a modern Tokyo nightclub, where, flanked by a loud jazz band, he is served sake by a Japanese hostess and red wine by a Caucasian. He first drinks the wine, but when he drinks the sake, the blaring jazz soundtrack is instantly replaced by a pastoral symphony, and Teruo nods approvingly to the Japanese hostess. As Teruo looks at the Caucasian hostess, her face dissolves into a montage of indiscriminant shots of dancing and drinking, set to an increasingly faint jazz melody. Unable to find his roots in the urban decadence of either Berlin or Tokyo, Teruo returns to his parents' farm, where he experiences an epiphany. Plunging his hands deep into the rice paddy, he intently smells a handful of earth as his father smiles approvingly and says: "It's good earth but . . . it's become very old." Teruo decides to remain in Japan and marry Mitsuko, and Gelda returns to Germany. In the final scene, Teruo and Mitsuko and their baby son have immigrated to Manchuria, where Teruo happily farms the "new earth" with a new tractor, under the protective gaze of an imperial Japanese soldier.

Upon his arrival in Japan, Fanck personally selected Itami Mansaku, father of the late film director Itami Juzo (*Tampopo, A Taxing Woman*), to coscript the film and serve as a consultant, based on the latter's work in period films. Ironically, Itami's films had until then humorously criticized precisely those sorts of government ideologies that Fanck wanted to propagate, and Itami was determined to prevent the film from becoming either an Orientalist travelogue or outright Nazi propaganda.[75] Itami's fears proved to be well founded, for it soon became clear that Fanck's vision of the "true" Japan bore very little resemblance to the one in which most Japanese lived.[76] Fanck's obsession with exterior shots of the natural beauty of Japan's countryside contrasted with his slipshod, uneven representation of the urban metropolises of Tokyo and Osaka. Similarly, Fanck's treatment of his actors, in particular sixteen-year-old Hara Setsuko, who played the role of Mitsuko, is indicative of the sort of matter-of-fact racism that Fanck would later be accused of. In a lecture to the Japan Motion Picture Foundation, Fanck stated that he had Hara speak her lines in German "in her own style," which he suggested was grammatically incorrect but produced an "inexpressible charm for us [Germans] when we heard her pronouncing the German language with a foreign accent. In other words, she made a better impression than if she had spoken German fluently."[77]

Fanck once said that he liked Japanese actors because he did not have to talk to them; they "just understood" what he wanted.[78] Considering that most of Fanck's work until that time was in the mountain film genre, where human actors are often relegated to a secondary status below the iconic status of natural settings, which were the true protagonists, his fascination with natural landscapes and relative inattention towards his actors does not seem unusual. But Fanck's attitude created friction between himself and the Japanese crew, who felt that Fanck's vision of Japan and the Japanese was demeaning as well as symptomatic of Western stereotypes. This friction eventually led the Japanese producer to demand that the film be reshot in two separate release versions, a "German version" shot and edited by Fanck and an "international version" edited and partially reshot by Itami. This only complicated matters. Some critics complained that Itami's version was not Japanese enough, while others argued that it was more "inconsistent, conceptual, and unfocused," but still felt like a Japanese film, where Fanck's definitely did not.[79]

Japanese critics were disturbed by Fanck's apparently indiscriminate application of Nazi ideology (particularly regarding blood and earth) to the Japanese case. At first glance Fanck's representation of the Japanese soil as almost divine seem an apt interpretation of the importance of land to Japan's farmers, who were then struggling with crop failure and crushing poverty. This was a familiar topic with Japanese left-wing "tendency film" filmmakers of the late 1920s and 1930s. Within two years, Uchida Tomu would begin filming *Earth* (*Tsuchi*, 1939), which was based on Nagatsuka Takashi's novel of the destitute lives of Meiji-era farmers, and after that Toyoda Shiro would produce *Ohinata Village* (*Ohinata mura*, 1940), a film about the mass immigration of a Japanese agricultural colony to Manchuria.[80] It is not difficult to see how Fanck and his crew might have linked Manchuria, and the emotional investment in land that it represented, with the Nazi aesthetic of soil. But the implication that Nazi aesthetics were interchangeable with Japanese aesthetics profoundly disturbed the Japanese press.

> The scenery that appeared onscreen was definitely Japanese, but the way it was shown was Western [*bata kusai*], exhibitionist, and queer. Holding up a Buddhist *manji* to resemble a Nazi swastika, he [Fanck] portrayed temples as if they were the sole repository of the Japanese spirit. Great Buddhist statues were treated as if they wielded an absolute power. He applied the Nazi spirit of self-sacrifice indiscriminately to the Yamato spirit . . . while claiming to praise the samurai spirit he was really praising the German spirit. He openly recognized Manchuria, but it is Germany that is requiring this New Order.[81]

Stylistically, *The New Earth* looks like a German film. Even its opening sequence recalls the opening of *Triumph of the Will*, where the camera moves through the mists of ages, gradually revealing the mythic islands of Japan through the clouds. Fanck's use of graphic matches between a Nazi swastika and a Buddhist *manji*, which was roundly criticized in the Japanese press, was simply an attempt to apply his visual style to Japanese material in order to articulate a Fascist aesthetics linking Nazi and Japanese iconography. Ironically, it was precisely the exterior shots of the countryside of Japan for which Japanese critics reserved their greatest praise and criticism. They praised their technical beauty but were disappointed at Fanck's inability to see Japan's "true essence" as being anything more than picturesque representations of cherry blossoms and Mt. Fuji. Certainly, Orientalist film representations of Japan were nothing new. Japanese audiences had endured similarly exotic images from Hollywood *and* Germany for decades.[82] But when seen in the light of fostering Japanese-German goodwill, *The New Earth* seemed to question the very possibility of mutual understanding among Axis nations.

Japanese film critic Iwasaki Akira suggested that the fault was not entirely that of Fanck or his crew: "It is almost an impossible task for anybody to describe proportionally and properly a complex country like Japan, which contains all of the complications and contradictions that result from the juxtaposition and harmony of the past and the present, East and West, nature and modern science." Understood in this context, Fanck's inability was symptomatic of a universal problem facing any "foreigner, however understanding and sympathetic" who similarly attempted to represent Japan.[83] Iwasaki's language may be diplomatic, but his critique is clear: the film was a failure not because of any insurmountable cultural divisions between East and West, but rather due to the impossibility of the Germans' understanding the Japanese experience of modernity. The same argument might have been made about the production of *Condottieri*, which was also plagued with similarly fatal intercultural misunderstandings, but in which no East/West division could be blamed for the breakdown among Axis allies.

Iwasaki's cultural exclusivist attitude can be understood within the context of a history of indignity over what many Japanese felt were repeatedly patronizing misrepresentations of Japan by the West. Ironically, however, it was also at this time that the Japanese film industry was similarly Orientalizing other Asian races under the auspices of building a new order in East Asia, one to be led by the Japanese and ruled with mutual understanding and goodwill. Japanese representations of bilateral goodwill towards their Asian brothers were no more legitimate than Fanck's vision of a "pure" Japanese ally.[84]

With all the noise of the great debate in the Japanese film press over German misrepresentations of contemporary Japan in *The New Earth*, the subplot of Manchuria as Japan's new earth was almost ignored. Critics were far more upset by continuity mistakes, such as Fanck's inexplicably editing shots of Osaka's Hankyu Department Store with shots of downtown Tokyo, than they were by the theme of a Japanese return to a nativist past, not in the Japanese countryside but rather in the semicolonial space of Manchuria. Only critic and screenwriter Sawamura Tsutomu speculated on what possible political effects the setting of the story in Manchuria might have on the film's marketability in non-Axis territories:

> At the end of the film Teruo and Mitsuko leave the narrow rice fields of Japan to go to Manchuria where, under the protection and peace guaranteed by the Japanese army, they joyously plough the earth of a new continent with a tractor. This is one of the most important themes of the film. But won't showing this be a problem in countries that do not officially recognize Manchuria?[85]

The completion of the film and the controversy over it did not create any of the political problems Sawamura anticipated, but it did spark a boom of interest in Nazi cultural policy and filmmaking in Japan.[86] It also led to numerous translations of articles and monographs, such as director Karl Ritter's "Theory of Nazi Film Aesthetics," and the publication of original essays by influential film critics offering detailed discussions of how the German system might best be adapted for use in Japan.[87] *The New Earth* was not a box-office failure in Japan or Germany, but after failing to live up to expectations, its international marketing campaigns (the most ambitious ever planned for a Japanese film until then) had to be drastically scaled down.[88] Given the large production budget, the high-profile cast, and official backing by both governments, it would have been difficult, if not impossible, for *The New Earth* to ever have lived up to the hype.

CHAPTER FIVE

The Emperor's Celluloid
Army Marches On

Japan's surrender to the Allies in 1945 marked an end to the physical reality of Japanese empire, but Japanese filmmakers continued to struggle with the loss of empire in the years after the war. For those who had lived their entire lives under the reality of Japanese empire—many of them outside the home islands of Japan—the question of how the newly decolonized Japanese nation fit in Asia was anything but self-evident. Not surprisingly perhaps, filmmakers often turned to the past, and cinematic representations of Japan's Asian empire continued unabated throughout the U.S. Occupation of Japan (1945–1952), intensifying during and after the Korean conflict, when Japan became a critical base of operations for the United States. Postwar films had to come to terms with the causes of Japan's crushing defeat and offer possible explanations as to why its loyal imperial subjects-turned-citizens were suffering. Occupation officials were eager to reeducate the Japanese so that they turned away from the empire-building of the past and retooled themselves into a modern democracy (after the American model). Films about the war (in the immediate postwar period, this generally referred to the years between 1941 and 1945) proliferated. After the Occupation, filmmakers enjoyed greater freedom to explore themes of Japanese wartime victimhood, which produced a genre of films that critics called the "postwar antiwar film." Japanese filmmakers routinely denounced war, but none ever challenged the underlying imperialist impulse. As a result, Japanese filmmakers and audiences would reclaim their empire onscreen time and again. The mix of guilt and nostalgia in these films created a formula that was strikingly similar to that of the films produced before the war.

Postwar melodramas such as *Bengawan River* (1951, *Bungawan soro*) or *Woman of Shanghai* (1952, *Shanghai no onna*) are tragic love stories set in Japan's former imperial territories that pair Japanese men with Asian women (played by Japanese

Yamaguchi Yoshiko/Ri Koran at the peak of her career in
the Manei-produced film *Beautiful Sacrifice* (1941).

actresses) in what is perhaps an instinctive revival of the goodwill film genre popular in the late 1930s. *Bengawan River* tells of a romance between a Japanese deserter and an Indonesian woman during the last weeks of the Pacific War, while *Woman of Shanghai* is about two ethnically Japanese spies who have grown up in China and fall in love with each other in Japanese-occupied Shanghai.[1] It is unclear how either film escaped the attention of Occupation censors, given that their subject matter appears to violate censorship directives against representing Japan as a militarist power. Whatever the case, it is clear that there was a strong demand for such films. While it should not surprise us that filmmakers would turn to proven genres, it is instructive that audiences still suffering the affects of war could be nostalgic for retreaded plots about "misunderstood" Japanese working selflessly for the benefit of unappreciative Asian populations. The war may have ended, but empire was a separate matter, and a relevant one. The Japanese desire for films about their empire, however, was no longer predicated on the actual physical possession of imperial territories, and prewar genres such as the goodwill film continued to provide a useful model for how to interpret Japan's pre-1945 role in Asia in a contemporary context.

Other Asians in these postwar films were not always romantic partners; indeed, they often became either comic foils or simply ungrateful competitors. The kind of representation of imperial territories seen in Western films are also apparent in these films. Examining the different interrelations of Japan and America, Japan and Europe, and Japan and its own past reveals the durability and usefulness of these images of Asia, highlighting their transhistorical and transnational hybridity. Japanese cinema is neither dependent on nor wholly independent of the international context in which it exists. The lure of the exotic and the appeal of the foreign in Japan's cinema of empire must be seen in relative, not absolute, terms.

Defeat and National Downsizing

> When I walked home after listening to the imperial proclamation . . . people on the shopping street were bustling about with cheerful faces as though preparing for a festival. . . . I don't know whether this was a sign of Japanese adaptability or a fatal character flaw, but I had to accept that both of these sides were part of the Japanese character. Both sides exist within me as well.[2]

At the time of the surrender in 1945, when Kurosawa Akira experienced these perceptions about the Japanese character, the Japanese film industry was nearly in ruins, and its top talent, barely managing to survive, was scattered throughout the far-flung reaches of the Japanese empire. Ozu Yasujiro was a communications officer in Singapore; Yoshimura Kozaburo was in preproduction for a film in Bangkok; Shibuya Minoru was filming in Canton, China. In Indonesia, Kurata Bunjin and Hinatsu Eitaro were both actively producing films for the Imperial Japanese Army in cooperation with local film production companies. Toyoda Shiro and Imai Tadashi were in Korea working on separate film projects in collaboration with two Korean directors. Yamamoto Satsuo and Uchida Tomu were shooting films in Manchuria, and Kimura Sotoji was finishing a Chinese-language feature film in southern China.[3]

Ironically, for the estimated 6.5 million imperial Japanese subjects stranded throughout Japan's former empire, defeat in the Pacific War represented less a break with the past, or even a new beginning, than a daily struggle for survival. It took years for most Japanese living abroad to repatriate to the home islands; some would never return. The many who did return faced widespread shortages of food, clothing, and shelter; existence there was just as severe, or perhaps even more so, than being caught outside Japan in the aftermath of empire. Contemporary Japan historian John Dower writes that many of these people struggled with adjusting their sense of national identity: "[Japan] had been obsessed with becoming a . . . country of the first rank. Indeed, fear that such status was being denied Japan was commonly evoked with great emotion as the ultimate reason for going to war with the West. Japan would be relegated to 'second-rate' or 'third-rate' status . . . if it failed to establish a secure imperium in Asia. Like a reopened wound, the term 'fourth-rate country' (*yonto koku*) immediately gained currency as a popular catchphrase in post-surrender Japan."[4]

It was in this milieu of defeat, decolonization, and American Occupation that Japanese filmmakers and audiences struggled to redefine and reaffirm what being Japanese meant in the absence of empire. Some Japanese filmmakers, like Kurosawa Akira, felt that life and work after the defeat resumed with an almost vexing continuity. For filmmakers and audiences, the loss of empire coagulated with war guilt, resulting in a need for films that attempted to explain what had happened. Questions of responsibility for Japan's demoralized postwar state became a popular subject for films and a topic of intense debate in the Japanese film press.

War Guilt vs. Imperial Nostalgia

In 1945, almost immediately after the surrender, filmmakers in Japan began churning out the first of what would be a long line of films that attempted to explain the cause of Japan's war in Asia.[5] *Who are the Criminals? (Hanzaisha wa dare ka*, 1945) was shot even before American Occupation officials issued the official directive of acceptable topics and suggested that the blame for war be placed fully on the shoulders of the wartime Japanese politicians, who willingly "deceived the people."[6] The following year *Enemy of the People (Minshu no teki*, 1946) took aim at heartless wartime factory managers for their blind support of the war and for "chasing after sake, women, bribery, and gambling, all in the name of powerful family-run financial cabals (*zaibatsu*)."[7]

Questioning the culpability of the emperor, the individual ultimately responsible for Japan's colonial wars in Asia, quickly became a topic prohibited by the Occupation as well. Documentary filmmaker Kamei Fumio learned this when he produced the 1947 documentary *A Japanese Tragedy (Nihon no higeki*), which condemned Japanese imperialist aggression in Asia and called for the emperor's prosecution as a war criminal.[8] Ironically, the Occupation film board initially approved the film but eventually deemed it too dangerous, both for its criticism of the emperor as well as for Kamei's pro-Communist leanings. The film was withdrawn one week after its release. This case reveals striking continuities between the imperial Japanese government's rigid media control and the similar approach adopted by Occupation officials. Many Japanese filmmakers felt that the war never really ended until the Occupation forces pulled out in 1952, taking the film censors with them.[9]

With the Japanese emperor absolved of any possible blame, Japanese filmmakers and critics had little to debate with regards to how they, as Japanese, could have been so deceived by their leaders into waging such a "hard struggle in a bad war" (akusen kuto). At the same time that the International War Crimes Tribunal in Tokyo were trying Japan's wartime leaders for crimes against humanity, the Japanese film industry was busy "purging" itself with the encouragement of the American Occupation Forces.[10] Most of those listed as war criminals were never fully purged from the film industry but rather were admonished to "reflect" on their actions. The exact nature of this self-reflection is not entirely clear considering the fact that several outspokenly anti-Anglo-American film critics and writers, such as Tsumura Hideo, worked consistently throughout the American Occupation and afterward. The majority of the accused returned to the industry within a year or two, often finding work producing and directing films that questioned war guilt.[11]

Film critic Shimizu Akira, who spent most of the war working in the Japanese film industry in Shanghai, claimed that the Japanese lacked any inherent sense of war guilt:

> Not only did the average Japanese at that time lack any sense of what invasion meant, they also had absolutely no sense of guilt . . . for the leaders of an island nation, imperialism was seen as the only way toward progress and material enrichment. . . . to the Japanese whose government had taken every opportunity to interfere in China's internal affairs, often using military force, the invasion [of China] seemed nothing out of the ordinary; in fact, it seemed almost commonsensical.[12]

By 1950 questions of Japan's role as an aggressor in Asia took a back seat to a topic that concerned most of the Japanese audience—Japanese suffering. Perhaps it was less that the Japanese lacked a sense of guilt, but rather that their sense of suffering outweighed that of guilt. Hear the Voices of the Sea (Kike wadatsumi no koe, 1950) and The Bells of Nagasaki (Nagasaki no kane, 1950) are films that emphasized the idea that the Japanese had been victimized at least as much, perhaps even more, than any other nation during the war. These films assaulted the senses of Japanese audiences by presenting them with something they had never seen onscreen before—the sight of dead or horribly mutilated Japanese soldiers. Scenes of war dead were prohibited under wartime censorship laws. By invoking powerful images of Japanese suffering, and especially of nuclear destruction, the weight of Japanese war responsibility in Southeast Asia, China, and Korea seemed to pale in comparison.[13]

"Victimization" films recognized that the Japanese military had been wrong to advance into China, but they also subsumed Asian suffering into the larger cauldron of human suffering, relieving individual Japanese of the need to remember themselves as aggressors in Asia. Japanese film critic Yamada Kazuo denounces this type of thought as rationalization and describes the process by invoking the Japanese proverb "in a fight, both sides lose" (*kenka ryoseihai*). In other words, Yamada argues that showing Japanese soldiers murdering or committing other horrid acts in Asia is tantamount to saying that "Japan was wrong, but so was America."[14] Every action is made relative. Actually, convenient villains based on prewar models like the Chinese or the Americans were no longer relevant. After the defeat, the new enemy in Japanese cinema became war itself. War was personified and referred to in the third person, in a codified way. Much as Japanese ideologues throughout the first half of the twentieth century had demonized the West in a plethora of visual media as the symbol of pure evil, so critics and filmmakers after 1945 personified war itself as pure evil.[15]

Reclaiming the Empire Onscreen

By 1950 representations of Japanese war guilt and suffering gave way to a wave of nostalgia for the lost Japanese empire in Asia. Often set in Japanese-occupied territories before the end of the Pacific War, these films put a post-defeat spin on Japan's imperial past that came to resemble a new Japanese history of the war. *Desertion at Dawn* (*Akatsuki no dasso*, 1950) and *White Orchid of the Desert* (*Nessa no byakuran*, 1951) helped revive nostalgia for the Japanese empire by taking audiences back to the prewar era, not to commiserate or atone, but rather to watch and sing. The connections to the prewar goodwill films (*shinzen eiga*) genre were obvious—familiar motifs of misunderstood Japanese and uncomprehending Asians were back with a vengeance.[16]

In the case of *White Orchid of the Desert*, the connection with goodwill films is made all the more obvious by its very title, which is an amalgamation of *Song of the White Orchid* and *Vow in the Desert*. This film reworks the story of *Desertion at Dawn*, but the lead character of *White Orchid of the Desert* is a Chinese "comfort woman" named Byakuran (literally, "White Orchid," and played by the Japanese actress Kogure Michiyo). The time frame is immediately after Japan's surrender in 1945. Byakuran travels on a transport truck with a group of Japanese who are crossing the Chinese continent to the coast to repatriate to Japan. On the way, their group encounters every possible adversity (including Chinese bandits!), and several Japanese are killed. Byakuran hates the Japanese for forcing her into a life of prostitution. But when she sees the Japanese corpses strewn mercilessly across the road, she experiences a miraculous transformation and is suddenly filled with pity for them. This change of heart motivates her to offer herself as a sacrifice to the marauding Chinese in exchange for the safety of the remaining Japanese passengers.[17]

These films were made partly in response to the Japanese defeat, partly to the American Occupation, and partly to the Korean War. The shock and demoralization many Japanese felt after the defeat and subsequent Occupation traumatized former imperial Japanese subjects, now citizens of a democratic Japan, who identified themselves in relation to their new and radically downsized nation. Politically and culturally Japan was under the control of the United States, but the outbreak of the Korean War put Japan's economy on the path to recovery much more quickly than anticipated. America's involvement in the Korean War buttressed Japan's status as a strategic geopolitical stronghold in Asia. The Korean War became the engine that kick-started a Japanese economy stalled by decades of war and then went on to sustain over two decades of unprecedented high economic growth. Japan's newfound financial confidence came at the expense of its former colony Korea and also stabilized the Japanese film industry. The postdefeat Japanese film industry set about making films for a truly domestic national audience for the first time in decades. Unburdened from any responsibility to consider the sensibilities of other Asian audiences, Japanese filmmakers now had to worry only about whatever constraints the American Occupation authorities placed on them. In keeping with the spirit of the U.S.-drafted Japanese Constitution, Japanese filmmakers renounced war (and particularly the war fought with America). But the confidence of the postwar economic upturn inspired filmmakers to reappropriate the visual geography of the Japanese empire in infinitely more benign terms. Reclaiming the empire, at least onscreen, helped lighten the burdens of post-defeat Japanese life by reaffirming Japan's status as a nation that had had an imperial history. Even films with contemporary settings and themes seemingly unrelated to the war were informed at a significant level by power relationships based on Japan's colonial history in Asia and were subsequently fueled by Japanese economic imperialism.[18]

French film scholar Panivong Norindr writes about a similar wave of nostalgia for empire in France in the 1990s, in which he recounts how popular narratives in film and television employ romantic melodrama as a metaphor for colonial relationships. Popular French television news anchor Bruno Masur describes the historical ties that bound France and Indochina for almost a century as "an old love story." [19] One thing that both 1990s France and 1950s Japan share is the trope of miscegenetic melodrama to replace and obscure the brutal realities of imperial rule with erotic fantasy. In fact, even today Japanese filmmakers still produce—and audiences still attend—films set in the era of Japanese empire in Asia.[20] The pedigree of these contemporary films that reassert national identity by invoking Japan's imperialist past can be traced back to the time when the Japanese economy began to revive during the Korean War.

Goodwill Again

Miscegenetic pairings between a masculine Japan and a feminized China were not uncommon in the prewar cinema of Japanese empire, but *Bengawan River* represents the first Japanese attempt ever to pair a masculine Japan with a feminized Indonesia on film.[21] *Bengawan River* owes its existence in large part to the runaway success of *Desertion at Dawn*, released the year before in 1950 and based on Tamura Taijiro's bestselling novel *Story of a Prostitute* (*Shunpuden*).[22] Given the bitter censorship struggles between the filmmakers and the American Occupation film censors, it is provocative that this film and its several adaptations could be produced at all during the American Occupation.[23]

Bengawan River is set in a small farming village near Java in August of 1945 weeks before the end of the war. Fukami (Ikebe Ryo), Noro (Ito Yonosuke), and Take (Morishige Hisaya) are three Japanese deserters on the run from the Japanese military police. They come to the house of an Indonesian family (all played by Japanese performers) seeking medicine and shelter for their malaria-stricken comrade Noro. The Indonesian family reluctantly agrees to let them stay in the stable until Noro is healthy. Sariya (played by Kuji Asami), the oldest daughter in the family, clearly despises the Japanese soldiers because her brother was killed in a Japanese bombing raid.

Over time, however, she begins to experience a change of heart and takes pity on the sick Noro. Unknown to the others, Sariya goes to the neighboring village and sells her prized necklace to buy medicine for him. Fukami and the others gradually become familiar with the family, and Sariya begins to fall in love with Fukami. This film not only banked on the popularity of Ikebe Ryo by reprising his role as a handsome deserter in an ill-fated love affair, but it also created a successful tie-in with the song "Bengawan River" (Bungawan soro) that was a huge hit in Japan at that time.

Based on the rhythm of a popular Indonesian song, "Bengawan River" was imported into Japan after the war and set to Japanese lyrics around 1948. Because the melody came from Indonesia, "Bengawan River" had a far greater sense of native authenticity than other popular songs about the South Seas such as "The Chieftains' Daughter."[24] The practice of grafting Japanese lyrics onto a native melody is paralleled in the film by the miscegenetic pairing of the two love interests. In his 1988 essay, Japanese cultural critic Tsurumi Shunsuke recalls his fondness for the film, commenting especially on the musical aspects.

> For me . . . *Bengawan River* was most memorable. That sort of film was rare during the occupation period. It was the story of Japanese soldiers stationed in Java who responded to the music that flowed in the villages outside the auspices of the army. It understands the war as being caught between the

music within the Japanese army and the music that surrounded the Japanese army. It was a wonderful film.[25]

Bengawan River draws on many racial and sexual stereotypes in the Japanese imperialist imagination. In particular, its representations of Sariya's sexuality, and to a lesser degree of her younger sister Kaltini's as well, are the most obvious. Throughout the film Sariya is photographed from angles that emphasize her physical sexuality, and she is often involved in activities that require her bending over or squatting toward or away from the camera. Her sarong is meant to evoke a sense of native "authenticity," by conjuring up preexisting fantasies in the minds of the audience of "bare-breasted women of the South Pacific."[26] Her clothing is styled to emphasize her shoulders, hips, buttocks, and breasts rather than to accurately represent the appearance of an Indonesian farmer. These camera angles and costuming choices become all the more apparent in the festival scenes, where other native women (also played by Japanese) are wearing sarongs, but of a distinctly less suggestive cut. As in prewar films set in the South Seas, Sariya, and all of the "Indonesian" characters perform in brownface to make them stand out from the Japanese characters.

Fukami, the male love interest, is less obviously sexualized; however, his good looks immediately distinguish him from his two comrades. What attracts Sariya most to Fukami is the strength of his character. His actions, such as searching for a horse to help move his sick friend and his selfless devotion, are as attractive as his physical appearance. His physical sexuality is represented partially through the use of costuming; his shirt is constantly unbuttoned lower than the others and his movements, like those of Sariya, suggest a sexual physicality. But as a deserter, Fukami lacks the absolute, infallible purity that prewar Japanese leading men like Hasegawa or Sano projected. In this sense his character clearly comes from a postwar sensibility. However, his conquest and domination of Sariya are unmistakable expressions of imperialist fantasies that link him in spirit, if not in deed, to his *shinzen eiga* predecessors. Fukami's death at the end of the film suggests the futility of any permanent relationship between the two protagonists (and their cultures). Much like the miscegenetic love melodramas that Hollywood was producing at this time, Fukami and Sariya's relationship ultimately has to be punished because it violates the postwar sexual taboo against interracial sexual love.[27]

Two fundamental contradictory Japanese assumptions regarding racial difference are evident in *Bengawan River*. The first is that Southeast Asians are racially different from Japanese and as such essentially unknowable. Production elements—the melody of the theme song, the setting, the costumes, the language, the gestures—all combine to create a Japanese imagined sense of Southeast Asian Otherness. Viewers are not expected to identify with these different sights, sounds, and gestures; they exist only to establish an exotic atmosphere markedly different from that of Japan. Within this synthetic foreign atmosphere, characters act according to different rules of behavior (sexual and otherwise), and viewers are liberated from normal Japanese conventions of behavior and permitted to indulge in voyeuristic fantasies.

In opposition to this assumption that foreign characters are always and irrevocably different, the second assumption takes for granted that Japanese are similar enough racially to masquerade as Southeast Asians. Private Noro decides to dress in native costume in the hope that he can avoid being detected as a deserter until the end of the war so he can return to Japan. The first time he appears dressed as an Indonesian, his comrade Take is shocked.

Take: What the hell's that get-up?
Noro: You don't think it looks good on me?
Take: (sarcastically) . . . you look great.
Noro: My uniform stands out.
Take: They'll all take you for a native.[28]

Director Ichikawa Kon would return to the theme of Japanese assimilation of the Asian several more times in *Ye lai xiang* (*Yaraika*, 1951) and *Harp of Burma* (*Biruma no tategoto*, 1956/1985). Characterizations of Southeast Asians progressed very little from the representations of Southeast Asians by Japanese character actors like Saito Tatsuo (*Southern Winds II*) or Sugai Ichiro (*Forward, Flag of Independence*). Japanese performers still applied brownface and supplemented their representations with gimmicky gestures such as ticks or excessive scratching. In addition, they used verbal incongruities like consistent mispronunciation of certain words or unintelligible verb suffixes to evoke an atmosphere that Japanese audiences would recognize as stereotypical of Southeast Asians. Consider the following scene when Take and Fukami try to keep Kaltini from entering the river while they bathe. In the process of the conversation, it becomes clear that Kaltini understands Japanese.

Take: . . . huh? You can speak Japanese?
Kaltini: (Happily nods) A leetle.
Take: (parodying) A "leetle"?
Kaltini: Father know a leetle. Mother know nothing. Sariya, ve—ry good![29]

One Japanese film critic remarked that *Bengawan River* was a good attempt at authenticity in that the characters spoke quite acceptable Malaysian.[30] To be sure, many of the Japanese actors playing Indonesian characters attempt to speak Indonesian, but this is nothing new. We have already seen numerous examples of prewar Japanese films where Japanese actors playing Asian characters speak in other languages. Moreover, Fukami and the other Japanese soldiers do not treat as natural the fact that the native characters in *Bengawan River* can speak Japanese.

The choice to cast Japanese for all the Indonesian roles also assumes an attitude that negates the importance of racial difference. Casting decisions are made at the production level, but the results are complex and often ideological. Casting a Japanese actress in a romantic leading role allows Japanese spectators to suspend reality just enough to identify with the characters, without actually alienating them. However, maintaining her racial difference frees the narrative from having to adhere to Japanese sexual norms of behavior and titillates the viewers. For example, when Sariya confronts Fukami and gives herself to him in the jungle, the camera stays on her naked back for several long extended takes as she slowly lets down her hair. The director avoided the conventional choice of shooting Sariya's and Fukami's love scenes in medium shots opting instead to use bust shots of Sariya or close-ups that emphasized various parts of her body. Even more pronounced are the scenes in which the Japanese sergeant (played by Japanese film icon Fujita Susumu) lustfully looks at Sariya's behind and bends down to rub it. Before he touches her, we are shown a close-up of her back and buttocks in a tight-fitting sarong as she squats on a rock washing clothes in the river. The viewer is made to gaze at the unwitting Sariya's body along with the sergeant, literally taking his point of view. The scene resonates with the many real-life accounts of Japanese soldiers raping local women.[31] Much like its prewar counterparts, *Bengawan River* has little to do with either goodwill or romance.

Singing the Same Songs

Although virtually ignored by contemporary scholarship, *Woman of Shanghai* is a remarkable postwar interpretation of Japan's imperialist past. Produced in 1952, one year after *Bengawan River*, *Woman of Shanghai* concerns issues of war guilt, identity, and Japanese victimization. Director Inagaki Hiroshi recalled that the idea for the film came in 1944, when he was in Shanghai shooting a Japanese/Chinese coproduction called *Remorse in Shanghai* (*Noroshi wa Shanhai ni agaru*, 1944). Inagaki was looking for a project for Ri Koran (Yamaguchi) partially due to his attraction to her "big, beautiful eyes" and also because "she spoke Japanese clearly and quickly with a Mandarin accent—just perfect for a Japanese/Chinese coproduction."[32] In preliminary negotiations Yamaguchi demonstrated a willingness to participate in the picture that left a lingering impression on Inagaki:

> I was very impressed when she said: "If I can be of any help, I'll gladly do anything. Nothing would please me more than to serve as a bridge for China." You couldn't find any Japanese actresses in those days that were that well spoken.[33]

Ultimately Inagaki was unable to cast Ri in the film due to her status as a "Manchurian" actress, while his film was intended to be a Japanese/Chinese coproduction. After the war, Inagaki made a Japanese period film with Yamaguchi, but his desire to produce the Chinese-themed film together only intensified. He explained: "I wanted her to sing all her [famous] songs in that beautiful Mandarin of hers."[34] What resulted was a fictionalized film biography of Yamaguchi that is just one of her many attempts to justify her role as an imperial icon as victimhood. Yamaguchi successfully reinvented her iconic status for a new generation of filmgoers, this time not as a model of smiling assimilation but rather as a misunderstood, long-suffering heroine. The mix of remorse for war (defeat) and nostalgia for empire tapped into the prevailing mood in Japanese postwar cinema.

In *Woman of Shanghai*, Yamaguchi plays Li Lili, a Japanese raised by Chinese foster parents in China who becomes a singer in a popular Shanghai nightclub. Li falls in love with Lieutenant Manabe, a bilingual Japanese spy who was also raised in China. The plot involves spies from Chongqing, Nanjing, and Japan all mixed together in the cosmopolitan milieu of Shanghai, but the focus of the narrative is the couple's love affair. Li and Manabe's love is thwarted by Ting, a Chinese underground subversive in league with the Japanese and also in love with Li.

Manabe and Ting are assigned by the Japanese government to infiltrate the Chinese spy ring where Li's adopted father works. Manabe's struggle between duty and love are mirrored by Li's split loyalties for China and Japan. Li is under constant surveillance by both sides, not due to any actions on her part, but because of her father's activities. Obvious parallels with Yamaguchi's own life can be found in Li's character, who, when asked which country she feels most loyalty for pleadingly responds: "Which do you love more, your natural or your adopted parents? I love Japan just the same as I love China. I love my Chinese friends. It's not just something that one can logically explain. . . . Oh, how I hate this war!" The personification of war as the ultimate source of her suffering is not unique to this film, but is, rather, a recurring motif in postwar war films. Li's usefulness as both a source of information and a propaganda tool is a device by which the Japanese military characters monitor and gain information about subversive Chinese activities. As they say:

> Her father is Li Kokumei, one of the top men in the Nanking [sic] government . . . his daughter, if you can call her that, is actually Japanese. I guess that's a sign of the age we live in. There's a story behind it, but the short of it is that no one suspects her identity. I guess it's because she's such a good singer . . . anyhow, she's Japanese by blood but raised and educated in Shanghai and Peking. If we could get her, she'd be a most convenient woman. But never let your guard down . . . she's a beauty.

Emphasizing Li's exotic beauty and musical ability is a direct link to her prewar persona, but the idea that her songs are covertly anti-Japanese at first appears to be a new wrinkle. With only one exception, every one of the unusually large number of songs in this film were popularized during Yamaguchi's days as Ri Koran, prompting one Toho executive to wryly remark: "What is this, a Ri Koran concert?"[35] The potential for resistance to Japanese rule in her songs is emphasized in a tearoom sequence. When the Chinese owner plays a record of one of Li's popular songs, the Japanese police burst into the store, beat up the owner, and arrest him, saying: "You were warned never to play that song." Li is inconsolable. Speaking out in a way the actress Yamaguchi never could, Li berates the Japanese military for misunderstanding her motives and mistreating China:

> I can't believe they think that's an anti-Japanese song, it's not! Everything sounds that way to them. Even if it were, what do they think they'll do—stop everyone from singing? . . . it makes me miserable that Japanese all turn their backs on Chinese like that. I wonder how many Japanese there are in the world who really understand the Chinese.

Li's and Manabe's suffering is complex, the result of her liminal position as a literal orphan of empire. While not everyone in the audience was born or raised abroad, dislocation and loss were certainly recognizable to many in the audience who had lost either family or friends in some former imperial territory. What the film's characters ultimately reaffirm, however, is a national Japanese identity informed by its imperial past. Thus, when Li confides in her stepfather that she has fallen in love with a Japanese spy, he tells her to handle the situation as a Japanese: "When you see him say, 'I'm sorry.' That's the Japanese way. And when you part, do it with a smile—the Japanese way."

Li becomes involved in a shootout at an orphanage among the Japanese, pro-Japanese Chinese, and anti-Japanese factions and is eventually arrested for treason (just as Yamaguchi herself was). Unable to stay her execution, Manabe visits her cell to profess his love for her one last time. In dialogue that eerily mirrors Keiran's transformation into a "good" imperial Japanese subject in *China Nights*, Li explains to Manabe: "I'm not sad at all, I'm happy. You taught me about the homeland that I never knew. I have no regrets. Now I can die in China as a Chinese, embracing my homeland of Japan." At the execution ground, Manabe asks for permission to execute Li as he cannot bear the thought of anyone else killing her. Ultimately, he is unable to kill her, and both are shot holding hands—almost an exact replication of the ending of *Desertion at Dawn*. Yamaguchi's links with Japan's imperial past are not only a direct connection to Japanese war guilt but also relate to the cinematic reclamation of the Japanese empire as a reaffirmation of a national Japanese identity.

The continuity in representations of Japan's empire in Asia did not end with what Japan scholars have termed the "collapse of empire."[36] The tremendous social and political changes resulting from the Potsdam Declaration and Japan's unconditional surrender, as epoch-making as they were, did not spell the end of the Japanese empire onscreen as I have shown.

The Emperor's Army Keeps Laughing

One year before the 1964 Tokyo Olympics, Shochiku released a war-themed comedy entitled *Dear Mr. Emperor* (*Haikei tenno heika-sama*).[37] Directed by veteran Nomura Yoshitaro[38] and based on Muneta Hiroshi's[39] popular novel of the same name, the film became an instant box-office smash that inspired two successful sequels, *Dear Mr. Emperor II* (*Zoku haikei tenno heika-sama*, 1964) and *Dear Mr. Prime Minister* (*Haikei soridaijin-sama*, 1964). Film critics hailed the series calling it "the most overlooked postwar antiwar war films," and certainly the first two installments of the *Dear Mr. Emperor* (hereafter *Emperor*) series broke ground by addressing topics that had been either completely ignored or glossed over until that time.[40] Unlike the melodramas discussed above, the *Emperor* series offers a fascinating and often humorous illustration of grassroots support for Japanese expansionism into China as well as representations of Chinese nationals living in Japan during and after the empire.

One of the most striking aspects of the *Emperor* series is its positive portrayal of army life as a viable alternative for lower-class Japanese peasants in the 1930s. In an early sequence in *Emperor II*, a third-person narrator informs viewers just how desperate conditions were for Zensuke, (played by Atsumi Kiyoshi)—the fact that he even survived puberty is suggested as a minor miracle:

> In those days of terrible depression, our little troublemaker Zensuke was often made to go without supper as a punishment. That year when his family unknowingly ate a rotten fish that they had found somewhere, everyone died except Zensuke, who was being punished.

The series created its main comic effect by deviating from typical "service comedy" narrative conventions that invariably portrayed the army as a hell on earth. The protagonist (Yamada Shosuke, or "Yamasho" in the first film and in the second film, Yamaguchi Zensuke, a night-soil man whom the village children nickname "Shitty Zen") is a dimwitted, illiterate, and sometimes violent country farmer who wholeheartedly welcomes the prospect of army life. As the voiceover narration explains:

> Most people hated the army, but for [Zen] it was heaven. On the outside everyday he was threatened with poverty, destitution, and near starvation. Here, he had no worries about where the next meal would come from; he

even got paid every ten days and never had look for a place to stay. Yes, it was heaven! But after two years passed, and his time was up, he was out of the army and back to collecting shit.[41]

Compared with the severity of his prewar life, the hard training and regular beatings in the army does not faze Shitty Zen. The possibility of dying on the Chinese continent never seems to concern Zen, but the prospect of peace absolutely petrifies him. In a clever montage depicting his literally having to be forced out of the army at the end of his term, the voiceover narration ironically explains that "the worst thing that ever happened to him was peacetime." So in order to try and save his beloved job, he attempts to write a letter to the Showa Emperor (hence the title), asking him not to end the war. Ironically, the rapid succession of military "incidents" on the Chinese continent renders his fear of an early peace moot. The real challenges come after defeat and repatriation back to Japan. Zen is unable to adjust to the changes of postwar Japan and just before he is to be married, he is struck down and killed by an American truck hauling supplies for the Korean War.[42]

Even given its decidedly ironic tone, *Emperor* illustrates that in poverty-stricken 1930s Japan, the army might not have seemed as some might imagine. *Emperor* recognizes, albeit comically, that not everyone had to be tricked or coerced into the army—there had, in fact, been a base of popular support for the war. Zen is obviously quirky, and his options are limited, but we also suspect that there were many others like him. Even viewers who had served in the war could experience a sort of nostalgia for their experiences through film series like *Emperor*. The army did not necessarily only represent the hellish dead end for everyone below the rank of officer, so memorably portrayed in darker series such as *Yakuza Soldier (Heitai yakuza)* and *Desperado Outpost (Dokuritsu gurentai)*.[43] *Emperor* suggests that for uneducated peasants, the army also provided a place to learn skills and interact with other socioeconomic classes in ways inconceivable "on the outside."

In the first installment of the *Emperor* series, the army transforms into a substitute family for Yamasho (called Zen in the later installment). He becomes friends with people from all walks of life. Though most would have had nothing to do with Yamasho in civilian life, in the army they treat him as a comparative equal. The paternal side of army life is epitomized by the kind, fatherly company commander, who makes it a point to see that Yamasho receives more than food, clothing, and shelter, but that he also gains an education. Army hierarchy is reversed when the illiterate Yamasho is taught to read and write by a first-year soldier. He begins reading primary school texts and gradually advances to popular serialized war stories, such as *300 Miles Behind Enemy Lines (Tekichu odan sanbyakuri)* and comic strips such as *Blackie the Stray Pup (Norakuro)*.[44] Both Yamasho and

Tagawa Suiho's phenomenally popular cartoon character *Blackie* are uneducated, lovable orphans who may screw up, but who also share a dog-like loyalty to the army and the emperor.[45] Screenwriter Yamada Yoji clearly emphasized these parallels, lest the audience fail to make the connection, in explicit dialogue when Yamasho remarks: "That poor Blackie, he's a lot like me."

The link between this Sad-Sack-like character and dogs was illustrated even more clearly in the second installment of the series, where the protagonist, Zen, is assigned to be a trainer in a military dog unit. About the dog that he feeds and trains in preparation to fight on the Chinese continent, Zen states that they are brothers. As with *Blackie the Stray Pup*, or even characters like Chaplin's tramp, viewers are asked to identify with this lovable misfit precisely because of his deficiencies—his low-class background, poor education, and short temper— all aspects that would have been seriously detrimental to "normal" socialization in 1960s middle-class Japanese society.

Zen's love of the army appears ironic, especially when juxtaposed with the other soldiers' distaste for it. We learn that the army calls soldiers like him—who stay in the army for six years, yet remain buck privates—*mosakure*, which means a type who never learns. But the *Emperor* series producers did this on purpose. They realized the power of Zen's underdog status and kept him a buck private (*nitohei*) throughout the series. Zen moved viewers not only because he was an underdog but because he did not seem to mind being one. With no chance of promotion in the army and a prison record on the outside, civilian society holds little appeal for Zen. Viewers feel a sense of pathos about his character precisely because he does not (or cannot) exercise control over his circumstances. Forsaking the possibility of wreaking righteous vengeance on his oppressors, this character does nothing on his own and gets by solely on the good graces of the kindly Japanese around him.

In this sense Zen is much less a figure to be lamented than one that reminds or instructs modern audiences of what seems to have been lost from the Japanese spirit by the 1960s. His unquestioning loyalty, perseverance, and honesty regarding the army and the emperor are never seriously mocked or critiqued so much as gently chided. While the presence of the emperor is central in both films, he is directly represented in only the first installment. The protagonist (here, Yamasho) is on maneuvers with his battalion in Okayama one day in 1932 when the Showa Emperor arrives to inspect the troops. The narrator explains (after the fact) that "of course none of us had actually ever seen the emperor before that day, but Yamasho hadn't even seen his photo!" This statement reaffirms the protagonist's lack of formal education by calling attention to the fact that he is unfamiliar with photos of the emperor that were found in classrooms in any national school (*kokumin gakko*). The emperor appears suddenly, announced by the company commander just before we see him. In fact, we never actually see him, but only his icons—flags with the imperial chrysanthemum crest, his white horse, and his boots in stirrups. In a traveling shot that passes Yamasho, presumably from the point of view of the emperor, we hear Yamasho's interior monologue in a voiceover:

> So that's the emperor? Hmm . . . who does he remind me of . . . no, not him . . . he doesn't look like a god . . . but he sure looks like someone else. What a kind face . . . he isn't a bit scary! From that day on Yamasho felt a distinct affinity for the emperor.

The soldiers are ordered not to look at the emperor, as it is a punishable offense (*fukeizai*). The "problem" of looking at the emperor seems to have extended to the actual filming of this scene. Japanese film critic Iwasaki Akira explained that not only was care taken in whom to cast in the role of the emperor, but also that director Nomura avoided directly showing the actor playing the emperor throughout the entire sequence. Even Iwasaki, a former diehard leftist critic/screenwriter who was once arrested during the war for opposing the 1939 Film Law, approved of the film's "sufficiently obtuse" representation of the emperor.[46] A certain *humanizing* of the emperor is achieved in this film, however. The music selected for each key scene dealing with the emperor is very light, music-box music, which undercuts the heavy atmosphere of the imperial entourage. And although ordered not to, all the soldiers, not just Yamasho/Zen, look at the emperor—his is the object of their individual gazes at the same time that he collectively inspects them.

Elsewhere in the film, the emperor is conspicuous by his absence. For instance, when Yamasho decides to write a letter to the emperor, he never suspects that it is a crime to do so. The logic of the situation is so far removed from what he can understand that it must be literally knocked into him by his friend. Yamasho asks: "Hey, you think if I address this "Emperor, Tokyo" it will make it there?" To which his friend replies incredulously: "What're ya, nuts?" The structuring absence of the emperor in the film's narrative becomes even more obvious in the second installment of the series. Here the emperor is set to make two appearances, but viewers never see him in anything other than newsreel footage. The first time occurs when the protagonist (Zensuke) is a child; the entire community shows up and waits for three hours, but the emperor never comes.[47] The second time, after the war, Zensuke is surrounded by a crowd and cannot see over the (American) heads. By not directly revealing the emperor, Iwasaki mused that viewers could keep whatever image they personally had of him in their hearts— ostensibly adding more personal depth to the criticism. Iwasaki explained that "for prewar folk that would have created extremely profound or at the very least complex emotions. A disagreeable feeling [followed by] a vaguely bittersweet familiar feeling that stirred up nostalgia. Together they . . . leave one in a terribly contradictory state of mind."[48]

Iwasaki went on to praise director Nomura's handling of what it meant to be a Japanese man in the closed space of the army by explaining that this film succeeded in surpassing the author's original work. In Muneta Hiroshi's original novel, the protagonist continues to nurture his worship of the emperor until his death in the postwar period. His faith shows none of the criticism or cynicism about the war found in other postwar novels such as Noma Hiroshi's *Zone of Emptiness* (*Shinku chitai*, 1952). Iwasaki and others have criticized Muneta for writing elsewhere about how *model* Japanese soldiers dealt with the harshness of war.[49] Iwasaki was impressed by the subtle way in which the film questioned the emperor's war responsibility. For Iwasaki, what makes the film so excellent, profound, and powerful is that, without screaming or confessing, it takes the image of the emperor and asks the Japanese to look at their modern history.

Iwasaki seems to be suggesting that history is far more knowable and accessible than the ambiguous representations in novels and films that constantly reconstruct and reimagine the past. At its foundation, Muneta's novel and Nomura's film are less a criticism of wartime Japan or even emperor worship than they are of the lingering effects of the Allied Occupation and the war in Korea. Zen's love, respect, and devotion for the emperor are not what kill him—he survives the war in China only to return to Japan and become a victim of Japan's former enemies.

The *Emperor* series recognizes the multiethnic fabric of the Japanese empire in which the war took place. We see that all Japanese, not just the upper class or even the highly educated, mixed with non-Japanese *because they had to.* Just as Korea remained central to the Japanese after the war, and just before Vietnam became a similar reality, the *Emperor* series seems to be stating that Asia—and particularly China—has always been an important space for Japan and that Asians have always been in Japan.

In *Emperor II*, the Chinese continent provides Zen the opportunity to stay in (or return to) his beloved army. For the Chinese characters in the film, the issue of war in China is more problematic. The effect of the wars is something like a protracted loyalty test in which they have to prove their solidarity with, and longing for, the Japanese empire. In the following sequence, night-soil man Zen, dubbed Shitty Zen by the town children, has just gotten the "good news" about the 1937 China Incident and rushes to the local Chinese barbershop for a military hair cut.

Zen: My gawd, you two, this place is filthy. (to Wang) Trim it all around n' make it tidy.
Wang: What's the occasion?
Zen: No occasion, 'cept I got my draft notice.
Fan: Zen-san . . . you're going to war?

Zen: You bet! It took them forever but now everything's gonna be okay. Startin' tomorrow my new boss is the emperor so there won't be no more trouble findin' somethin' to eat.

Wang: That's why you want your hair cut?

Zen: Uh-huh.

Wang: Do you mind *someone like me* cutting your hair? I'm Chinese. I mean I've always treated all Japanese as friends. But Japan's at war with China and no one comes in my store anymore.

Fan: And everyone calls us, "Chink, Chink."

Wang: She's right. Sure you want a *Chink* like me to cut the hair of a man going to war?

Zen: Uh, yeah . . . I guess so.

Wang: Zen-san! (grabbing Zensuke) Oh, Shitty Zen-san—Zen-san!! Shitty, shitty!!

Zen: Say, would ya knock off that *shitty* stuff? You gotta shit too, doncha?

Wang: Okay. Xie-xie, *arigato*. Your heart . . . my heart . . . same. You know? You're the only Japanese who understands my heart. Makes me happy. (to wife) Bring a hot towel!

Zen: Uh, how about just makin' it cheaper instead? I'm a little short.

Wang: What? I don't want money! We're *peng-you*. See? In Chinese, that means "friend."

Zen: (gets hot towel thrown on his face) Ow! Damn, pun-yo! That's hot![50]

In this sequence Zen's obliviousness to his surrounding conditions is misunderstood as a political act on behalf of Wang (played by Japanese comedian Ozawa Shoichi)[51] and Fan. This scene marks the beginning of a friendship between the two male characters that lasts from 1931 to 1950. Initially, the scene seems to be reviving stereotypical prewar Japanese notions of the Chinese as unclean, by having Zen comment on the obvious dirt, but then it changes direction to associate Zen with filthiness. Viewer expectations are subtly manipulated when we learn why Zen has come—the pause creates tension between the Japanese Zen and the Chinese Wang, and we anticipate that Wang may refuse to cut the hair of a man going to war to kill other Chinese. This fear dissipates, however, when Wang and his wife shed tears of joy to think that any Japanese would come to patronize their shop during the war. If Zen's obliviousness makes him comical, then Wang's and Fan's thankfulness seems downright farcical. Wang's characterization appears to rise above simple cheap stereotypes when the question of money is raised— despite their obviously desperate financial situation, Wang refuses payment on the basis of friendship.

Much of the credit for this attempt at an evenhanded representation should go to the film's assistant director and coscreenwriter Yamada Yoji. Yamada was no stranger to the Japanese empire. He had firsthand experience that came from living in the Japanese-occupied Manchuria as a child when his father worked for Mantetsu, the Japanese-run Southern Manchuria Railway. In a 1977 interview Yamada recalled how some of his stereotypical expectations of the Chinese had been subverted immediately after Japanese defeat in Manchuria. "Then along came the Eighth Army [with] red-capped pistols, and I remember thinking to myself what a disheveled bunch of soldiers they looked like. But actually they were quite an army and real gentlemen. I was [in] junior high school then and had always been taught that the Eighth Army was simply a bunch of bandits . . . that they were to be feared. But they turned out to be such a gentlemanly army. The [repatriation] ships didn't make it to Dalian right away so we were there for about two and one-half years. Those Japanese who didn't repatriate soon often couldn't find enough to eat. Towards the end, we nearly starved to death. Some of our neighbors did; it was horrible."[52]

The struggle to survive in a foreign environment was something that Yamada could understand, and for the most part he treats liminal characters living under wartime conditions in Japan sensitively. But the treatment of such characters—especially Wang and Fan—in Occupied Japan is somewhat less sensitive. *Emperor*'s vision of everyday life in postwar Japan under U.S. Occupation is presented as being more hellish than life in the army ever was. In the post-surrender society, prewar order, logic, and nearly everything else is represented as having been turned upside down, inside out. Likewise, the fortunes of the Japanese and non-Japanese have been turned almost entirely around.

Zen, an out-of-work repatriate, eventually runs across Wang, who is now separated from Fan and runs a restaurant with his new Japanese wife in Tokyo. Fan runs a black-market operation selling contraband American PX goods to Wang and others. For the remainder of the film, the gap visibly widens between the "haves," represented almost entirely by "third-class foreigners" (*daisan kokujin*), and the "have-nots," represented by Zen and other Japanese repatriates. The "third-class foreigners" in the film appear to be less the victims of the Greater East Asian War and its aftermath but rather postwar parasites responsible for rampant war profiteering. In stark contrast to the poor but humble Japanese who are barely able to eke out a living, the Chinese in the film are made out to be opportunists. Familiar stereotypes of "miserly Chinese" who do anything for money are an integral part of the representation of Wang and Fan in the postwar period. As Wang's restaurant prospers, he expands into the *pachinko* business.[53] Fan reveals that she has left Wang because of his infidelity with a Japanese woman, but she still sells goods (Lucky Strikes, beer) to his store because, after all, "business is business."

On the other hand, viewers are reminded that certain behavior, acceptable for Japanese during the war, is no longer appropriate in the postwar period. For example, when Zen is invited to his former war buddy's house, he "appropriates" (*chohatsu*) a chicken to bring as a gift. His friend, sensing that something is wrong, asks where Zen got the chicken:

> Friend: For god's sake, don't tell me that you thought you were back on the battlefield?
> Zensuke: Well, yeah, I . . . uh . . . "appropriated" it.
> Friend: You idiot! What do you mean you "appropriated" it? What sort of Japanese would steal from other Japanese!? You fool!

The moral of the scene is regardless of what may have happened on the Chinese continent during wartime, Japanese do not steal from Japanese—but apparently "any fool" did not know this. In the *Emperor* series, viewers are not asked simply to believe that soldiers could long for the simpler but painful life of a buck private—rather, there is a clear longing for a return to "normative" (that is, prewar) colonial power relationships. Despite the financial hardship and social ostracizing that they had to endure in the prewar Japanese countryside, Wang and Fan were represented as "pure" in the era of Japanese imperial rule. In the postwar beyond Japanese control, their values appear to be as counterfeit as the American contraband they sell.

Post-imperial Pan-Asia

Historian Eric Hobsbawm reminds us of the need to "demystify" the Age of Empire because we "are no longer in it, but do not know how much of it is still in us."[54] The amount of imperial rhetoric and ideology of empire that still finds its way into contemporary discourse is astounding. Politicians such as Tokyo governor and former cabinet minister Ishihara Shintaro claimed in 2003 that Japan "did not militarily invade" Korea, but that it was the Koreans who "sought the help of the modernized Japanese people . . . and annexation was conducted by a consensus of the world's nations."[55] Such attitudes however, are not limited to the political arena, but can be located within a broader right-wing historical revisionist movement that includes such scholars as Fujioka Nobukatsu and Hata Ikuhiko. Popular *manga* writers like Kobayashi Yoshinori and Yamano Sharin continue to publish series of best-selling cartoon essays that take a decidedly revisionist stance on the effects of Japanese colonialism in Okinawa, Taiwan, and Korea, so that Japanese "children can feel pride rather than shame for what their ancestors did in the war."[56]

In fact, one of the most commercially successful Japanese feature films of 1998, a high-profile attempt to recuperate lost Japanese pride, was appropriately entitled *Pride, the Fateful Moment* (*Puraido: unmei no toki,* 1998). The governments of the People's Republic of China, North Korea, and South Korea almost immediately denounced *Pride* for its sympathetic portrayal of former Army Minister Tojo Hideki, its denial of the Nanjing Massacre, and its insistence that Japan waged war in its own self-defense as well as for the (*successful*) liberation of Asia.[57] Filmmakers throughout South Korea, Hong Kong, Taiwan, and other former imperial territories are increasingly challenging historical views of the legacy of Japanese imperialism in Asia like those presented in *Pride*. In South Korea, director Lee Si-Myung's big-budget science-fiction fantasy *2009: Lost Memories* questions what would happen if Japan used a time machine to return to the past to erase the shame of defeat and regain its Asian empire.[58] This modern-day struggle over "correct" interpretations of history is reminiscent of the Hollywood/Japanese film wars of the 1930s and 1940s, as theaters across Asia have once again become sites where films almost literally shoot back to each other.

Negative representations of Japanese imperialism in East and Southeast Asian cinema are nothing new. Filmmakers have been coming to terms with the legacy of Japanese empire there since 1945. The last ten years have seen a definite shift from industry-wide dependency on the documentary, art-house, or period-film genres to lighter, more popular ones that were previously considered comparatively trivial and inappropriate for representing serious historical "facts." Contemporary action films, comedies, sci-fi, and sports films are all broaching the subject of empire, which suggests a liberalization of the generic boundaries for what constitutes politically and commercially viable films about the Japanese colonial era. In the increasingly global Asian film market, every film—including those that deal with empire—must reach multiple markets.

Over the past five years, government deregulation, the liberalization of Asian film markets, and global capital have all contributed to an increase in the number of Asian coproductions created for export throughout Asia and even North America and Europe.[59] Chinese films like *Purple Butterfly* (*Zi hudie*, 2003) and Japanese films such as *T.R.Y.* (2003) acknowledge emerging Asian markets by consciously using big budgets, multinational casting, and overseas locations to sell Asian stars to young "Pan-Asian" viewers in regional markets. Intriguingly, many of these coproductions are set in the era of empire. *T.R.Y.* tells the story of a Japanese con man named Izawa Shu, who lives in Shanghai in 1911. He runs a Robin Hood-like multiethnic band of swindlers that includes a Korean, Park Chengik, and a Chinese, Chen Siping. Izawa helps a Chinese revolutionary group sting the Imperial Japanese Army out of a trainload of weapons to aid a budding Chinese revolution. The film's producers sought to break into the "Asian film market" by casting Japanese actor Oda Yuji, with supporting actors from China, such as Shao Bing, Yang Ruoxi and Peter Ho, and Korean actor Sohn Chang-Min.[60] Oda's large fan base and "crossover appeal" in China and other Asian markets came from the success of his popular TV series *Tokyo Love Story*.[61] The producers believed that in the globalized markets of China and Korea Oda's Japanese-ness would not be associated with the history of colonization so much as with TV dramas, J-pop music, and fashion magazines. The idea was that linguistic, cultural, and regional divisions could be mediated by tapping into "intra-Asian flows of popular culture."[62]

In a 2002 interview in the Japanese film journal *Cinema Bi-weekly* (*Kinema junpo*), Sohn Chang-Min spoke about the future of Pan-Asian coproductions: "For this generation, I think Asia *is* one. Japan, Korea, and China are already one and so is the market. I also believe that there will be many more projects like this one [*T.R.Y.*] in the future, at least, I hope there will. At first I worried whether or not staff from three countries would be able to work well together on this project, but now I think it went very well."[63] Producers of Pan-Asian films often stress that these films are made possible due to the shared "cultural proximity" among the Asian staff and cast members. Joseph Straubhaar explains the notion of cultural proximity as connoting what was a "seemingly natural—and thus, power neutral—recognition by audiences of primordial cultural similarities."[64] Despite repeated claims of shared cultural affinities, staff also expressed anxiety over the threat that cultural and linguistic differences pose to film production, some even fearing that the film would never be completed because of these differences. Notions such as cultural proximity and crossover appeal are never as self-evident as they appear to be.

What makes the image of Japanese empire an attractive one over half a century since its official demise? The variety of representations of the "sentiment, rationale, and imagination" of empire should help us to understand its enduring appeal.[65] The Japanese empire has now ceased to exist for longer than it originally existed physically, yet each year it still is the topic of numerous films, books, video games, songs, theatrical plays, and CDs. Even events ostensibly meant to commemorate the end of the Japanese imperial project, such as *Ri Koran, the Musical* and the release of a thirty-volume video set of Manchurian films, function to recirculate and reconfigure its myth.[66] Many images in film and other popular media today draw their power from the legacy of prewar stereotypes and the ideology examined in these chapters. The availability of these products inspired by the age of Japanese empire, as well as their marketability, suggest that while there are shifts in the representations of Japan's empire in Asia, there are no endings, happy or otherwise.

Selected Filmography

What follows is a selected chronological filmography of empire-themed films produced in Japan and/or its formal and informal imperial territories. It includes crucial information regarding directors, screenwriters, cast, and production companies while sampling key cinematic expressions of Japan's imperial project throughout Asia. All film titles are taken from their original Japanese release title. Official English translations did not exist for the majority of these films, and secondary English sources are not always in agreement regarding translation. Thus, most English translations included here are my own.

The Village at Twilight (Yuhi no mura, 1921)

Production	Shochiku
Direction	Henry Kotani
Screenplay	Ito Daisuke
Cast	Henry Kotani, Hide Yuriko, Katsumi Yotaro

The Chieftain's Daughter (Shucho no musume, 1930)

Production	Towa Kyoto
Direction	Ishihara Eikichi
Screenplay	Fukuda Toshio
Cast	Takekawa Iwao, Miyagi Naoki

Manchurian March (Manshu koshinkyoku, 1932)

Production	Shochiku
Direction	Shimizu Hiroshi
Screenplay	Noda Kogo
Cast	Arai Jun, Ryu Chishu

Shanghai Bombardiers (Shanhai bakugekitai, 1932)

Production	Nikkatsu
Direction	Ina Seiichi
Screenplay	Hatamoto Shuichi
Cast	Nanbu Shozo, Oki Etusji

Manchurian Girl (Manshu musume, 1932)
Production   Shinko Kinema
Direction   Watanabe Shintaro
Screenplay   Yahiro Fuji
Cast   Asada Kenji, Mizuhara Reiko, Yamaji Fumiko

Dawn of the Foundation of Manchuria-Mongolia (Manmo kenkoku no reimei, 1933)
Production   Shinko Kinema
Direction   Mizoguchi Kenji
Screenplay   Masuda Shinji
Cast   Takako, Nakano Eiji, Matsumoto Taisuke

Forward! To Jehol (Yukeyo Nekka e, 1933)
Production   Shinko Kinema
Direction   Kiyosuke Takuaki
Screenplay   Takei Makoto
Cast   Asada Kenji, Mochizuki Ayako

Asia Screams (Sakebu Ajia, 1933)
Production   Tsukamoto Yoko
Direction   Uchida Tomu
Screenplay   Ito Daisuke
Cast   Fujiwara Yoshie, Shima Koji, Chiba Sachiko

Dancing Girl from the Peninsula (Hanto no maihime, 1936)
Production   Shinko Kinema
Direction   Kon Hidemi
Screenplay   Kon Hidemi
Cast   Sai Shoki, Senda Koreya, Sugai Ichiro, Urabe Kumeko

The New Earth (Atarashiki tsuchi, 1937)
Production   J. O. Studios (Toho)
Direction   Arnold Fanck (German version);
                Itami Mansaku (international version)
Screenplay   Arnold Fanck
Cast   Hayakawa Sessue, Hara Setsuko, Kosugi Isamu, Ruth Eweller

Karayuki-san (Karayukisan, 1937)
Production   P. C. L./Toho
Direction   Kimura Sotoji
Screenplay   Hatamoto Shuichi
Cast   Irie Takako, Roger Shigeno, Maruyama Sadao

The Journey (Tabiji, 1937)

Production	Chosen Eiga
Direction	Suzuki Shigeyoshi
Screenplay	Li Gyu-hwan
Cast	Wang Pyeong, Lin Sai-haeng, Mun Un-bong

Piercing Through the Northern China Sky (Hokushi no sora o tsuranuku, 1937)

Production	P. C. L./Toho
Direction	Watanabe Kunio
Screenplay	Yazumi Toshio
Cast	Irie Takako, Oka Kenji, Okawa Heihachiro

Break the Waves! (Doto o kette, 1937)

Production	P. C. L./Toho
Producer	Matsushima Keizo
Direction	Shirai Shigeru
Narration	Tokugawa Musei

Five Scouts (Gonin no sekkohei, 1938)

Production	Nikkatsu
Direction	Tasaka Tomotaka
Screenplay	Aramaki Yoshiro
Cast	Kosugi Isamu, Izawa Ichiro, Izome Shiro, Hoshi Hikaru

Shanghai (Shanhai, 1938)

Production	Toho
Producer	Noda Shinkichi
Direction	Kamei Fumio
Narration	Matsui Shusei

Nanjing (Nankin, 1938)

Production	Toho
Producer	Noda Shinkichi
Direction	Akimoto Ken
Narration	Tokugawa Musei

The Road to Peace in the Orient (Toyo heiwa no michi, 1938)

Production	Towa Shoji
Direction	Suzuki Shigeyoshi
Screenplay	Suzuki Shigeyoshi
Cast	Xu Tsung, Bai Guang, Li Feiyi, Li Ming, Zhang Erzi

Mabo's Unexplored Continent Expedition (*Mabo no tairiku hikkyo tanken*, 1938)
Production   Sato Sen
Animation   Sato Ginjiro, Chiba Hiromichi

Karayuki War Song (*Karayuki gunka*, 1938)
Production   Shinko Tokyo
Direction   Mieda Shintaro
Screenplay   Murakami Tokusaburo
Cast   Kawazu Seisaburo, Shiga Etsuko, Hirai Kiyoko, Tanano Yumi

Troop Train (*Gunyo ressha*, 1938)
Production   Hanto Eiga
Direction   Seo Gwang-je
Screenplay   Cho Yeong-pil, Kikuchi Morio
Cast   Wang Pyeong, Lin Sai-haeng, Jeong Sun-hui, Sasaki Nobuko

Beijing (*Pekin*, 1938)
Production   Toho
Producer   Matsuzaki Keiji
Direction   Kamei Fumio
Narration   Matsuda Shusei

International Spy Ring (*Kokusai supai ami*, 1938)
Production   Daito Eiga
Direction   Yatsushiro Atsushi
Screenplay   Yatsushiro Atsushi
Cast   Fujima Rintaro, Matsukaze Chiaki, Nakano Eiji, Oyama Debuko

Enoken Busts Through to the Continent (*Enoken no tairiku tosshin*, 1938)
Production   Toho
Direction   Watanabe Kunio
Screenplay   Watanabe Kunio
Cast   Enomoto Kenichi, Tsukijima Haruko, Kisaragi Kanta

Daughter of Asia (*Ajia no musume*, 1938)
Production   Shinko Kinema (Tokyo)
Direction   Tanaka Shigeo
Screenplay   Yoda Yoshitaka
Cast   Kawazu Seizaburo, Aizome Yumeko, Niida Minoru

Continental March (*Tairiku koshinkyoku*, 1938)
Production   Nikkatsu (Tamagawa)
Direction   Taguchi Tetsu
Screenplay   Taguchi Tetsu
Cast   Todoroki Yukiko, Kosugi Isamu

My Nightingale (*Watakushi no uguisu*, 1938)
Production   Manchurian Film Co. (Manei)/Toho
Direction   Shimazu Yasujiro
Screenplay   Shimazu Yasujiro
Cast   Ri Koran, Gregorii Sayapin, Chiba Sachiko, Basil Tomskii

Continental Bride (*Tairiku no hanayome*, 1939)
Production   Daito Eiga
Direction   Yoshimura So
Screenplay   Kita Reito
Cast   Nakano Eiji, Fujima Rintaro, Oyama Debuko

Fighting Soldiers (*Tatakau heitai*, 1939)
Production   Toho
Producer   Matsuzaki Keiji
Direction   Kamei Fumio
Camera   Miki Shigeru

Continental Bride (*Tairiku no hanayome*, 1939)
Production   Shochiku
Direction   Hirukawa Iseo
Screenplay   Saito Ryosuke
Cast   Miura Mitsuko, Tokudaiji Noboru, Sakamoto Takeshi,
              Yoshikawa Mitsuko

Shanghai Landing Squad (*Shanhai rikusentai*, 1939)
Production   Toho
Direction   Kumagai Hisatora
Screenplay   Sawamura Ben
Cast   Ohinata Den, Saiki Hideo, Hara Setsuko

China Doll (*Shina ningyo*, 1939)
Production   Takarazuka Eigasha
Production details unknown

The Han River (*Kanko*, 1939)
Production   Hanto Eiga
Direction   Pang Han-sun
Screenplay   Kim Hyeok, Li Yi
Cast   Li Geum-ryong, Hyeon Sun-yeong

Earth and Soldiers (*Tsuchi to heitai*, 1939)
Production   Nikkatsu (Tamagawa)
Direction   Tasaka Tomotaka
Screenplay   Sasahara Ryozo
Cast   Kosugi Isamu, Izome Shiro

Song of the White Orchid (*Byakuran no uta*, 1939)
Production   Toho
Direction   Watanabe Kunio
Screenplay   Kimura Chieo
Cast   Hasegawa Kazuo, Saito Tatsuo, Ri Koran

Yaji and Kita: On the Road to the Continent (*Yaji kita tairiku dochu*, 1939)
Production   Shochiku
Direction   Kono Eisaku
Screenplay   Yanai Takao
Cast   Takada Hiroyoshi, Fushimi Nobuko, Tsuboi Tetsu, Masuda Kiton

Karafuto (*Karafuto chiho*, 1940)
Production   Kyoikuyo Jisha
Production details unknown

Blossoming on the Continent (*Daichi ni saku*, 1940)
Production   Nikkatsu (Tamagawa)
Direction   Kiyose Eijiro
Screenplay   Toyama Tetsu
Cast   Nakata Koji, Izawa Ichiro, Todoroki Yukiko

Karafuto and Fox Culturing (*Karafuto to yoko*, 1940)
Production   Morimoto Yoyoyoshi
Production details unknown

Okiku from Siberia (*Shiberia okiku*, 1940)
Production   Daito Eiga
Direction   Yoshimura So, Wada Toshizo
Screenplay   Tsuchida Kohei
Cast   Mizuhara Yoichi, Tsushima Keiichiro, Matsukaze Chieko,
              Kumoi Saburo

10,000 Leagues of Exotic Land (Yodo banri, 1940)
Production   Nikkatsu (Tamagawa)
Direction   Kurata Bunjin
Screenplay   Kurata Bunjin
Cast   Egawa Ureio, Izumo Tatusko, Kazami Masako

A Journey to the East (Toyuki, 1940)
Production   Toho/ Manchurian Film Co. (Manei)
Direction   Oya Toshio
Screenplay   Takayanagi Haruo
Cast   Ri Koran, Xu Tsung, Fujiwara Kamsoku, Kishii Akira, Hara Setsuko

A Record of Building a New Continent (Shin tairiku kensetsu no kiroku, 1940)
Production   Domei Tsushinsha
Direction   Kuwano Shigeru
Narration   Kitamura Atsushi

Glimpses of the Canton Advance (Koton shingunsho, 1940)
Production   Nihon Tampen Eigasha
Direction   Takagi Toshiro
Screenplay   Hino Ashihei

The Yang-tze River (Yosuko, 1940)
Production   Ministry of the Navy
Direction   Mie Shintaro
Camera   Yahagi Hoji, Kitamura Kojiro

China Nights (Shina no yoru, 1940)
Production   Toho
Direction   Fushimizu Osamu
Screenplay   Oguni Hideo
Cast   Hasegawa Kazuo, Ri Koran, Hattori Tomiko

The Continent Smiles (Tairiku wa hohoemu, 1940)
Production   Daito Eiga
Direction   Yato Kenji
Screenplay   Tsuchida Kohei
Cast   Tsushima Keiichiro, Terumoto Setsuko, Misora Hibari

Dawn's Light (Reimei kokyo, 1940)
Production   Manchurian Film Co. (Manei)/Shochiku
Direction   Yamauchi Eizo
Screenplay   Aramaki Yoshiro
Cast   Xu Tsung, Ryu Chishu, Ju Chou

Ohinata Village (Ohinata mura, 1940)
Production   Tokyo Hassei Eiga
Direction   Toyoda Shiro
Screenplay   Yagi Koic
Cast   Kawarazaki Chojuro, Sugimura Haruko, Nakamura Meiko

The Monkey King (Songoku, 1940)
Production   Toho
Direction   Yamamoto Kajiro
Screenplay   Yamamoto Kajiro
Cast   Enomoto Kenichi, Kishii Akira, Hattori Tomiko, Ri Koran,
              Wang Yang

Women Head South (Nanshin josei, 1940)
Production   Shinko Kinema
Direction   Ochiai Yoshito
Screenplay   Shindo Kaneto
Cast   Mihato Mari, Wakahara Masao

Vow in the Desert (Nessa no chikai, 1940)
Production   Toho/Kahoku Denei
Direction   Watanabe Kunio
Screenplay   Watanabe Kunio
Cast   Hasegawa Kazuo, Ri Koran, Egawa Ureio, Wang Yang

Seoul (Keijo, 1940)
Production   Dai Nippon Bunka Eiga
Producer   Takahashi Tadao
Director   Shimizu Hiroshi
Camera   Atsuta Yuharu

Pray for the Continent (Daichi ni inoru, 1941)
Production   Tokyo Hassei Eiga
Direction   Murata Takeo
Screenplay   Otsu Shinzo
Cast   Honma Kazuko, Satomi Aiko, Chiba Sachiko

A Song of New Life (Shinsei no uta, 1941)
Production   Shinko Kinema
Direction   Numanami Katsuo
Screenplay   Ichinoki Akira
Cast   Mayama Kumiko, Kaga Kunio

Moon Over Shanghai (*Shanhai no tsuki*, 1941)
Production   Toho/Zhonghua Dianying
Direction   Naruse Mikio
Screenplay   Yamagata Yusaku
Cast   Yamada Isuzu, Wang Yang, Satomi Aiko

Arctic Lights (*Hokkyoko*, 1941)
Production   Shinko Kinema
Direction   Tanaka Shigeo
Screenplay   Murakami Genzo
Cast   Mayama Fumiko, Koshiba Kanji, Mihato Mari, Kuroda Noriyo

Beautiful Sacrifice (*Utsukushiki gisei*, 1941)
Production   Manchurian Film Co. (Manei)
Direction   Yamauchi Eizo
Screenplay   Takayanagi Haruo
Cast   Ri Koran, Sui Yi-fu, Lau En-Sheng

The Land of Cherry Blossoms (*Sakura no kuni*, 1941)
Production   Shochiku/Kahoku Denei
Direction   Shibuya Minoru
Screenplay   Ikeda Tadao, Tsuro Yoshiro
Cast   Uehara Ken, Takamine Mieko, Mito Mitsuko, Saito Tatsuo,
               Ryu Chishu

Joindo (1941)
Production   Hanto Eiga
Direction   Pang Han-sun
Screenplay   Ri Yi
Cast   Hyeon Sun-yeong, Choe Un-bong, Li Baek-su, Jeon Taek-i

You and I (*Kimi to boku*, 1941)
Production   Chosen Gunhodobu
Direction   Hinatsu Eitaro
Screenplay   Iijima Tadashi, Hinatsu Eitaro
Cast   Mizuta Genjiro, Kosugi Isamu, Ohinata Den, Kawazu Seizaburo,
               Ri Koran

Suzhou Nights (*Soshu no yoru*, 1941)
Production   Shochiku
Direction   Nomura Hiromasa
Screenplay   Saito Ryosuke
Cast   Sano Shuji, Saito Tatsuo, Ri Koran, Mito Mitsuko

Spring on the Peninsula (*Hanto no haru*, 1942)
Production   Meiho Eiga
Direction   Li Byeong-il
Screenplay   Han Gyeong-ho
Cast   Kim Il-hae, Kim So-yeong, So Wol-yeong, Baek Nan

Mabo's Record of Fighting South Sea Savages (*Mabo no nankai bansenki*, 1942)
Production   Sato Eiga
Producer   Sato Ginjiro
Direction   Chiba Hiromichi
Animation   Chiba Hiromichi

Mabo's Continent Pacification Squad: Exterminating Bandits
(*Mabo no tairiku senbutai: Hizoku taiji no maki*, 1942)
Production   Sato Eiga
Producer   Sato Ginjiro
Direction   Chiba Hiromichi
Narration   Makino Shuichi

Early Blossoming Flower (*Geshunka*, 1942)
Production   Manchurian Film Co. (Manei)
Direction   Sasaki Yasushi
Screenplay   Nagase Kihan
Cast   Ri Koran, Qun Wei, Zhang Min, Kogure Michiyo, Konoe Toshiro

The Green Earth (*Midori no daichi*, 1942)
Production   Toho
Direction   Shimazu Yasujiro
Screenplay   Yamagata Yusaku
Cast   Irie Takako, Egawa Ureio, Fujita Susumu, Hara Setsuko, Ikebe Ryo

Spies Don't Die (*Kancho imada shisezu*, 1942)
Production   Shochiku
Direction   Yoshimura Kimisaburo
Screenplay   Tsuro Yoshiro, Kinoshita Keisuke
Cast   Saburi Shin, Uehara Ken, Saito Tatsuo, Mito Mitsuko,
              Kogure Michiyo

He Returned from the South (*Minami kara kaetta hito*, 1942)
Production   Toho
Direction   Saito Torajiro
Screenplay   Oguni Hideo
Cast   Furukawa Roppa, Watanabe Kaoru, Takamine Hideko, Irie Takako

Bouquet of the South Seas (*Nankai no hanataba*, 1942)
Production   Toho
Direction   Abe Yutaka
Screenplay   Abe Yutaka, Yagi Koichiro
Cast   Ohinata Den, Kawazu Seizaburo, Okawa Heihachiro,
              Maki Jun Tsukida Ichiro

The Water Margin (*Suikoden*, 1942)
Production   Toho
Direction   Okada Kei
Screenplay   Kishi Matsuo
Cast   Enomoto Kenichi, Shiomi Yo, Takamine Hideko, Tokugawa Musei,
              Kishii Akira

Mulan Joins the Army (*Mulan jugun*, 1942)
Production   Zhongguo lianhua yingye gongsi: Huacheng Film
Direction   Bu Wangcang
Screenplay   Ouyang Yuqian
Cast   Chen Yunchang, Xi Mei, Han Langen, Liu Jiqun, Huang Naishuang

Malay War Diary (*Mare senki*, 1942)
Production   Nihon Eigasha
Screenplay   Iijima Shinbi

Southern Winds (*Minami no kaze*, 1942)
Production   Shochiku
Direction   Yoshimura Kimisaburo
Screenplay   Ikeda Tadao
Cast   Saburi Shin, Ryu Chishu, Takamine Mieko

Burma War Diary (*Biruma senki*, 1942)
Production   Nihon Eigasha

The Clan of the Sea (*Umi no gozoku*, 1942)
Production   Nikkatsu (Kyoto)
Direction   Arai Ryohei
Screenplay   Katado Katsuo
Cast   Arashi Kanjuro, Sawamura Kunitaro, Hara Kensaku, Okura Chiyoko

Southern Winds II (*Zoku Minami no kaze*, 1942)
Production   Shochiku
Direction   Yoshimura Kimisaburo
Screenplay   Ikeda Tadao
Cast   Saburi Shin, Ryu Chishu, Takamine Mieko, Saito Tatsuo, Mito Mitsuko

Attack on Hong Kong: The Day England Fell
(*Honkon koryaku: Eikoku kuzururu hi*, 1942)
Production   Daiei
Direction   Tanaka Shigeo
Screenplay   Toyama Tetsu, Koiwa Hajime
Cast   Usami Jun, Kuroda Noriyo

Genghis Khan (*Jingasu kan*, 1943)
Production   Daiei
Direction   Ushiwara Kiyohiko, Matsuda Teiji
Screenplay   Hisa Yoshitake
Cast   Togami Jotaro, Takiguchi Shintaro, Kagawa Ryosuke, Kita Ryuji

The Eve of War (*Kaisen no zenya*, 1943)
Production   Shochiku
Direction   Yoshimura Kimisaburo
Screenplay   Tsuro Yoshiro, Takei Shohei
Cast   Tanaka Kinuyo, Uehara Ken, Kogure Michiyo, Ryu Chishu

The Opium War (*Ahen senso*, 1943)
Production   Toho
Direction   Makino Masahiro
Screenplay   Oguni Hideo
Cast   Kosugi Isamu, Sugai Ichiro, Maruyama Sadao, Takamine Hideko

City of War (*Tatakai no machi*, 1943)
Production   Shochiku
Direction   Hara Kenkichi
Screenplay   Uchida Gisaburo
Cast   Uehara Ken, Ri Koran, Miura Mitsuko, Tokudaiji Shin

Our Music on the March (*Ongaku daishingun*, 1943)
Production   Toho
Direction   Watanabe Kunio
Screenplay   Kisaragi Bin, Yamazaki Kenta
Cast   Hasegawa Kazuo, Furukawa Roppa, Oka Kenji, Kishii Akira,
    Takamine Hideko

Momotaro's Sea Hawks (*Momotaro no umiwashi*, 1943)
Production   Geijutsu Eigasha
Supervision   Navy Info Division
Direction   Seyo Mitsuyo
Screenplay   Kurihara Arishige

Suicide Troops of the Watchtower (*Boro no kesshitai*, 1943)

Production	Toho/Chosen Eiga
Direction	Imai Tadashi
Screenplay	Yamagata Yusaku, Yagi Ryuichiro
Cast	Takada Minoru, Saito Tatsuo, Sugai Ichiro, Hara Setsuko

Singapore All-out Attack (*Shingaporu sokogeki*, 1943)

Production	Daiei
Direction	Shima Koji
Screenplay	Nagami Koji
Cast	Murata Koju, Nanbu Shozo, Nakata Koji

The Tiger of Malay (*Marai no tora*, 1943)

Production	Daiei
Direction	Koga Masato
Screenplay	Kimura Keizo
Cast	Nakata Koji, Nanbu Shozo, Ueda Kichijiro, Murata Koju

Bell of Sayon (*Sayon no kane*, 1943)

Production	Shochiku/Taiwan Colonial Govt./Manchurian Film Co. (Manei)
Direction	Shimizu Hiroshi
Screenplay	Ushida Hiro, Saito Torajiro
Cast	Ri Koran, Oyama Kenji

The Promised Chorus (*Chikai no gassho*, 1943)

Production	Toho/Manchurian Film Co. (Manei)
Direction	Shimazu Yasujiro
Screenplay	Shimazu Yasujiro
Cast	Ri Koran, Kurokawa Yataro, Toba Yonosuke

Maria Ruze Slave Ship Incident (*Maria Ruzu jiken doreibune*, 1943)

Production	Daiei
Direction	Marune Santaro
Screenplay	Marune Santaro
Cast	Ichikawa Utaemon, Ichikawa Haruyo, Tachibana Kimiko

Our Planes Fly South (*Aiki minami e tobu*, 1943)

Production	Shochiku
Direction	Sasaki Yasushi
Screenplay	Yanai Takeo
Cast	Saburi Shin, Nobu Chiyo

On to Victory in the Skies (Kessen no ozora e, 1943)
Production   Toho
Direction   Watanabe Kunio
Screenplay   Yazumi Toshio
Cast   Takada Minoru, Hara Setsuko, Kodaka Masaru

Torrid Winds (Neppu, 1943)
Production   Toho
Direction   Yamamoto Satsuo
Screenplay   Yazumi Toshio
Cast   Fujita Susumu, Numazaki Tsutomu, Hara Setsuko

Onward, Flag of Independence (Susume dokuritsuki, 1943)
Production   Toho
Direction   Kinugasa Teinosuke
Screenplay   Yazumi Toshio, Yamagata Yusaku
Cast   Hasegawa Kazuo, Irie Takako, Todoroki Yukiko, Mori Masayuki

The Man from Chungking (Jukei kara kita otoko, 1943)
Production   Daiei
Direction   Yamamoto Hiroyuki
Screenplay   Ishida Yoshio
Cast   Mizushima Michitaro, Aiba Chieko, Hoshi Hikaru, Urabe Kumeko

Figure of Youth (Wakaki sugata, 1943)
Production   Chosen Eiga/Toho/Daiei/Shochiku
Direction   Toyoda Shiro
Screenplay   Hatta Naoyuki
Cast   Maruyama Sadao, Tsukigata Ryunosuke, Saburi Shin, Huang Kou,
              Wen Yiyuen

Blast the Pirate's Flag (Kaizokuki Futobu, 1943)
Production   Shochiku (Kyoto)
Direction   Tsuji Kichiro
Screenplay   Makino Shinzo, Takizawa Hajime
Cast   Takada Hirokichi, Sawamura Kunitaro, Miyagi Chikako

Fire on that Flag! [aka *Dawn of Freedom*] *(Ano hata o ute!,* 1944)
Production   Toho
Direction   Abe Yutaka
Screenplay   Yagi Koichiro, Oguni Hideo
Cast   Ogochi Denjiro, Kawazu Seizaburo, Tsukida Ichiro, Fernando Po,
              Leopold Celecdo

Captain Kato's Fighting Hawk Squadron (*Kato hayabusa sentotai*, 1944)

Production	Toho
Direction	Yamamoto Kajiro
Screenplay	Yamazaki Kenta, Yamamoto Kajiro
Cast	Fujita Susumu Kurokawa Yataro, Numazaki Tsutomu, Takada Minoru, Ogochi Denjiro

International Smuggling Ring (*Kokusai mitsuyunyu dan*, 1944)

Production	Daiei (Kyoto)
Direction	Ito Daisuke
Screenplay	Ito Daisuke
Cast	Ichikawa Utaemon, Terajima Mitsugu

Mr. Sailor (*Suiheisan*, 1944)

Production	Shochiku
Direction	Hara Kenkichi
Screenplay	Yanagawa Shinichi
Cast	Hoshino Kazumasa, Mito Mitsuko Ryu Chishu, Iida Choko

Lifeline Harbor (*Inochi no minato*, 1944)

Production	Toho
Direction	Watanabe Kunio
Screenplay	YamagataYusaku
Cast	Hasegawa Kazuo, Takehisa Chieko, Yamane Yasuko, Tsukida Ichiro

Storm Over Bengal (*Bengaru no arashi*, 1944)

Production	Daiei
Direction	Nobuchi Akira
Screenplay	Nobuchi Akira
Cast	Ramon Mitsusaburo, Usami Jun

Celebes (*Serebes*, 1944)

Production	Nihon Eigasha
Direction	Akimoto Ken
Camera	Kogura Kinya

Though the Enemy Numbers Millions (*Teki wa ikuman aritotemo*, 1944)

Production	Toho
Direction	Saito Torajiro
Screenplay	Yamagata Yusaku, Fushimi Akira
Cast	Furukawa Roppa, Hanai Ranko, Tsukida Ichiro

Frontline Brass Band (*Yasen gunrakutai*, 1944)
Production   Shochiku (Kyoto)
Direction   Makino Masahiro
Screenplay   Noda Kogo
Cast   Ri Koran, Kosugi Isamu, Saburi Shin, Uehara Ken, Sano Shuji,

Thus Blows the Divine Wind (*Kakute kamikaze wa fuku*, 1944)
Production   Daiei (Kyoto)/Imperial Army/Imperial Navy
Direction   Marune Santaro
Screenplay   Matsuda Inosuke
Cast   Bando Tsumasaburo, Katayama Akihiko

The Army (*Rikugun*, 1944)
Production   Shochiku
Direction   Kinoshita Keisuke
Screenplay   Ikeda Tadao
Cast   Ryu Chishu, Nobu Chiyo

Blitz Squad Moves Out (*Raigekitai shutsudo*, 1944)
Production   Toho
Direction   Yamamoto Kajiro
Screenplay   Yamamoto Kajiro
Cast   Ogochi Denjiro, Fujita Susumu, Kono Akitake, Tsukida Ichiro,
               Haida Katsuhiko

Signal Fires in Shanghai [aka *Remorse in Shanghai*]
(*Noroshi wa Shanhai ni agaru*, 1944)
Production   Daiei/Zhonghua Dianying
Direction   Inagaki Hiroshi
Screenplay   Yahiro Fuji
Cast   Bando Tsumasaburo, Li Luhua, Tsukigata Ryunosuke

Invisible Enemy (*Sugata naki teki*, 1945)
Production   Daiei
Direction   Chiba Yasuki
Screenplay   Ogawa Norimasa
Cast   Usami Jun, Murata Chieko

Momotaro Divine Soldiers of the Sea (*Momotaro umi no shinpei*, 1945)
Production   Shochiku
Direction   Seyo Mitsuyo
Animation   Kumaki Kiichiro

A Japanese Tragedy (*Nihon no higeki*, 1946)
Production   Nichiei
Direction   Kamei Fumio
Editing   Kamei Fumio

Coming Home (Damoi) (*Kikoku [damoi]*, 1949)
Production   Shin Toho
Direction   Sato Takeshi
Screenplay   Kishi Matsuo
Cast   Inoue Masao, Ohinata Den, Ikebe Ryo, Yamaguchi Yoshiko,
               Fujita Susumu

Escape at Dawn (*Akatsuki no dasso*, 1950)
Production   Shin Toho
Direction   Taniguchi Senkichi
Screenplay   Taniguchi Senkichi, Kurosawa Akira
Cast   Ikebe Ryo, Yamaguchi Yoshiko, Ozawa Ei, Tanaka Haruo

Hear the Voices of the Sea (*Kike wadatsumi no koe*, 1950)
Production   Toyoko Eiga
Direction   Sekigawa Hideo
Screenplay   Funabashi Kazuro
Cast   Izu Hajime, Hara Naomi, Sugimura Haruko, Kono Akitake

The Bells of Nagasaki (*Nagasaki no kane*, 1950)
Production   Shochiku
Direction   Oba Hideo
Screenplay   Shindo Kaneto
Cast   Wakahara Masao, Tsushima Keiko, Takizawa Shu

Fragrance of the Night [aka *Ye lai xiang*] (*Yaraika*, 1951)
Production   Shin Toho
Direction   Ichikawa Kon
Screenplay   Matsuura Toshio, Ichikawa Kon
Cast   Uehara Ken, Kuji Asami

Bengawan Solo (*Bungawan soro*, 1951)
Production   Shin Toho
Direction   Ichikawa Kon
Screenplay   Wada Natto
Cast   Ikebe Ryo, Ito Yunosuke, Fujita Susumu, Kuji Asami

White Orchid of the Desert (*Nessa no byakuran*, 1951)

Production	Daiichi Kyodan
Direction	Kimura Keigo
Screenplay	Shindo Kaneto
Cast	Kogure Michiyo, Yamamura So, Ikebe Ryo, Sugai Ichiro

Woman of Shanghai (*Shanhai no onna*, 1952)

Production	Toho
Direction	Inagaki Hiroshi
Screenplay	Tanada Goro, Inagaki Hiroshi
Cast	Yamaguchi Yoshiko, Mikuni Rentaro, Araki Michiko

Buck Privates (*Nitohei Monogatari*, 1955)

Production	Shochiku
Direction	Fukuda Seiichi
Screenplay	Funabashi Kazuro
Cast	Ban Junzaburo, Hanabishi Achako, Miyagino Yumiko

Desperado Outpost (*Dokuritsu gurentai*, 1959)

Production	Toho
Direction	Okamoto Kihachi
Screenplay	Okamoto Kihachi
Cast	Sato Makoto, Uemura Sachiyuki, Mifune Toshiro

Dear Mr. Emperor (*Haikei tenno heika-sama*, 1963)

Production	Shochiku
Direction	Nomura Yoshitaro
Screenplay	Nomura Yoshitaro
Cast	Atsumi Kiyoshi, Nagato Hiroyuki, Nakamura Meiko

Dear Mr. Emperor II (*Zoku haikei tenno heika-sama*, 1964)

Production	Shochiku
Direction	Nomura Yoshitaro
Screenplay	Nomura Yoshitaro, Yamada Yoji
Cast	Atsumi Kiyoshi, Sada Keiji, Iwashita Shima

Yakuza Soldier (*Heitai yakuza*, 1965)

Production	Daiei
Direction	Masumura Yasuzo
Screenplay	Kikushima Ryuzo
Cast	Katsu Shintaro, Tamura Takahiro, Awaji Keiko

Notes

Lost Histories

1. *2009: Lost Memories* (*2009: Lostu memoriju*) was one of the most expensive South Korean feature films ever produced, costing an estimated US$6 million. *Lost Memories* remained in the top ten for six weeks, gaining a total of 2,263,800 paid admissions nationwide. See Korean Association of Film Art and Industry and the Korean Film Commission (KOFIC) website http://hyunfilm.tripod.com/2002.htm. Novelist Bok Geo-il was reportedly so dissatisfied with the film adaptation of his book that he successfully sued the production company to have his name removed from the credits.

2. This appears to be a misspelling of the derogatory Japanese term *futei senjin*, which was historically used to refer to "insubordinate (or lawless) Koreans."

3. Goguryeo (37 BC–668 CE) was a kingdom in northern Korea and a large part of Manchuria. Along with Baekje and Silla, it was one of the Three Kingdoms of Korea.

4. Dialogue in Japanese and Korean from *2009: Lost Memories*.

5. Examples of Korean movies popular in Japan include *Asako in Ruby Shoes* (*Sunaebo*, 2000, dir. Lee Je-Yong); *Seoul* (2002, dir. Nagasawa Masahiko); *KT* (2002, dir. Sakamoto Junji); *Run 2U* (*Ron tu yu*, 2003, dir. Kang Jeong-Su); and *Hotel Venus* (*Hoteru biinasu*, 2004, dir. Takahata Shuta). There have also been numerous collaborations on such television drama productions as *Fighting Girl* (2001, Fuji-TV); *Friends* (2002, MBC/TBS); and *Sonagi* (2002, MBC/Fuji-TV). *Winter Sonata* (broadcast on NHK in 2003) was not a coproduction, but is considered to be one of the most important breakthroughs in creating a broad audience base for the Korean Wave.

6. Stephen Howe, *Empire: A Very Short Introduction* (Oxford University Press, 2002), 10.

7. These include action films such as *Phantom: The Submarine* (*Yuryong*, 1999, dir. Min Byung-Chun); comedies such as *YMCA Baseball Team* (*YMCA Yagudan*, 2002, dir. Kim Hyeon-Seok); and historical melodramas like *Thomas Ahn Jung-geun* (*Doma Ahn Jung-geun*, 2004, dir. Seo Se-won); *Fighter in the Wind* (*Paramui paito*, 2004, dir. Yang Yun-ho); *Han Gil-su* (2005, dir. Lee In-su); *Rikidozan* (2005, dir. Song Hae-sung); *Blue Swallow* (*Cheong yeon*, 2005, dir. Yun Jong-chan); and *With a Blue Sky* (*Changgong uro*, 2006, dir. Lee In-Su).

8. "[Japan] most certainly did not militarily invade [Korea]. Rather, it was because the Korean peninsula was divided and could not be consolidated that by their own collective will [the Koreans] chose between Russia, China (*Shina*), and Japan. They sought the help of the modernized Japanese people, who shared the same facial color as their own and

annexation was conducted by a consensus of the world's nations. I do not intend to justify Japanese annexation 100 percent. From their [the Koreans'] emotional point of view, it probably was annoying, maybe even humiliating. But if anything, it was the responsibility of their ancestors." *Mainichi shinbun*, Oct. 29, 2003.

9. Notable examples include: *Nanking 1937* (1995, Hong Kong, dir. Wu Ziniu); *Devils on the Doorstep* (*Guizi lai le*, 2000, China, dir. Jiang Wen); *Purple Butterfly* (*Zi hudie*, 2003, China, dir. Lou Ye); *City of Sadness* (*Beiqing chengshi*, 1989, Taiwan, dir. Hou Hsiao Hsien); *A Borrowed Life* (*Duo-sang*, 1994, Taiwan, dir. Wu Nien-Jen); *Boys Will Be Boys, Boys Will Be Men* (2000, Thailand, dir. Euthana Mukdasanit); *Behind the Painting* (*Khanglang phap*, 2001, Thailand, dir. Cherd Songsri); *In the Bosom of the Enemy* (*Gatas: Sa dibdib ng kaaway*, 2001, Philippines, dir. Gil Portes); *Aishite imasu* (Mahal kita) *1941* (2004, Philippines, dir. Joel Lamangan); *Embun* (2002, Malaysia, dir. Erma Fatima); *Budak nafsu* (1983, Indonesia, dir. Syuman Djaya).

10. Edward Said, *Culture and Imperialism* (New York: Vintage, 1993), 12.

11. A 1938 U.S. Department of Commerce report on foreign film markets explained: "It has frequently been pointed out that Japan has the reputation of being the largest producer of motion pictures for home consumption in the world. This reputation has been built up by a 'grinding out' policy of production, with quality of secondary consideration and decidedly inferior to that of American and European productions. In spite of the large meterage of film produced, Japanese producers cannot make sufficient quality feature films to supply the domestic market." The report also suggests that Japan's massive newsreel production contributes to the inflated numbers. See U.S. Department of Commerce, Motion Picture Division, ed., *Review of Foreign Markets* (Washington, DC, U.S. Department of Commerce, 1938), 305. The Japanese Home Ministry reported that Japan produced 580 films to America's 548 (compare with Britain, 150; Germany, 125; France, 121; China, 75; and Italy, 37) quoted in *Eiga bunka tenrankaiki* (Dainippon eiga kyokai, 1940), 69 [chart 10].

12. Joseph Nye, *Bound to Lead: The Changing Nature of American Power* (Basic Books, 1990), 32–33.

13. Daniel Headrick *The Tools of Empire* (New York: Oxford University Press, 1981), 4.

14. Paul Virilio *War and Cinema: The Logistics of Perception* (New York: Verso, 1989).

15. Ella Shohat and Robert Stam, *Unthinking Eurocentrism* (London: Routledge, 1994), 100.

16. John MacKenzie *Propaganda and Empire* (Manchester: Manchester University Press, 1986), 72–73. Guido Convents, "Film and German Colonial Propaganda," in *Prima di Caligari* (Biblioteca dell'Immagine, 1990), 58–76. Sabine Hake, "Mapping the Native Body," in Friedrichsmeyer, ed., *The Imperialist Imagination* (Ann Arbor: University of Michigan Press, 1998), 163–187.

17. Koga Futoshi, ed. *Hikari no tanjo Lumière!* (Asahi Shinbun, 1995); and Yoshida Yoshishige et al., *Eiga torai-shinematogurafu to [Meiji no Nihon]* (Iwanami Shoten, 1995).

18. Other Lumière films include: *Japanese Actors: Trying on Wigs* (*Acteurs japonais: Exercice de la perruque*, 1898); *Japanese Dances: 1–3* (*Danse japonaise: 1–III*, 1899); *Japanese Woman Puts on Make up* (*Japonaise faisant sa toilette*, 1899). Freres Pathé, Edison, and later Vitagraph also produced Japan-themed films within a year or two of 1897.

19. Hazumi Tsuneo, *Eiga gojunenshi* (Masu Shobo, 1942), 24.

20. MacKenzie, *Propaganda*, 70–71.

21. Virilio, *War and Cinema*, 68.

22. Li Narangoa and Robert Cribb, eds., *Imperial Japan and National Identities in Asia, 1895–1945* (London: Routledge, 2003), 1–22.

23. Tanaka Junichiro, *Nihon kyoiku eiga hattatsushi* (Kagyusha, 1979), 23–24.

24. H. D. Harootunian "A Sense of an Ending and the Problem of Taisho," in Harootunian et al., *Japan in Crisis: Essays on Taisho Democracy* (Princeton, NJ: Princeton University Press, 1974), 3–28.

25. Akutagawa Mitsuzo, "Manei o choshu suru," *Eiga junpo*, Aug. 1, 1942, 20.

26. Ichikawa Sai, *Ajia eiga no sozo oyobi kensetsu* (Kokusai eiga tsushinsha, 1941); Hazumi Tsuneo, *Eiga gojunenshi* (Masu Shobo, 1942); Tsumura Hideo, *Eigasen* (Asahi shinsensho, 1944); Shibata Yoshio, *Sekai eiga senso* (Toyosha, 1944).

27. Martin Greene, *Dreams of Adventure, Deeds of Empire* (New York: Basic Books, 1979), 11.

28. Ibid.

29. Iijima Tadashi, *Nihon eigashi*, vol. 2. (Hakusuisha, 1955), 66.

30. "All domestic industries were treated the same and the film industry was no exception. We went from a free economy to a controlled economy just like a rabbit being hunted by a dog." Tanaka, *Nihon eiga hattatsushi*, vol. 3, 20.

31. Some notable exceptions include: Iwamoto Kenji, ed., *Eiga to daitoa kyoeiken* (Shinwasha, 2004); Yomota Inuhiko *Ri Koran to higashi Ajia* (Tokyo daigaku shuppankai, 2001); Tamura Shizue *Hajime ni eiga ga atta* (Chuokoron shinsha, 2000); Peter B. High, *Teikoku no ginmaku* (Nagoya: Nagoya University Press, 1995), translated and revised in English as *The Imperial Screen* (Madison: University of Wisconsin, 2003); Shimizu Akira, *Shanhai sokai eiga shishi* (Shinchosha, 1995); Yamaguchi Takeshi *Maboroshi no kinema Manei* (Heibonsha, 1989); Sato Tadao, *Kinema to hosei* (Riburopoto, 1985).

32. Elsewhere I have written on the links between postwar Japanese "victim" narratives and an underlying imperialist desire in the so-called postwar antiwar film genre. See Michael Baskett, "Dying for a Laugh: Japanese Post-1945 Service Comedies," *Historical Journal of Film, Radio, & Television* 23, no. 4 (Oct. 2003), 291–310.

33. In this sense, my book shares many of the assertions made by Robert Rydell's in his research on world's fairs. See particularly, Robert W. Rydell, *World of Fairs* (Chicago: University of Chicago Press, 1993).

34. Amakasu, Masahiko. "Manjin no tame ni eiga o tsukuru." *Eiga junpo*, Aug. 1, 1942, 3.

35. Eric Hobsbawm *The Age of Empire* (New York: Vintage, 1987), 151.

Chapter One: From Film Colony to Film Sphere

1. Ichikawa Sai, *Ajia eiga no sozo oyobi kensetsu* (Kokusai Eiga Tsushinsha, 1941), 86–88. Taiwan film historian Tamura Shizue speculates that Takamatsu also screened *Hokusei jihen katsudoshashin*; Tamura Shizue, *Hajime ni eiga ga atta* (Chuo Koron Shinsha, 2000), 54.

2. Tamura, *Hajime ni*, 88.

3. Ibid., 90.

4. Kobayashi Katsu, "Taiwan eigakai no insho," *Eiga junpo*, May 1, 1942, 40–42.

5. Tamura, *Hajime ni*, 97.

6. Sawamura Kunitaro, "Taiwan hodan," *Eiga* (Apr. 1942): 75–76.

7. Ibid.

8. Patricia Tsurumi argues that this was the primary goal of Japanese-language policies in Taiwan during the era of Japanese colonialism; see her *Japanese Colonial Education in Taiwan* (Cambridge, MA: Harvard University Press, 1977), 2.

9. Hung Ya-wen, "Nihon shokuminchi shihai ni okeru Taiwan eigakai ni kansuru kosatsu" (MA thesis, Waseda University, 1997).

10. Shimizu Kogakko Eiga Kenkyubu, ed., *Eiga kyoiku no jissai* (Tokyo: self-published, 1941), 19–27.

11. Hung Ya-wen, "Sotokufu ni yoru eiga seisaku." *Eigagaku*, vol. 12 (Sept. 1998), 120.

12. Taichushu Kyoikukai, "Eiga annai ichi taichushu gakko eiga renmei shincho firumu shokai," *Taichushu kyoiku* 4, no. 7 (1937): 24–27.

13. Production data unknown. This film was screened in Japan at the Yamagata International Documentary Film Festival 1997.

14. Ichikawa, *Ajia eiga*, 86–98.

15. Ibid., 86.

16. Jo Fukkan, "Eiga to engeki kankeisha zadankai," cited in Hung, *Nihon shokuminchi*, 132.

17. Hung, "Sotokufu," 138; Chen Fei-Bao, *Taiwan dianying shihua* (Beijing: Zhongguo Dianying Chubanshe, 1988), 1–30.

18. American consular records report: "Japanese films lead . . . but of imported films, American pictures are in the greatest demand at 20% of the total [630]. At present, following Japanese and American films, come German, French, Italian, and British in order of popularity. Chinese films imported from Shanghai have enjoyed popularity in the past among Formosan Chinese, but these shows have been prohibited since the outbreak of the 'China Incident' in July, 1937"; United States Department of Commerce, Motion Picture Division, ed., *Review of Foreign Markets* 1938 (U.S. Department of Commerce, 1938), 136.

19. Lee Young-il and Choe Young-choi, *The History of Korean Cinema* (Jimoondang International, 1988), 19–24. Japanese historians have stated that in October 1898 an Englishman named Angst Haus screened several French Pathé films in a warehouse rented from a Chinese merchant on south Daimon street; Ichikawa, *Ajia eiga*, 99. Lee and Choe also discuss Haus but state that the original citation cannot be verified. Recently Cho Hee Moon stated that films were first introduced in 1899 when Oscar Bennett Dupue and Elias Burton Holmes shot scenes in Korea and that the first public showing was at the Seoul Electric Company in 1903; Cho Hee Moon, "A Study of Early Korean Film History: Introduction and Reception of Motion Pictures 1896–1923" (PhD diss., Chungang University, 1992), 25–30.

20. In 1915, Nikkatsu owned the Kirakukan and the Taishokan, Tenkatsu held the Ogonkan and foreign exhibitors managed the Danseisha, the Chosen Gekijo, and the Yubikan. By 1920, Shochiku had acquired the Ogonkan, Teikine built the Taishokan,

Nikkatsu kept the Kirakukan, and Makino Films owned the Chuokan. Ichikawa, *Ajia eiga*, 100–101. See also Lee and Choe, *History*, 19–24.

21. Japanese censors banned *Thunder over Mexico!* (1933), *Geronimo* (1939), and *Gunga Din* (1939) from screening in Korea; Ikeda Kunio, "Eiga kenetsujo no tokushu jijo," *Eiga junpo*, July 11, 1943, 28.

22. Kokusai Koryu Forum, ed. *Ajia eigashi hakkutsu shirizu*, vol. 2: *Kankoku no sairento eiga to katsubenshi no sekai* (Kokusai Koryu Kikin, 1996). J. L. Anderson, "Spoken Silents in the Japanese Cinema; or, Talking to Picture: Essaying the *Katsuben*, Contextualizing the Texts," in Nolletti and Desser, eds., *Reframing Japanese Cinema: Authorship, Genre, History* (Terre Haute: Indiana University Press, 1992), 259–311. W. Stephen Bush, "The Human Voice as a Factor in the Moving Picture Show," *Katsudo shashinkai*, Jan. 23, 1909, 86.

23. See Lee Gu-yong, "Film History Through Incidents," *Eiga geijutsu* (Seoul) December 1970, cited in Lee Yong-il "Nitei Shokuminichi Jidai no Chosen Eiga," in Imamura et al., eds. *Koza Nihon eiga*. vol. 3: *Tooki no jidai* (Iwanami Shoten, 1986), 313–314.

24. As no such intertitle appears in the original film, the dialog that Lee quotes was most likely spoken by the *pyon'sa*. Lee Yong-il, "Nitei," 316.

25. *Chosen sotokufu kinema* (Chosen Sotokufu, 1938), 1.

26. Ibid., 2.

27. Ichikawa, *Ajia eiga*, 110. Ichikawa states that from 1922 to 1941 the film industry in Korea employed over 10,000 people in fifty production companies and produced 200 films at a total cost of 700,000 yen.

28. Lee Yong-il, "Nitei," 317. Other Koreans in Japan include Sim Hun (director of *Mondong-i*) and Kang Hong-sik (who acted under the Japanese name of Ishii Teruo); Lee and Choe, *History*, 55. Monma Takashi, *Ajia eiga ni miru Nihon II* (Shakai Hyoronsha, 1996), 24–25. For Japanese "passing" as Koreans, see Lee Yong-il, "Nitei,"; Monma, *Ajia eiga II*, 160–163.

29. Kino-dramas were one reel long and depicted outdoor scenes that were integrated at various intervals into a regular stage performance. The Japanese performance mentioned here was *The Boat Captain's Wife* (*Sencho no tsuma*), performed for the second anniversary of the building of the Ogonkan Theater in Keijo (Seoul) by the Japanese troupe Setonaikai. LeeYong-il, *Nitei*; Joseph L. Anderson and Donald Richie, *The Japanese Film: Art and Industry* (Princeton, NJ: Princeton University Press, 1982), 27–28.

30. Lee Yong-il, "Nitei," 321–326.

31. Lee Yong-il and Sato Tadao, *Kankoku ega nyumon* (Gaifusha, 1990), 51–53.

32. *Arirang* was first submitted to the censors on December 22, 1926 (censor record # A-2683). Naimusho Keihokyoku, ed., *Firumu kenetsu jiho* no. 33 12/21/26–12/31/26, 818.

33. Monma, *Ajia eiga II*, 16–17.

34. Ichikawa, *Ajia eiga*, 104. Reprinted in "Chosen eiga sanjunenshi," *Eiga junpo*, July 11, 1943, 16.

35. *Arirang* tells the story of Yong-jin, a young man who becomes mentally ill after being arrested by the Japanese colonial police in Korea for leading protesters in the March 1st protest. After returning home, he is constantly bullied by his Korean landlord, who collaborates with the Japanese. Yong-jin kills the landlord's servant and is immediately

rearrested. In 1995 film historian Kim Yong-sun suggested that *Arirang* was possibly a Japanese production, which might explain why it was exported to Japan.

36. The three reels referred to in the text are: *Prince Takamatsu Visits Mt. Kongo and Keishu* (*Takamatsumiya denka kongosan, keishu onari*, 1926), *Korean Flood Damage* (*Chosen suigai*, 1926), and *French Indo-China Colonial Governor General Melfan* (*Fukkoku indo sotoku merufan taisho*, 1924), which are listed in *Chosen sotokufu kinema*, 4–5.

37. "Chosen eiga no genjo," *Eiga hyoron* (July 1941): 44.

38. Saito Torajiro, "Chosen Koki," *Eiga* (July 1941): 73–74.

39. Ibid., 74. Kono Kiyoichi, ed., *Kigeki eiga no osama: Saito Torajiro kantoku* (Akita: self-published, 1989).

40. Takashima Kinji, *Chosen eiga toseishi* (Keijo: Chosen Eiga Bunka Kenkyujo, 1943).

41. Niwa Fumio, "Hanto eiga ni tsuite," *Eiga no tomo* (Oct. 1940): 78.

42. Jeong Hyakuchu, "Hanto eigakai ni okuru kotoba," *Eiga no tomo* (Dec. 1940): 78.

43. Ibid.

44. Ibid.

45. Karafuto was another formal Japanese colony, but it did not develop into a distribution or production market for Japan, and with the exception of a handful of Japanese films set there, it remained a fairly isolated and obscure territory. For a discussion of *Northern Lights* (*Hokkyokuko*,1941, directed by Tanaka Shigeo), one of the few Karafuto-themed feature films, and a general discussion of Karafuto colonial subjects, see Tessa Morris-Suzuki, "Northern Lights, the Making and Unmaking of Karafuto Identity," *Journal of Asian Studies* 60, no. 3 (Aug. 2001): 645–672.

46. *The Village at Twilight* is lost, but a reviewer in *Kinema junpo* praised Ito Daisuke's subtle script and Kotani's technological virtuosity while criticizing the acting as lacking "sincerity"; *Eiga junpo*, Nov. 21, 1921, 8; Tanaka Junichiro, "Koya no adabana manshu eiga," in *Bessatsu ichiokunin no showashi-Nihon shokuminchi*, vol. 2 (Mainichi Shinbunsha, 1978), 286–290. Henry Kotani was born in Hiroshima. His parents moved to Hawai'i when he was a baby, and he later moved to San Francisco where he studied theater in high school. After graduation he went to Hollywood and became an assistant cameraman under Alvin Wyckoff, Cecil B. DeMille's cinematographer. Kotani became a cinematographer at Paramount in 1917, where he worked on several dozen Hollywood pictures; Masumoto Kinen, *Jinbutsu-shochiku eigashi* (Heibonsha, 1987), 34–36; Sato Tadao, "Hariuddo no Nihonjin tachi" in Imamura Shohei et al., eds., *Koza Nihon eiga*, vol. 1: *Nihon eiga no tanjo* (Iwanami Shoten, 1985), 267.

47. *The Sheik* (1921), *Queen of Atlantis* (*L'Atlantide*, 1921), and *The Indian Tomb* (*Das Indische Grabmal*, 1921) are considered by film historians to be three representative colonial-themed films set in exotic locals; Pierre Boulanger, *Le cinema colonial de "L'Atlantide" a "Lawrence d'Arabie"* (Paris: Seghers, 1975), 31–41; Jeffrey Richards, *Visions of Yesterday* (London: Routledge, 1973), 156.

48. Ichikawa, *Ajia eiga*, 128–131; Yamaguchi, *Maboroshi*, 41–48.

49. *Manchurian Motion Picture Corporation* (no date listed), 5.

50. *Motion Pictures in Manchuria* (undated, unpaginated).

51. Amakasu Masahiko, "Manjin no tame ni eiga o tsukuru," *Eiga junpo*, Aug. 1, 1942, 3.

52. Muto Tomio, *Manshukoku no danmen: Amakasu Masahiko no shogai* (Kindaisha, 1956), 223–234.

53. Negishi was head of Nikkatsu's Tamagawa studios and produced a spate of so-called humanistic war films in the late 1930s, including *Five Scouts* (*Gonin no sekkohei*, 1938) and *Mud and Soldiers* (*Tsuchi to heitai*, 1939); Iwasaki Akira, ed., *Negishi Kanichi* (Tokyo: self-published, 1969).

54. Ibid., 3.

55. Amakasu, "Manjin," 3.

56. Uchida Tomu and Iwasaki Akira are two well-known examples. Iwasaki, an active member of the Japanese Proletariat Film Movement (Prokino), was the only film critic ever jailed for opposing the war. Since the war, both men have remained silent about their collaboration with the imperial regime.

57. Stefan Tanaka, *Japan's Orient* (Berkeley: University of California Press, 1993), 253–258.

58. Kuwano Choka, "Manshu no eiga jigyou kairan," *Eiga junpo*, Aug. 1, 1942, 28–31.

59. Amakasu Masahiko, "Making Films for the Manchurians," *Eiga junpo*, Aug. 1, 1942, 3.

60. Yamaguchi, *Maboroshi*.

61. Amakasu, "Making Films," 3.

62. Hu Chang and Gu Quan. *Manying: Guoce dianyin mianmian guan* (Beijing: Zhonghua Shujuchu, 1990).

63. Ibid., 3.

64. Mitsukichi Kaya, "Mannin no warai," *Eiga hyoron* (Jan. 1943), 35.

65. Ibid., 34–35; Yahara Reisaburo, "Manei sakuhin e no danso," *Eiga hyoron* (Dec. 1942), 48–51; Sato Tadao, *Nihon eigashi*, vol. 2 (Iwanami Shoten, 1995), 128–142.

66. Iijima Tadashi, *Senchu eigashi-shiki* (M. G. Shuppan, 1984), 254–255, 309–310.

67. Joyce Lebra, *Japan's Greater East Asia Co-Prosperity Sphere in World War II* (New York: Oxford University Press, 1975).

68. Iijima Tadashi, *Kagaku eiga no shomondai* (Hakusuisha, 1944).

69. Hazumi Tsuneo, "Dai toa eiga no arikata," *Eiga hyoron* (Feb. 1942), 21–24; Murao Kaoru, "Dai toa eiga no koso," *Eiga hyoron* (May 1942), 42–46.

70. Iijima, *Shomondai*, 203.

71. Ibid., 207.

72. Tsumura Hideo, "Daitoa eiga ni kansuru noto," *Eiga hyoron* (Apr. 1942), 18.

73. Ella Shohat, "Gender and the Culture of Empire," in Bernstein and Studlar, eds., *Visions of the East: Orientalism in Film* (New Brunswick, NJ: Rutgers University Press, 1997), 34–35.

74. Lu Xun, "Preface to *Call to Arms*," in *Lu Xun: Selected Works*, vol. 1 (Beijing: Foreign Languages Press, 1956), 35.

75. Sun Yu, *Dalu zhihua* (Beijing: Yuen Liang Chubanshe, 1990).

76. Abe Mark Nornes, "*Dawn of Freedom*," in Nornes and Yukio, eds., *Nichibei Eigasen: Media Wars Then & Now* (Yamagata: Yamagata International Documentary Film Festival, 1991), 260.

77. Silverberg, "Remembering Pearl Harbor, Forgetting Charlie Chaplin, and the

Case of the Disappearing Western Woman: A Picture Story" *Positions* 1, no. 1 (Spring 1993); Peter High, Teikoku no *ginmaku* (Nagoya: Nagoya Daigaku Shuppan, 1995); Freda Freiberg, "China Nights," *Historical Journal of Film, Radio, and Television* 14, no. 4 (Oct. 1994): 353–478; and Shelly Stephenson, "Her Traces Are Found Everywhere," in Yingjin Zhang, ed., *Cinema and Urban Culture in Shanghai, 1922–1943* (Stanford, CA: Stanford University Press, 1999).

78. Ibid.

Chapter Two: Media Empire

1. Benedict Anderson, *Imagined Communities* (London: Verso, 1983), 35.

2. U.S. educator and scientist Dr. William Smith Clark cofounded Hokkaido University in the Meiji era and is still celebrated for his contributions to progress in the region as well as for this famous admonition: "Boys, be ambitious! Be ambitious not for money or for selfish aggrandizement, nor for that evanescent thing which men call fame. Be ambitious for knowledge, for righteousness, and for the uplift of your people. Be ambitious for the attainment of all that a man ought to be."

3. John L. Fell, *Film and the Narrative Tradition* (Berkeley: University of California Press, 1986), 9; Donald Crafton, *Emil Cohl, Caricature, and Film* (Princeton, NJ: Princeton University Press, 1990), 222; David Kunzle, *History of the Comic Strip* (Berkeley: University of California Press, 1973).

4. Fell, *Narrative Tradition*, 184–185.

5. Noma Seiji, *Noma of Japan: The Nine Magazines of Kodansha* (New York: Vanguard, 1934), 184.

6. Ibid., 184.

7. Ibid., 184. Kathryn Castle, ed., *Britannia's Children* (St. Martin's Press, 1996); Jeffrey Richards, *Imperialism and Juvenile Literature* (Manchester University, 1989).

8. Richards, *Juvenile*, 1.

9. Tagawa Suiho, *Norakuro jijoden* (Kojinsha, 1983); Tagawa Suiho, "Mokenrentai Norakuro niheisotsu" in Tagawa, ed., *Norakuro mangashu*, vol. 1 (Kodansha, 1975), 39.

10. Yoshimoto Sanpei, *Pokopen Taisho, Boys' Life* (Dec. 1934).

11. Shabana Bontaro, *Hokushi sensen-kaisoku Heichan butai: Totsugeki!* (Nakano Shoten, 1937), 44–53.

12. Kawamura Minato, "Taishu orientarizumu to ajia ninshiki" in Oe Shinobu et al., eds., *Kindai Nihon to shokuminchi*, vol. 7, *Bunka no naka no shokuminchi* (Iwanami Shoten, 1993), 107–111.

13. "Boken Dankichi no koto" in Shimada Keizo, ed., *Boken Dankichi*, vol. 2 (Kodansha, 1967), 186–187.

14. Kawamura, "Orientarizumu," 135.

15. Yano Toru, *"Nanshin" no keifu* (Chuo Koronsha, 1975), 154; Kawamura, "Orientarizumu," 109.

16. Shimada, *Boken Dankichi*, vol. 4, 167.

17. Gregory Kasza, *The State and the Mass Media in Japan, 1918–1945* (Berkeley: University of California Press, 1988), 61–71.

18. Kubota Tatsuo, *Bunka eiga no hohoron* (Daichi Bungeisha, 1940); Aikawa Haruki, *Bunka egaron* (Kasumigaseki Shobo, 1944); Tanikawa Yoshio, *Nihon no kagaku eigashi* (Yuni Tsushin, 1978); and Okano Kaoruko, *Kagaku eiga ni kaketa yume* (Soshisha, 1999).

19. A reel of film was 1,000 feet, and lasted, depending on projection speed, approximately ten minutes; Yamaguchi Katsunori et al., eds., *Nihon animeshon eigashi* (Yubunsha, 1977).

20. William Moritz, "Resistance and Subversion in Animated Films of the Nazi Era," in Jayne Pilling, ed., *A Reader in Animation Studies* (London: John Libbey and Co., 1997), 228–240.

21. Imamura Taihei, *Manga eigaron* (Dai'ichi Geibunsha, 1941), 113.

22. *Princess Iron Fan* (*Tie shan gong zhu*, 1941, Wan Laiming and Wan Guchan) was produced in China by the Japanese capitalized China Film Company. Contemporary Japanese reviews praised the film as a technical wonder, but did not claim it as a Greater East Asian Film. The film was said to have taken three years, 237 artists and 350,000 yuan to make. The story was based on part of the popular Chinese folktale *Journey to the West*. Sixteen-year-old Tezuka Osamu saw the film in Japan and cited it as an influence in his becoming a comic artist.

23. John Dower, *War Without Mercy* (New York: Pantheon Books, 1987); Abe Mark Nornes and Yukio Fukushima, eds., *The Japan/America Film Wars* (Langhorne, PA: Harwood, 1994).

24. *The Adventures of Prince Achmed* (Germany, 1923–1926, dir: Lotte Reiniger). William Mortiz on *Lotte Reiniger*, http://www.awn.com/mag/issue1.3/articles/moritz1.3.html.

25. Historian John Dower refers to this hierarchy in prewar Japanese society as "proper place," in *War Without Mercy*, 205–206, 210–211.

26. "Ongaku eiga ni kokyo nashi," *Eiga no tomo* (July 1942): 34.

27. Hosokawa Shuhei, "Seiyo ongaku no Nihonka-taishubunka 42," *Myujikku magajin* (Sept. 1992): 153.

28. Utasaki Takahiko, ed., *Shogen Nihon yogaku rekodoshi senzenhen* (Ongaku no Tomosha, 1998); Enomoto Yasuko, *Gakunin no miyako-shanhai* (Kenbun Shuppan, 1998); and Tonoshita Tatsuya, "Senjitaiseika no ongakkai," in Akazawa Shiro, ed., *Bunka to fashizumu* (Nihon Keizai Hyoronsha, 1993).

29. "Natsukashi no eigakan," *Gekkan tosa* 21, nos. 4–5 (1986); Endo Noriaki, ed., *Eiga ogonki koya to meisaku no fukei* (Kokusho Kankokai, 1989).

30. *Hollywood: A Celebration of the American Silent Film*, (1980, dir. Kevin Brownlow).

31. The dearth of scholarship on the *gakushi* should not suggest that they were a negligible part of film history. *Gakushi* organized large unions, second in power only to the *benshi*. With the advent of sound pictures, many *gakushi* were able to find employment as studio musicians; Sasaki Jun et al., eds., *Utaeba tengoku* (Tokyo: Media Factory, 1999); Akiyama Kuniharu, *Nihoneiga ongakushi* (Tabata Shoten, 1974); and Yoshida Chieo, *Mohitotsu no eigashi: Katsuben no jidai* (Jiji Tsushinsha, 1978).

32. Kevin Brownlow, *The Parade's Gone By* (New York: Knopf, 1968), 338–341.

33. Benshi Tokugawa Musei described his sense of "fear" as singer Nakayama Utako

performed before an audience at the Aoi Theater for the film *Until the Dawn* (*Asahi sasu mae*, 1919, Nikkatsu); Tokugawa Musei, *Musei handaiki* (Shibundo, 1929).

34. Kurata Yoshihiro, *Nihon rekodo bunkashi* (Tosho Sensho, 1992), 123–127; Komota Nobuo et al., eds. *Shinpan Nihon ryukoakashi*, vol. 1 (Shakai Shisosha, 1994). An early example was the theme song for *Bird in a Cage* (*Kago no tori*, 1924).

35. "Shucho no musume" (1930, Nippon Polydor) sung by Osaka Nanji and Tomitaya Kikuji. Music historian Komota Nobuo claims the original melody was a Taisho era dormitory song; Komota, *Shinpan Nihon ryukokashi*, vol. 1, 253.

36. *The Chieftain's Daughter* (*Shucho no musume*, 1930, Toa Kyoto) was directed by Ishihara Eikichi and starred Takekawa Iwao, Chishu Yuriko, and Miyagi Naoe.

37. Paul Whiteman, Ronnie Munroe, Eddie Cantor. *White Shadows in the South Seas* (1928, dir.: W. S. Van Dyke); *Aloma of the South Seas* (1926, dir.: Maurice Tourneur); and *The Pagan* (1929, dir.: W. S. Van Dyke).

38. Shima, Koji. "Ongaku eiga ni kokyo nashi." *Eiga no tomo*, July 1942, 34.

39. Hosokawa Shuhei, "Seiyo ongaku no Nihonka-taishubunka, 43," *Myujikku magajin* (Oct. 1992), 146.

40. The number of songs that reference Manchuria/China in their title mushroomed from 9 in 1931 to over 100 in 1932. Similarly, after the 1937 China Incident, the number of songs with references to China in their title almost tripled; Fukuda Shunji, *Shashin de miru showa no kayoshi senzen-senchuhen* (Takushoku Shobo, 1991), 96–149.

41. Hattori Ryoichi, *Boku no ongaku jinsei* (Chuo Bungeisha, 1982), 292.

42. Fukuda Shunji and Kato Masayoshi. *Showa kayo soran: senzen, senchuhen.* (Takushoku Shobo, 1994), 78–140.

43. Ogawa Chikagoro, *Ryukoka to sesso* (Nihon Keisatsu Shinbunshahan, 1941), 179.

44. Ibid.,188–189.

45. The Three Human Bullets (sometimes called Human Bombs) was the name the Japanese press gave to three Japanese soldiers who blew themselves up in order to penetrate the Chinese front line during the Shanghai Incident of 1932. For more, see Louise Young, *Japan's Total Empire* (Berkeley: University of California Press, 1998), 75–78.

46. Before *The Neighbor's Wife and Mine* (*Madamu to Nyobo*) previous experiments with Japanese sound films included *Daybreak* (*Reimei*, 1927) and Mizoguchi's *Hometown* (*Furusato*, 1930). *Reimei* used a domestic sound-on-disc system known as Mina-Tokii named after its inventor Minakawa Yoshizo but synchronization problems eventually led to the film being shelved before ever being shown publicly; Akiyama Kuniharu, *Nihon no eiga ongakushi* (Tabata Shoten, 1974), 15.

47. John Mundy, *Popular Music on Screen* (St. Martin's Press, 1999), 55.

48. Kobayashi Hideo, *The Literature of Lost Home* (Stanford University Press, 1995), 52–53.

49. Salary expenditures for *Enoken the Magician* (*Enoken no majutsushi*, 1934) were three times that of the entire budget for films like *The Actress and the Poet* (*Joyu to shijin*,1935); see the Makino collection, Tokyo.

50. Jippensha Ikku, *Tokai Dochu Hizakurige* (1802).

51. Singer Rokyo Tokuyama Tamaki (1903–1942) was also a vocal coach who trained

Watanabe Hamako, Nakano Tadaharu, and Matsudaira Akira. His hits included "Samurai Nippon" and "Manchurian March" (*Manshu Koshinkyoku*).

52. Kanagaki Robun, *Seiyo dochu hizakurige* (Bankyukaku, 1871); John Mertz, "Internalizing Social Difference: Kanagaki Robun's *Shanks' Mare* to the Western Seas" in Hardacre and Kern, eds., *New Directions in the Study of Meiji Japan* (Boston: Brill Academic Publishers 1997).

53. Hosokawa Shuhei, "Seiyo ongaku no Nihonka-taishuka: Tairiku," *Myujikku magajine* (Sept. 1992), 153.

54. John Mackenzie, *Orientalism: History, Theory, and the Arts* (Manchester: Manchester University Press, 1995), 142.

55. Seductive desert queens were a popular motif in pulp literature such as Pierre Benoît's *L'Atlantide* and Henry Rider Haggard's *She*, both of which inspired multiple film adaptations.

56. Mundy, *Popular Music*, 243.

57. Magazine articles on Ri Koran were frequently printed along side advertisements for her films; see *Manchurian Film* (*Manshu eiga*) (Dec. 1939), 85, and her endorsements of other products, *Eiga* (Feb. 1942), 56–57.

58. Takasaki Takaharu, *Senjika no zasshi* (Fubosha, 1976).

59. The greatest increase was in newsreel and *bunka* (culture) film production; Naimusho Keihokyoku ed. *Eiga kenetsu Jiho*, 40 vols. (Fuji Shuppan, 1985) vols. 14, 15, 29, 30, 31.

60. Tanaka Junichiro, *Nihon eiga hattatsushi*, vol. 3 (Chuo Koronsha, 1980).

61. Imamura Miyoo, *Nihon eiga bunkenshi* (Kagamiura Shobo, 1967), 173–174.

62. Ibid., 174. The Japanese Film Magazine Association consisted of critics and industry insiders Uchida Kisaburo, Suzuki Jusaburo, Iida Shinbi, Iijima Tadashi, Tsuda Tokihiko, Matsuda Masuzo, Mizumachi Seiji, and Shimazaki Kiyohiko.

63. "Nettai chiho ni okeru eigayo nega ni tsuite," *Eiga gijutsu* 17, no. 7 (July 1942), 17–21; Miki Shigeru, "Nanpo no shitsudo," *Eiga gijutsu* 17, no. 9 (Sept.1942), 44–45; Manshu eiga kyokai eiga kagaku kenkyusho, "Taikan satsuei shiken hokoku," *Eiga gijutsu* 18, no. 7 (July 1943), 2–9.

64. Taguchi Ryusaburo, "Daitoasen to eiga kikai," *Eiga gijutsu* 18, no. 1 (Jan. 1943), 42–43; Kaeriyama Norimasa, "Eiga kikai yuryo kokusanka no konpon hosaku," *Eiga gijutsu* 18, no. 1 (Jan. 1943), 43–44.

65. "Roketai minami e yuku," *Eiga no tomo* (Mar. 1943), 78–79; Aki Yoshi, "Ware ni saku ari," *Eiga no tomo* (Apr. 1943), 74–75.

66. Aki Kosei, "Satsueisho wa nanpo netsu," *Eiga no tomo* (May 1942), 68–69.

67. Ibid.

68. "Dai-ikkai *Eiga no tomo* yoron chosa: Watakushi wa ko kangaeru," *Eiga no tomo* (June 1941), 62.

69. Ibid.

70. "Dainikai *Eiga no tomo* yoron chosa: watakushi wa ko omou: eigakai no shintaisei o megutte," *Eiga no tomo* (Dec. 1941), 50–56.

71. "Dai-san *Eiga no tomo* yoron chosa: watakushi wa ko kangaeru: shintaiseigo no eigakai o megutte," *Eiga no tomo* (Sept. 1942), 32–39.

72. See the *Eiga no tomo* readers' polls cited above; "Kankyaku ni kiku," *Eiga junpo*, Aug. 21, 1942, 48–49.

73. Iijima Tadashi, *Nihon eigashi*, vol. 2 (Hakusuisha, 1955), 65–66; Tanaka, *Hattatsu-shi*, vol. 3, 83–84.

74. "Kankyaku ni kiku," *Eiga junpo*, Mar. 21, 1942, 49.

75. *Eiga junpo*, Mar. 21, 1942, 16.

76. *Katsudo gaho* (June 1917), 198, 200; *Kinema junpo*, May 21, 1920, 9.

77. "Nihon [eiga no uta] tosen happyo," *Eiga hyoron* (Apr. 1942), 37.

Chapter Three: Imperial Acts

1. *The Green Earth* (*Midori no daichi*, 1942), my translation, emphasis retained.

2. The popular American song "You Don't Have to Know the Language" (1947, James Van Huesen/Johnny Burke), written under the U.S. Good Neighbor policy, followed a similar pattern and demonstrates that this trope is commonly found in popular representations of colonial (and para-colonial) interactions.

3. Iijima Tadashi, "Japanese Films in Review 1938–9," in *Cinema Yearbook of Japan 1939* (Kokusai Bunka Shinkokai, 1939), 19.

4. Li Narangoa and Robert Cribb, eds., *Imperial Japan and National Identities in Asia, 1895–1945* (London: Routledge, 2003), 315–318.

5. For more on the idea of China and "Orient-studies" as Japan's archive during the early Meiji period, see Stephen Tanaka, *Japan's Orient* (Berkeley: University of California Press, 1993).

6. Shabana Bontaro, *Hokushi sensen-kaisoku heichan butai* (Nakano Shoten, 1937), 44–53.

7. "Tairiku eiga ni tsuite watakushi wa ko omou," *Eiga no tomo* (May 1942), 44–47.

8. Taguchi Masao, "Ri Koran ni okuru kotoba," *Eiga no tomo* (June 1941), 99.

9. Towa Shoji, ed. *Towashoji goshikaisha shashi* (Tokyo: self-published, 1942), 114. Producer Kawakita Nagamasa was educated in China and Germany and fluent in both languages. In 1928 Kawakita established Towa Shoji, part of which served as an importer and distributor of predominantly European films. Together with wife Kazuko, Kawakita helped to establish Japanese film's reputation internationally. The Kawakita Memorial Film Institute currently houses his original library and film collection; see Kawakita Kazuko, *Eiga hitotsujini* (Kodansha, 1973).

10. *Towashoji*, 117.

11. Ibid., 118. Tsuji Hisaichi, *Chuka denei shiwa: Ippeisotsu no nichu eigakaisoki* (Gaifusha, 1987), 42.

12. Peter B. High, *Teikoku no ginmaku* (Nagoya Daigaku Shuppan, 1995), 247.

13. Kawakita was very committed to introducing Japanese film to foreign audiences and had Japanese, English, and German versions of *The Road to Peace in the Orient* in the works in preparation for wide foreign distribution. He also had concluded a contract with the Brazil Art Film Company to handle South American distribution, but the poor reviews (and unrealized revenues) killed the plan; Kawakita Nagamasa, "Mazu rinpo no minshin o rikai subeshi" in *Eiga junpo* (Feb. 1, 1941), 24–25.

14. Ueda Hiroshi, "Shinajin o egake! Ueda Hiroshi o tazunete," in *Eiga no tomo* (Dec. 1940). Prior to the war, Ueda wrote novels about militarism in Asia and Japan: *Kojin* (*Yellow Dust*, 1938); *Kensetsu senki* (*Construction Battle Record*, 1939); *Chinetsu* (*Scorched Earth*, 1942); and *Shido monogatari* (*Tales of Leadership*, 1940). *Shido monogatari* was made into a successful film by Toho in 1941, and *Kensetsu senki* was cancelled in preproduction due to exorbitant production cost estimates.

15. Shimazu Yasujiro, "Tairiku eiga zakkan," *Eiga* (Mar. 1942), 33.

16. Murata Atsuro, "Shina eiga no kako to genzai," in Kubo Tensui, ed., *Dai Shina taikei*, vol. 12: *Bungaku-engekihen gekkan* (Bunrikaku Shobo, 1930), 631.

17. "Zadankai—Tairiku o kataru" *Eiga no tomo* (Jan. 1942), 33–34.

18. Fujiwara Sakuya and Yamaguchi Yoshiko, *Ri Koran: Watashi no hansei* (Shinchosha, 1987); Mainichi Shinbun, ed., *Ri Koran: Futatsu no sokoku ni yureta seishun* (Mainichi Gurafu Bessatsu, 1991); Miriam Silverberg, "Remembering Pearl Harbor, Forgetting Charlie Chaplin and the Case of the Disappearing Western Woman: A Picture Story," *Positions* 1, no. 1 (Spring 1993).

19. Taguchi Masao, "Ri Koran ni okuru kotoba," *Eiga no tomo* (Jun. 1941), 98–99. This was written just after it was discovered that Ri Koran was actually Japanese. Although her real identity was known, there is only one brief reference to it. Other articles about her likewise neither mention her dual identity nor call her Yamaguchi.

20. "Minzoku kyowa—Ri Koran no hendai" in *Manshu eiga* (Apr., Keitoku 7 [1940]).

21. Silverberg, "Remembering," 30, 56.

22. Yamaguchi Takeshi, *Aishu no Manshu eiga* (Santen Shobo, 2000), 47–72; Fujiwara Sakuya and Yamaguchi Yoshiko, *Ri Koran: Watashi no hansei*. (Shinchosha, 1987), 99–116.

23. Taguchi, "Ri Koran ni," 98.

24. Good Neighbor films also contained political messages, but North American directors understood that audiences were far more receptive to films that presented ideological messages in the form of musicals or comedies. In Japan, almost the complete opposite was true; melodramas were far more popular.

25. High, *Teikoku*, 248–249.

26. The British film *Pygmalion* (1938, released in Japan in 1939, Pascal Film Productions).

27. Yamaguchi, *Hansei*, 137–138.

28. In *Shanghai Landing Squad* (*Shanhai rikusentai*, 1938), Japanese actress Hara Setsuko plays a Chinese woman who is slapped by a Japanese soldier when she attempts to keep other "Chinese" women from taking food offered them. Here, too, the slap is the turning point in the woman's understanding of Japanese goodwill.

29. "Zadankai: tairiku o kataru," *Eiga no tomo* (Jan. 1942), 32–33.

30. "Pekin to Nihon eiga," *Eiga junpo* (Nov. 1, 1942), 24–25.

31. "Chugoku haikei toshita nihon eiga wa kore de yoi no ka," *Eiga hyoron* (Nov. 1941), 60–61.

32. Asai Shosaburo, "Chugokujin to nihon eiga," *Eiga junpo* (Nov. 1, 1942), 22.

33. Kurashige Shuzo, "Chosen eiga e no kibo," *Eiga hyoron* (July 1941), 8.

34. Narangoa and Cribb, *Imperial Japan*, 315–318.

35. Oguma Eiji, *Tanitsu minzoku shinwa no kigen* (Shinyosha, 1995); "*Nihonjin*" *no kyokai* (Shinyosha, 1998). Peter Duus *The Abacus and the Sword* (Berkeley: University of California Press, 1995).

36. David Mesler, "Korean Resistance Literature," in Andrew Nahm, ed., *Korea Under Japanese Colonial Rule* (Kalamazoo: Western Michigan University, 1973), 220–230; Andrew Nahm, "Themes of Popular Songs and Poems of the Koreans as Oppressed People," in Eugene Kim and Doretha Ellen Mortimore, eds., *Korea's Response to Japan: The Colonial Period 1910–1945* (Kalamazoo: Western Michigan University, 1977), 188–230; and Oh Kon Cho, "Resistance Theatres and Motion Pictures," also in Kim and Mortimore, eds., *Korea's Response*, 231–240.

37. While this sort of image was being constructed by the cultural producers in imperial Japanese film culture, diplomatically the exact opposite image was being generated; see Peter Duus, *The Abacus and the Sword*; Barbara Brooks, *Japan's Imperial Diplomacy* (Honolulu: University of Hawai'i Press, 2000).

38. Oguro Toyoji, "Chosen eigako (1)," *Eiga hyoron* (Sept. 1941), 75.

39. *Naisen ittai* literally meant Japan (*nai*) and Korea (*sen*) as one unit (*ittai*). Minami Jiro, governor general of the Korean Colonial Government said the process was responsible for "making Koreans good and faithful imperial subjects"; Miyata Setsuko, *Chosen minshu to kominka seisaku* (Miraisha, 1985), 148.

40. Miyata, *Chosen minshu*, 94–114. Sasaki Yuko, *Jugun ianfu-naisen kekkon* (Miraisha, 1992), 82.

41. Yoshida Seiji, *Watakushi no senso hanza: Chosenjin kyosei renko* (Sanichi Shobo, 1983); *Chosenjin Ianfu to Nihonjin* (Shinjinbutsu Oraisha, 1977).

42. Iijima Tadashi and Hinatsu Eitaro, "Shinario: *Kimi to boku,*" *Eiga hyoron* (July 1941), 132–145.

43. Miyata writes that Japanese imperialization policies directed at the Koreans began after the China Incident in 1937 when the *shiganhei* system was first implemented; Miyata, *Chosen minshu*, 50–55; Oguma Eiji, *Nihonjin no kyokai* (Shinyosha, 1998), 417–418.

44. Jennifer Robertson, *Takarazuka Sexual Politics and Popular Culture in Modern Japan* (Berkeley: University of California Press, 1998), 92–93.

45. Ibid., 134.

46. Ibid., 100.

47. Ibid., 139.

48. Ibid., 145.

49. Tasaka Tomotaka, in a letter dated July 16, 1941; see Makino collection, Tokyo, Japan.

50. Two hit singles were released from the film's soundtrack: "Kimi to boku," sung by Nam In-soo and Chang Sei-jung, and "Nakhwasamchun," sung by Kim Jung-goo (1941, Okeh Records). Park Chan-ho, *Kankoku kayoshi 1895–1945* (Shobunsha, 1987), 325–356.

51. French historian Henry Rousso has called this phenomenon in French history "the Vichy Syndrome" and makes a compelling argument for a more nuanced understanding of occupation histories; see Henry Rousso *The Vichy Syndrome: History and Memory in France Since 1944* (Cambridge, MA: Harvard University Press, 1991).

52. Lee and Choe, *Korean Cinema*, 75–82; Sato, *Nihon eigashi*, vol. 2, 70, 120.

53. Utsumi Aiko and Murai Yoshinori, *Shineasuto kyoei no Showa* (Gaifusha, 1987), 29–34.

54. Interview with Tanabe Masatomo in *A Filmmaker with Three Names* (1997, director: Kim Jae-bum).

55. This group included propaganda squad leader Machida Keiji, cultural critic Oya Soichi, *manga* artist Yokoyama Ryuichi (creator of the Fuku-chan series), *benshi* (film narrator) Matsuda Shunsui, and film director Kurata Bunjin. Oya Soichi regarded this period in Java working for the propaganda corps as being the "high point and main event" of his life; see Machida Keiji, *Tatakau bunka butai* (Hara Shobo, 1967), 2. Curiously any mention of Hinatsu is completely absent in Machida's otherwise meticulous chronicle of the Japanese cultural activities on Java. Sakuramoto Tomio mentions Hinatsu in passing as being part of a cultural unit representing Nichei, the newsreel company; see Sakuramoto Tomio, *Bunkajin no daitoa senso* (Aoki Shoten, 1993), 125.

56. The film is preserved at the National Film and Sound Archive, Australia.

57. Utsumi and Murai, *Shneasuto kyoei no Showa*, 125.

58. Ibid., 191.

59. China Film Archive, ed., *Joris Ivens and China* (Beijing: New World Press, 1983).

60. Imai Tadashi, "Senso senryo jidai no kaiso," in Imamura Taihei et al., *Koza Nihon eiga*, vol. 4, *Senso to eiga* (Iwanami Shoten, 1986), 202–205. The 1926 silent and 1939 sound versions of *Beau Geste* were both very successful in Japan, as were most Foreign Legion films, including *Lives of a Bengal Lancer* (Paramount, 1935), *Under Two Flags* (20th Century Fox, 1936), and *Gunga Din* (RKO, 1939).

61. Brian Taves, *The Romance of Adventure* (Jackson, MS: University of Mississippi Press, 1993), 177.

62. The advertising taglines were: "1750 to 1! Always out-numbered! Never out-fought! These are the Bengal Lancers, heroes all, guarding each other's lives, sharing each other's tortures, fighting each other's battles. Set in mystic India with its glittering mosques, oriental palaces, queer music, bronze skinned dancers" (*Lives of a Bengal Lancer*, 1935). "Out of the stirring glory of Kipling's seething world of battle they roar—red-blood and gunpowder heroes all!" (*Gunga Din*) "Three against the world . . . brothers and soldiers all!" (*Beau Geste*). Compare these with the tagline for the Japanese film *Boro no kesshitai*: "This war action drama portrays the brave border police protecting our northern border in the cruel cold!"

63. For more on the Name Law (*soshi kaimei*), see Miyata Setsuko, *Soshi kaimei* (Akaishi Shoten, 1992), 80.

64. Ibid.

65. Tsurumi, *Japanese Colonial Education*.

66. Cited in Silverberg, "Remembering," 34.

67. Sayama Atsushi (only his Japanese name is given) and other Korean actors in this film were well known in the Korean film industry from the late 1930s through the mid-1940s. The teacher in this scene (played by Korean character actor Kinoshita Akira—only his Japanese name is given) also speaks Japanese with a slight, but obvious, Korean accent.

68. Iijima and Hinatsu, "Shinario: *Kimi to boku*," 145.

69. See Oguma Eiji, *Nihonjin no kyokai* (Shinyosha, 1998), 156–157.

70. Mark Peattie, *Nanyo: The Rise and Fall of the Japanese in Micronesia, 1885–1945* (Honolulu: University of Hawai'i Press, 1988), 39–41.

71. Ichikawa, *Ajia eiga*, 289.

72. Approximately two-thirds of the newsreels produced by Nichiei between 1940 and 1945 have Nanyo-related content; *Nihon nyusu eigashi* (Mainichi Shinbun, 1977).

73. This term referred to Japanese women sold as sex workers into Southeast Asian brothels. A reworking of this phrase, Japayuki-san or Japan-bound women, was used to refer to Southeast Asian women who came to work in Japan during the bubble economy in the 1980s.

74. Sameshima Rintaro, "Karayukisan ni tsuite," *Eiga hyoron* (Special issue 1937), 210–211.

75. *Kara modori* or *kara agari* (returning from the South) were similarly derogatory terms for Japanese prostitutes returning to Japan from Southeast Asia. Prostitutes returning to Japan from Shanghai were similarly called Shanghai Returnees (Shanhai gaeri); Fujikawa Chisui "Karayuki eiga no keifu," in *Eigashi kenkyo*, no. 5 (1974), 21–35, 56.

76. Sawamura Tsutomu, "Karayuki-san," *Eiga hyoron* (Apr. 1937), 129. Sawamura was also a noted screenwriter whose best-known wartime film was *Kaigun* (Navy) (1942, Shochiku).

77. Hatamoto Shuichi and Tobo Shirocho "Karayukisan," *Eiga hyoron* (Special issue 1937), 51.

78. Ibid., 24.

79. Ueno Ichiro, "Karayuki-san," *Eiga hyoron* (Apr. 1937), 125.

80. Ibid., 125–129; Sawamura Tsutomu, "Karayuki-san," *Eiga hyoron* (Apr. 1937), 129–131.

81. *Hanasaku minato*, *Eiga kyakuhon* (Apr. 1943), 54–87.

82. *Marai no tora*, *Eiga kyakuhon* (Apr. 1943), 7.

83. The legend of Harimao has been resurrected over the years across a variety of media, including a live-action children's TV show *Kaiketsu Harimao* (1960–1961, NTV, 65 episodes), comic strips, and a feature film entitled *Harimao* (1989, Shochiku); *Tokushu: Harimao Densetsu Sixteen Club* no. 10, 1989.

84. Oyama Takashi, "Kyomi to kokusaku no konzen taru kessho," *Eiga* (July 1943), 34.

85. Yamamoto Akira, "Jugonen sensoka, Nihon no senso eiga," in Imamaura et al., eds., *Koza Nihon eiga*, vol. 4, *Senso to eiga* (Iwanami Shoten, 1986), 76–77.

86. In a 1943 internal Toho Studio document entitled "Shabestu Fugiri Seiseki Juni Ichiranhyo," *Tiger of Malay* (*Marai no tora*) was ranked as the second-highest-grossing film of all the film studios. The top five were *Heiroku's Dream Tales* (*Heiroku yume monogatari*, Toho), *Tiger of Malay* (*Marai no tora*, Daiei), *Singapore All-out Attack* (*Shingaporu sokogeki*, Daiei), *Daughter* (*Musume*, Shochiku) and *Suicide Troops of the Watchtower* (*Boro no kesshitai*, Toho); see the Makino Collection, Tokyo.

87. *Marai*, *Eiga kyakuhon*, 7.

88. This film, a Japanese/Philippine coproduction, had Gararado de Leon as its Filipino director.

89. Terami Motoe, "Nihon senryoka no firipin eiga," in Imamura et al., eds., *Koza Nihon eiga*, vol. 4 (Iwanami Shoten, 1986), 291. For Yomota's remarks, see "Abe no Hari-

uddo, De Reon no Hariuddo," in *Herarudo de Reon kantoku o megutte hokokusho* (Koku-sai Koryu Kikin Senta, 1995), 33–34.

90. Saigo Takamori (1827–1877) was a major political and military figure of the Meiji period. He was the leader of the military forces that overthrew the Tokugawa rule and was also known for his support of a war with Korea. Saigo planned to send himself as an envoy to Korea under the pretense of demanding an apology for their failure to promote better relations with Japan, confident that the Koreans would murder the envoy and give Japan a justification for military invasion. His plan was rejected, and he was exiled to Satsuma (modern-day Kagoshima), where he died in the Sainan Rebellion (1877) against the Japanese government. Although he never went to Cambodia, the film plays on the possibility that he might have escaped and had progeny in Cambodia.

91. Heinz Morioka and Miyoko Sasaki, *Rakugo: The Popular a Narrative Art of Japan* (Cambridge, MA: Harvard University Press, 1990), 6–8; Barak Kushner, *The Thought War: Japanese Imperial Propaganda* (Honolulu: University of Hawai'i Press, 2005).

92. For a discussion of "blackface" in Hollywood, see Michael Rogin, *Blackface/White Noise* (Berkeley: University of California Press, 1996), 45–70.

93. Matsuda Atsushi, "Saito Tatsuo to iu Otoko: Suteki na sengakusha," *Eiga* (Nov. 1942), 84–85.

94. Ibid. The article praised Saito's "considerable improvement" as a character actor in films such as *Southern Winds II* (*Zoku minami no kaze*) compared with his "*nansensu*" roles in films like *Airplane Bride* (*Hikoki hanayome*, 1928, Shochiku).

95. Ikeda Tadao and Tsuro Yukio, "*Minami no kaze*," *Nihon eiga* 7, no. 6 (June 1942), 135–175.

96. Japanese dialogue from *Southern Winds II*.

97. Ibuse Masuji, "Hana no machi," in *Ibuse Masuji Zenshu*, vol. 3 (Chikuma Shobo, 1967), 31–118; Hino Ashihei, *Hito mindanshu* (Taiseishuppan, 1945).

Chapter Four: Competing Empires in Transnational Asia

1. Ian Jarvie, *Hollywood's Overseas Campaign: The North Atlantic Movie Trade, 1920–1950* (Cambridge: Cambridge University Press, 1992), xiv.

2. *Moving Picture World*, Dec. 21, 1918, 1398.

3. *The Film Daily Yearbook* listed the following data for American films on Asian screens from 1930–1934:

	Year				
Place	1930	1931	1932	1933	1934
British Malaya	71	74	76	72	63
Ceylon	85	85	85	65	60
China	83	83	80	80	75
Japan	22	22	12	13	11
Netherlands East Indies	n/a	n/a	n/a	n/a	50+
Philippines	95	90	80+	80+	n/a

(Table continued)

Note: Japanese reports on film conditions in the East Indies state that the between 1930 and 1940, American films accounted for approximately 65.72 percent, followed by Germany (10.47 percent), China (9.79 percent), and Japan (0.13 percent).
Source: Eiga Haikyusha Nanpokyoku Chosabu, ed. *Higashi Indo no eiga jijo* (Eiga Haikyusha, 1942), 10.

4. Shohat and Stam, *Unthinking Eurocentrism*, 113.

5. Kristin Thompson, *Exporting Entertainment: America in the World Film Market 1907–1934* (London: British Film Institute, 1985), 72–73; Tanaka Junichiro, *Nihon eiga hattatsushi*. vol. 3, 80–82.

6. Michael Walsh, "The Internationalism of the American Cinema" (PhD diss., University of Wisconsin, Madison, 1998), 79–86.

7. In 1924 the German trade paper *Lichtbildbuhne* wrote that "with the exception of the United States, no nation in the world is able to cover its [film] negative costs in its own country" (no. 23, March 1, 1924). Dependency on foreign revenues was seen as a weakness, and Murao Kaoru claimed that the Japanese market was self-sufficient in "Kahoku to nihon eiga" *Eiga junpo* (Nov. 1, 1942), 19.

8. Uchida Kisao, "Toa ni okeru beikoku eiga no eikyo," *Eiga hyoron* (Feb. 1942), 27–30.

9. Tsuji Hisakazu, "Shinajin to gaikoku eiga," *Eiga hyoron* (Nov. 1940), 62–63.

10. Ibid., 63.

11. Ibid., 63.

12. Yamaguchi Kaoru, *Zensen eishatai* (Matsukage Shorin, 1943).

13. Robert S. Ward, *Hong Kong Under the Japanese Occupation* (U.S. Bureau of Foreign and Domestic Commerce, Dept of Commerce, 1943), 94, 134–136; reprinted in Ward's *Asia for the Asiatics? The Techniques of Japanese Occupation* (Chicago: University of Chicago Press, 1945), 172.

14. In the Philippines, Japanese films held the third largest share of the market from the late 1930s through the early 1940s; Thompson, *Exporting*, 76; Clodualdo del Mundo, *Native Resistance: Philippine Cinema and Colonialism 1898–1941* (Manila: De La Salle University Press, 1998).

15. Cheng Ji-hua, Li Xiaobai, and Xing Zuwen, *Zhongguo dianying fazhan shi*, vol. 1 (Beijing: Zhongguo Dianying Chubanshe, 1980), 189.

16. *The Dragon Seed* was not screened in Japan until after the Pacific War, but Japanese film magazines wrote about the film frequently.

17. Dialogue from the film *Oil for the Lamps of China*.

18. In 1937 the number of Paramount-produced films declined from 46 to 10 in 1938, Columbia dropped from 39 to 20, MGM from 31 to 16, Warner Brothers from 31 to 7, RKO from 21 to 18, Universal from 20 to 6, Fox from 17 to 9, and United Artists from 17 to 8. Perhaps unsurprisingly Warner Brothers, known for producing antifascist films even before Pearl Harbor, suffered the greatest per capita loss; Tanaka, *Hattatsushi*, vol. 3, 65–66.

19. U.S. Dept. of Commerce, "The Japanese Motion Picture Market in 1938," in *Motion Pictures Abroad* (Dept. of Commerce, Dec. 1, 1938).

20. Kevin Brownlow, *The War, the West, and the Wilderness* (New York: Knopf, 1978), 6–8.

21. Japanese film studios periodically boycotted American films, such as when Nikkatsu Studios retaliated for litigation brought against them for film piracy and in response to the 1924 U.S. Immigration Act that made it illegal for Japanese to immigrate to the United States; Thompson, *Exporting*, 141.

22. Even drops in production brought about by rationing, shortages, or conscription of personnel did not diminish the large pool of films that Hollywood could—and did—re-release to cover shortfalls; Clayton Koppes and Gregory Black, *Hollywood Goes to War* (Berkeley: University of California Press, 1987).

23. These titles are included on the restored DVD version (Columbia TriStar, COL07639DVD).

24. Virilio, *War and Cinema*, 3.

25. Leo C. Rosten, *Hollywood: The Movie Colony, The Movie Makers* (New York: Harcourt, Brace and Co, 1941), 34–35.

26. Charlton Heston, interviewed in *California Here We Come* (History Channel, 2000).

27. Virilio argues that *The Adventures of Baron Munchhausen* (*Münchausen*,1943), a big-budget Agfacolor film with an impressive number of special effects, was produced in response to films like *Gone With the Wind*. He further states that Eisenstein shot a color sequence of *Ivan the Terrible* with captured Agfacolor stock; *War and Cinema*, 8.

28. Even during the ban, Japanese film journals regularly reported on Hollywood film projects; Takamatsu Koichiro, "Hariuddo bakugeki," *Eiga* (Dec. 1942), 29–32.

29. Taken from a 1947 *Cinema Bi-weekly* interview with Ozu conducted by Iida Shinbi and reprinted in Sato Tadao, *Ozu Yasujiro no geijutsu*, vol. 2 (Asahi Sensho, 1978), 104–105.

30. U.S. Office of Strategic Services, "Japanese Films: A Phase of Psychological Warfare," Report 1307 (U.S. Government, March 30, 1944), 13.

31. Muto Tomio, *Manshukoku no danmen: Amakasu Masahiko no shogai* (Kindasha, 1956), 54–55.

32. Works that provide meaningful instances of cultural exchange include *Fascism and Theatre* (Berghaus, 1996); Akazawa Shiro et al., eds., *Bunka to fuashizumu* (Nihon Keizai Hyoronsha, 1993); and Dojidai Kenchiku Kenkyukai, ed., *Hikigeki 1930 nendai no kenchiku to bunka* (Gendai Kikakushitsu, 1990).

33. Dower, *War Without Mercy*, 207.

34. Virilio, *War and Cinema*, 6–7.

35. Nicholas Reeves, *The Power of Film Propaganda* (London: Cassell, 2000), 4–6; Richard Taylor, *Film Propaganda* (London: I. B. Taurus, 1998), 35; Margaret Dickinson and Sarah Street, *Cinema and State* (London: British Film Institute, 1985), 19; Jean Gili, *L'Italie de Mussolini et son cinéma* (Paris: Henri Veyrier, 1985), 47–55.

36. The term "fascist" rarely appears in prewar Japanese film sources with regard to Japan. More often these sources differentiate between German *nachisu* (Nazis) and Italian *fashisuto* or *fasho* (Fascists). Postwar Japanese film journalists typically, and uncritically, apply the term to the Japanese military; Okada Susumu, *Nihon eiga no rekishi*

(Sanichi Shinsho, 1957), 196–210. Yomota Inuhiko's *Nihon eigashi 100nen* (Shueisha Shinsho, 2000) calls Hara Setsuko in *The New Earth* a "beautiful *fascist* maiden," without differentiating "Japanese fascism" from other "fascisms."

37. Kasza, *State and Mass Media in Japan*, 241; Uchikawa Yoshimi, ed., *Gendaishi shiryo*, vol. 41 (Misuzu Shobo, 1975), 234–236. The Anti-Comintern Pact was concluded between Germany and Japan in September 1936; Italy signed in November. The Tripartite Pact was ratified in Berlin on Sept. 27, 1940.

38. NHK Dokyumento Showa Shuzai, ed., *Dokyumento Showa* (Kadokawa Shoten, 1986), 111–120.

39. *Film Education in Japan* (Japan, Department of Education, 1937), 21.

40. Iwasaki Akira, *Hitora to eiga* (Asahi Sensho, 1975), 84.

41. Ibid., 85-87.

42. Tanaka Eizo, *Eiga haiyu junbi dokuhon* (Eiga Nihonsha, 1941).

43. Iwasaki, *Hitora*, 86. See Shibata Yoshio, *Sekai eiga senso* (Hokuryukan, 1944) on the "Jewish problem" and the monopolization of finance capital in the Western (predominantly U.S.) film industries.

44. Yamada examined the influences of Italy's Italian Film and Theater Law (Il cinematographo e il teatro nella legislazione fascsita) on the Japanese Film Law; Yamada, *Eiga kokusaku no zenshin* (Koseikaku, 1940), 76–77; Dai Nippon Eiga Kyokai, ed., *Itari eigaho* (Dai Nippon Eiga Kyokai, 1938).

45. One such diplomatic flap occurred over Cecil B. DeMille's *The Cheat* (1915); see Kevin Brownlow, *Behind the Mask of Innocence* (Berkeley: University of California Press, 1990), 348–349; and Sumiko Higashi, *Cecil B. DeMille and American Culture* (Berkeley: University of California Press, 1994), 101.

46. Andrew Higson and Richard Maltby, eds., *"Film Europe" and "Film America"* (Exeter: University of Exeter Press, 1999); Ruth Vasey, *The World According to Hollywood, 1918–1939* (Madison: University of Wisconsin Press, 1997).

47. John Harley, *World-wide Influences of the Cinema* (Los Angeles: University of Southern California Press, 1940), 154–155.

48. *Cinema Yearbook of Japan 1938* (Kokusai Bunka Shinkokai, 1938), 60.

49. Harley, *World-wide Influences*, 156.

50. Ibid., 157.

51. Ibid., 160.

52. Ibid., 174.

53. *Cinema Yearbook of Japan 1938*, 54. Tanaka Junichiro, *Nihon eiga hattatsushi*. vol. 3 (Chuo Koronsha, 1980), 65–70.

54. *The Motion Picture Herald*, June 3, 1939, 27.

55. For more on Pommer's success abroad, see Ursula Hardt, *From Caligari to California: Eric Pommer's Life in the International Film Wars* (Providence: RI: Berghahn Books, 1996).

56. Ibid.; Sato Tadao, *Kinema to hosei*, 20–26; Tsuji Hisaichi, *Chuka denei shiwa* (Gaifusha, 1987).

57. Towa Shoji, ed., *Towa shoji goshikaisha shashi* (Towa Shoji, 1942).

58. Ibid.

59. Other Italian winners included *Cardinal Messias* (*Abuna Messias*, 1939); *Siege of the Alcazar* (*L'assedio di Alcazar*, 1940); and *White Navy* (*La nave bianca*, 1941). See *Almanacco del cinema Italiano* vol. 1939–XVII (Rome: Carlo Bestetti, 1952).

60. *Luciano Serra, Pilot* emphasized the Fascist fascination with machines, especially airplanes, as the technological basis for victory in the Ethiopian war. Based on the life of national hero Amedeo Nazzari, *Luciano Serra, Pilot* presented a new sort of hero, a man who is part pioneer, part pilot, and part modern-day gladiator. After abandoning his family, he sets out to find his fortune in the exotic environs of South America. Reunited by chance with his son on the battlefields of Ethiopia, Luciano sacrifices his life to save his son. Japanese critics cite both *Luciano Serra, Pilot* and *Only Angels Have Wings* (1939) as major influences on *Bouquet of the South Seas* (*Nankai no hanataba*, 1942); Nozawa Tadashi, "Koku eiga no subete" in *Maru* (Nov. 1957), 43–47.

61. James Hay, *Popular Film Culture in Fascist Italy* (Princeton, NJ: Princeton University Press, 1987) 182–183.

62. Ibid.

63. Shibata, *Sekai eiga senso*, 144.

64. It was precisely this desire for the colonial and the modern that led Showa intellectuals such as writer Kobayashi Hideo to create a sense of "lost home" and that made young Japanese regard the deserts of Morocco that they have never seen as more familiar than the Ginza right before their eyes; see Seiji Lippit, *Topographies of Japanese Modernism* (New York: Columbia University Press, 2002).

65. Komoto Nobuo et al., eds., *Shinpan Nihon ryukokashi*, vol. 1.

66. Gian Piero Brunetta, ed., *L'ora d'Africa del cinema Italiano, 1911–1989* (Rovereto: Materiali di Lavoro, 1990). This process by which Japanese film distributors attempted to localize the alien to Japanese audiences recalls previous attempts by 1920s journalists who, when writing of their travels in China, naturalized Chinese place names by assigning them Japanese equivalents, such as "the Kyoto of (Hangkow)"; Joshua Fogel, *The Literature of Travel in the Japanese Rediscovery of China, 1862–1945* (Stanford: Stanford University Press, 1996).

67. When the Italian/German coproduction *Condottieri* premiered in Japan in 1937, it was released under the Japanese title *Arupus no sokihei* (*The Alps Lancers*). This was a reference to the Japanese release title for the American colonial-themed film *Lives of a Bengal Lancer* (*Bengaru no sokihei*), which had been released the year before.

68. Tsumura Hideo, *Zoku eiga to kansho* (Sogensha, 1943), 64–73

69. Ibid. Tsumura thought that films like *Luciano Serra, Pilot* compared favorably with "frivolous" Japanese films set in China such as *Moon over Shanghai* (*Shanhai no tsuki*, 1941, Naruse Mikio), *Song of the White Orchid* (*Byakuran no uta*, 1939, Watanabe Kunio), and *China Nights* (*Shina no yoru*, 1940, Fushimizu Osamu).

70. The German Kolonialfilm genre began with the 1896 colonial exhibition in Berlin, when the government integrated films that "instilled colonial spirit" into the education curriculum; Guido Convents, "Film and German Colonial Propaganda," in Lorenzo Codelli, ed., *Prima di Caligari* (Pordenonne: Edizioni Biblioteca dell'Immagine, 1990), 58–76; Sabine Hake, "Mapping the Native Body," in Sara Friedrichsmeyer, ed., *The Imperialist Imagination* (Ann Arbor: University of Michigan Press, 1998), 163–187.

71. Advertisement in *Eiga junpo*, Aug. 1, 1943, unpaginated.

72. Ozuka Kyoichi, "Tekisaishin koyo eiga ni nozomu," *Eiga hyoron* (Aug. 1944), 7.

73. Ibid.

74. Kawakita Kazuko, "Atarashiki tsuchi," *Eiga no tomo* (Dec. 1936), 67.

75. Tanaka, *Hattatsushi*, vol. 2, 350–356; *Towa shoji goshi kaishashi* (Towa Shoji, 1942), 93–103.

76. Janine Hansen, *Arnold Fancks Die tochter des samurai* (Berlin: Harrassowitz Verlag, 1997); Yomota Inuhiko, *Nihon no joyu* (Iwanami Shoten, 2000).

77. Arnold Fanck, "On the Exportation of Japanese Motion Picture Films," *Cinema Yearbook of Japan 1936–1937* (KBS, 1937), 30–31.

78. Hansen, *Tochter*, 62–86; Yomota, *Joyu*, 35–36.

79. Sawamura Tsutomu, *Gendai eigaron* (Tokei Shobo, 1941), 261–262.

80. Suzuki Naoyuki, *Uchida tomu den, shisetsu* (Iwanami Shoten, 1997).

81. Ibid.

82. China was a favorite setting for German filmmakers from the 1910s; see *Harakiri* (1919, Fritz Lang), *Loves of Pharaoh* (*Das weib des Pharao*, 1921, Ernst Lubitsch), and *The Indian Tomb* (*Das Indische grabmal*, 1921, Joe May). After the 1931 Manchurian Incident, German films took a political interest in Manchuria; see *Struggle in Manchuria* (*Kampf un die Mandschurei*, 1932), *Alarm in Peking* (1937), *The New Asia* (*Das neue Asien*, 1940), and *Secret Tibet* (*Geheimnis Tibet*, 1943); Alfred Bauer, ed., *Deutscher spielfilm-almanach 1929–1950* (Munich: Filmblatter Verlag, 1950).

83. Iwasaki Akira, "The Japanese Cinema in 1937," *Cinema Yearbook of Japan 1937* (KBS, 1937), 18.

84. Elsewhere I have argued that the Japanese goodwill film genre was unable to either locate or create true Japanese/Chinese mutual understanding precisely because the stereotypical attitudes underlying the representation of the characters was based on a colonial (or neocolonial) hierarchy that always found its way into the film; Michael Baskett, "Goodwill Hunting: Rediscovering and Remembering Manchukuo in Japanese 'Goodwill Films,'" in Mariko Tamanoi, ed., *Crossed Histories: Manchuria in the Age of Empire* (Honolulu: University of Hawai'i Press, 2005).

85. Sawamura, *Gendai*, 260.

86. Fanck returned to Germany after completing *The New Earth*, but cameraman Angst stayed to write *Oath of the Nation* (*Kokumin no chikai*,1938, Nomura Hiroshi) and direct *War Buddy's Song* (*Senyu no uta*, 1939).

87. *Doitsu eiga o ikani manabu bekika* (Aoyama Shoin, 1942); *Doitsu no eiga taisei* (Doitsu Bunka Shiryosha, 1941).

88. In 1936 the average Japanese film cost 50,000 yen to produce, less than one-tenth *The New Earth*'s 750,000 yen budget.

Chapter Five: The Emperor's Celluloid Army Marches On

1. Even before starring in *Woman of Shanghai*, Japanese filmmakers had tried to get Yamaguchi to perform in other similar projects. For example, in 1951 Ichikawa Kon was producing *Ye lai xiang*, based on the title of a melodramatic love ballad that Ri Koran

helped popularize in Japan in the late 1930s. He tried to get Yamaguchi as the leading actress, but she had already left for the United States to reinvent herself as "Shirley" Yamaguchi. In America, Shirley Yamaguchi starred in three Japanese-Occupation-themed American films: *Japanese War-Bride* (1952, 20th Century Fox), *House of Bamboo* (1955, 20th Century Fox), and *Navy Wife* (1956, Allied Artists).

2. Kurosawa Akira, *Gama no abura: Jden no yona mono* (Iwanami Shoten, 1984), 268–269; Kurosawa Akira, *Something like an Autobiography*, trans. Audie E. Bock (New York: Vintage Books, 1982), 145.

3. Tanaka Masazumi, *Ozu Yasujiro zenhatusgen, 1933–1945* (Tairyusha, 1987). Yoshimura Kozaburo, *Kinema no jidai* (Kyodo Tsushinsha, 1985), 299–301. Utsumi Aiko, *Shineasuto kyoei no showa* (Gaifusha, 1987), 179–190. Kimura Sotoji, *Shin chugoku* (Tomine Shobo, 1953), 19–23. Uchida Tomu, *Eiga kantoku gojunen* (Sanichi Shobo, 1968), chap. 2. Sato Tadao, *Nihon eigashi*, vol. 2 (Iwanami Shoten, 1995), 160–161.

4. John Dower, *Embracing Defeat: Japan in the Wake of World War II* (New York: W. W. Norton, 1999), 44.

5. *Who Are the Criminals?* (*Hanzaisha wa dareka* 1946, Daiei) and *Enemy of the People* (*Minshu no teki*, 1946, Toho) were two of the earliest attempts to recast the recent history of Japanese imperialist aggression in Asia as the result of a military cabal controlling the masses.

6. On Nov. 19, 1945, the American Occupation Army announced that thirteen topics would be prohibited in all films produced during the Occupation. Those topics were: militarism, revenge, nationalism, antiforeign chauvinism, distortions of historical fact, racial or religious discrimination, feudalism, suicide, the degradation of women, brutality, antidemocratic thought, the exploitation of children, and anything contrary to the "spirit or letter" of the Potsdam Declaration or SCAP (Supreme Commander of the Allied Powers) directives; see Hirano Kyoko, *Mr. Smith Goes to Tokyo: Japanese Cinema under the American Occupation, 1945–1952* (Washington, DC: Smithsonian Institution Press, 1992), 44–45.

7. Advertising copy in the pressbook for *Enemy of the People* (*Minshu no teki*, 1945, Toho).

8. In 1941, director/producer Kamei Fumio was arrested by the Japanese government for violating the Peace Preservation Law (*koan ijiho*) and jailed for allegedly "propagating Communism." He was released, however, and made one more documentary in 1941 before the end of the Pacific War.

9. *War and Peace* (*Senso to heiwa*, 1947), codirected by Kamei Fumio and Yamamoto Satsuo, was a significant exception before 1954; see Mark Nornes, *Japanese Documentary Film: The Meiji Era through Hiroshima* (Minneapolis: University of Minnesota, 2003), and Hirano, *Mr. Smith*, 124–145.

10. The following is the official list of people in the Japanese film industry charged with war crimes. "A" class war criminals included: Tatebayashi Mikio, Nakano Toshio, Kawamo Ryuzo, Fuwa Suketoshi, Amakasu Masahiko (Manei studio chief), Kido Shiro (Shochiku studio chief), Ozawa Masao, Ohashi Takeo, Masutani Rin, Uemura Taiji, Sasho Sesaburo, Hori Kyusaku, Kikuchi Kan (novelist and former Daiei chief), Nagata Masaichi, Ueda Takuzo, Saiki Eisuke, Shigeki Kyubei, and Tachibana Ryosuke. "B"

class war criminals included: Kawakita Nagamasa (Chuka Denei/Towa Shoji), Mori Iwao, Kumagai Hisatora (director), Manaji Heita, Kanezashi Eiichi, Isono Shinsei, Soga Masashi, Emori Seikiro, Negishi Kanichi (former Nikkatsu Tamagawa studio chief), and Aoji Chuzo. "C" class war criminals included: "everyone who worked or cooperated in the planning, writing, production, and marketing of the following films; *The War at Sea from Hawaii to Malay, Fire on that Flag!, Our Planes Fly South, Decisive Battle, Tank Commander Nishizumi, Singapore All-out Attack, Storm over Bengal, Mother of Eagles, Volunteer Human Bullets, Boy Soldiers, Nippon News*, etc.; see *Eiga geino nenkan 1947 nenban* (Jiji Tsushinsha, 1947), 48–49.

11. Ibid., 50.

12. Shimizu Akira, "Nihon ni okeru senso to eiga," in Nornes and Fukushima et al., eds., *Paru haba goju shunen: Nichibei eigasen* (Yamagata Kokusai Dokyumentari Eigasai, 1991), 5–6.

13. *Listen to the Voices of the Sea* (*Kike wadatsumi no koe*, 1950, Daiei); *Bells of Nagasaki* (*Nagasaki no kane*, 1950, Shochiku); and *Desertion at Dawn* (*Akatsuki no dasso*, 1952, Toho) are examples of this sort of film.

14. Yamada Kazuo, *Itsuwari no eizo: Senso o egaku me* (Shin Nippon Shuppansha, 1984), 113–116.

15. James Orr writes about a similar phenomenon occurring in postwar Japanese literature at this time; see *The Victim as Hero: Ideologies of Peace and National Identity in Postwar Japan* (Honolulu: University of Hawai'i Press, 2001). For the prewar period, see Barak Kushner, *The Thought War* (Honolulu: University of Hawai'i Press, 2005); John Dower, *War Without Mercy*.

16. Freda Freiberg, "China Nights (Japan, 1940): The Sustaining Romance of Japan at War," *Historical Journal of Film, Radio, and Television* 14, no. 4, (Oct. 1994), 36–41.

17. Miyagi Kenshu, *Sengo senso eigashi* (Bokuto Shunshusha, 1991), 84–87.

18. Miyoshi Masao, "A Borderless World?" in Rob Wilson et al., eds., *Global/Local: Cultural Production and the Transnational Imaginary* (Durham, NC: Duke University Press, 1996), 78–106; Shiraishi Takashi, "Japan and Southeast Asia," in Peter Katzenstein et al., eds., *Network Power: Japan and Asia* (Ithaca, NY: Cornell University Press, 1997), 169–194.

19. Panivong Norindr, *Phantasmatic Indochina* (Durham, NC: Duke University Press, 1996), 132.

20. *Merdeka 17805* (*Murudeka 17805*, 2001); *T.R.Y.* (2003); *Red Moon* (*Akai tsuki*, 2004); and *Spy Sorge* (*Supai Zoruge*, 2004). In *Spy Sorge* the Japanese man falls in love with a woman of mixed Caucasian-Chinese blood. Even contemporary dramas such as *Fireflies* (*Hotaru*, 2001), which are not set in the past, remain deeply influenced by human interactions (friendship, love, betrayal) that begin in the imperial era and remain unresolved in the present.

21. Ichikawa Kon, the director, returned to the theme of the Japanese in the Nanyo two years later in *Burmese Harp* (*Biruma no tategoto*, 1954), based on the phenomenally popular novel by Takeda Taijun. Thirty-one years later, in 1985, Ichikawa remade it, reshooting many of the same scenes verbatim and using some of the same actors; Association for the Diffusion of Japanese Film Abroad, ed., *Japanese Film 1985–6* (UniJapan Film, 1985).

22. The film tells the story of two lovers, Mikami, a Japanese soldier (Ikebe Ryo), and Harumi, a Japanese singer (Yamaguchi Yoshiko), who fall in love after Harumi and other singers come to the Chinese front to "comfort the troops" (*imon ryoko*). Mikami's superior officer (Ozawa Sakae) also falls in love with Harumi and, unable to cope with her rejection, brutalizes Mikami. Mikami and Harumi escape into the desert, where they are shot without mercy by the embittered commanding officer as deserters. *Story of a Prostitute* was also remade in 1965 by Japanese director Suzuki Seijun; Tamura Taijiro, *Shumpuden* (Kodansha, 1953).

23. Regarding the censorship of *Desertion at Dawn*, see Hirano, *Mr. Smith*, 87–95.

24. Tanaka Katsunori, "Ikoku shumi ga kakaeteita mono," in the CD liner notes of *Saihakken*-Nihon *no oto-gei*, vol. 7, *Ajian konekushon* (Teichiku: TECR 20177, 1995) 6–7.

25. Tsurumi Shunsuke, "Nihon eiga ni detekuru gaijin," in Imamura Shohei et al., eds., *Koza Nihon eigashi*, vol. 5, *Nihon eiga no tenbo* (Iwanami Shoten, 1988), 105.

26. Silverberg, "Remembering," 281.

27. On American interracial films with Asian and Caucasian casts, see Gina Marchetti, *Romance and the Yellow Peril* (Berkeley: University of California Press, 1993).

28. Japanese dialogue from *Bengawan River*.

29. Ibid.

30. Yamane Sadao, video liner notes for *Bungawan soro*, Toho Kinema Kurabbu, 1993. Although Yamane claims the dialogue is spoken in "acceptable Malaysian," when I showed this sequence at a conference, several Southeast Asian specialists laughed at the "horrible pronunciation" of the Japanese actors and actresses; most of which, they said, was nearly entirely unintelligible.

31. New Guinean women rape victims discuss their experiences in the 1989 documentary *Senso Daughters* (*Senjo no onnatachi*, 1989) directed by Sekiguchi Noriko.

32. *Noroshi wa Shanhai ni agaru* (1944, Daiei/China Film Company). For nearly fifty years since the end of the Pacific War, this film was thought to have been lost until its recent discovery in the Russian Film Archive, Gosfilmofund. On the production of this film, see Poshek Fu "The Ambiguity of Entertainment: Chinese Cinema in Japanese Occupied Shanghai, 1941–1945," in *Cinema Journal* 37, no. 1 (Fall 1997), 78–80. Tsuji Hisaichi, *Chuka denei shiwa 1939–1945* (Gaifusha, 1987).

33. Inagaki Hiroshi, *Nihon eiga no wakaki hibi* (Mainichi Shinbunsha, 1978), 203.

34. Ibid., 204.

35. Inagaki, *Wakaki*, 205.

36. Oguma Eiji, *Tanitsu minzoku shinwa no kigen* (Shinyosha, 1995), 325.

37. The *Haikei* series (1963–1964) produced a total of three titles: *Haikei tenno heika-sama* (1963), *Zoku haikei tenno heika-sama* (1964), *Haikei soridaijin-sama* (1964). The first film was based on the best-selling novel of the same name written by Muneta Hiroshi. All three installments were directed and cowritten by Nomura Yoshitaro. The second installment was coscripted by Taga Yosuke and Yamada Yoji, and Yamada also served as assistant director.

38. Nomura Yoshitaro was the son of Shochiku director and studio chief Nomura Hotei 1880–1934) and was raised on the Shochiku Studio backlot in Kamata Tokyo until the 1923 Great Kanto Earthquake. Drafted in 1942, he was sent to the Burmese front, where he

was one of the few who survived the grueling Impaal offensive. Repatriated back to Japan in 1946, he worked as an assistant director under Kurosawa Akira, Kobayashi Masaki, Kawashima Yuzo, and others. His film adaptations of Matsumoto Seicho's novels *Stakeout* (*Harikomi*, 1958) and *Castles of Sand* (*Tsuna no utsuwa*, 1966) were critical successes; Eiga Junpo, ed., *Nihon eiga terebi kantoku zenshu* (Eiga Junpo, 1988), 306.

39. Muneta Hiroshi was a corporal in the Japanese army at the time of the China Incident and was injured during the battle of Joshu. He won the Noma Literature Prize, as a war correspondent in Southeast Asia during World War II. After the war he continued to write about his experiences with an increasingly humorous touch.

40. *Nihon haiyu zenshu: Danyu hen* (Eiga Junpo, 1979), 17.

41. Japanese dialogue from *Dear Mr. Emperor II.*

42. Iwasaki Akira wrote that it was a common practice among Japanese screenwriters during the Occupation to use phrases like "large man" (*o-otoko*) to mean "Americans" in order to avoid censorship. He reveals that in the original script Zen is struck and killed by a "large truck" (*o-torakku*) and argues that at that time the only large trucks rushing around Japan were American military trucks transporting supplies for the Korean War; Iwasaki Akira, *Eiga no zensetsu* (Godo Shuppan, 1981), 22.

43. The popular film series *Desperado Outpost* (*Dokuritsu gurentai*, 1959–1965) was darker and more satirical rather than outright comical. Okamoto Kihachi directed the first three films, which were set on the Chinese continent and told of the exploits of a band of renegade Japanese soldiers. *Yakuza Soldier* (*Heitai yakuza*, 1965–1972) was another popular war-film series, which, like *Desperado* was also bitterly ironic in tone. In this series, Katsu Shintaro (*Zatoichi*) plays a *yakuza*-turned-soldier who alternately fights against and participates in the corrupt military hierarchy.

44. Yamanaka Minetaro's graphic novel 300 *Miles behind Enemy Lines* (*Tekichu odan sanbyakuri*, 1930) and Tagawa Suiho's *Blackie the Stray Pup* (*Norakuro*) comic strip (1931–1941) were both serialized in the popular youth-oriented magazine *Boys' Club* (*Shonen kurabu*), published by Kodansha.

45. Tagawa wrote in his memoirs that he wanted to end the strip earlier, but its popularity with young readers made it necessary to keep promoting Norakuro in rank in order to continue publication. Tagawa finally ended the strip, partially out of fear that Norakuro's success would ultimately alienate readers and partially due to criticism from the military that an uneducated, mongrel, troublemaker could be promoted to general. In the final installment, Norakuro quits the army to go to Manchuria to "do his duty" as a private citizen; see Suiho Tagawa, *Norakuro jijoden* (1983), 1–4.

46. Iwasaki, *Zensetsu*, 22.

47. "We waited for three hours, but all we saw was fog. Zensuke was impressed by how great the emperor was." Dialogue from *Dear Mr. Emperor II.*

48. Iwasaki, *Zensetsu*, 22.

49. Ibid, 23.

50. Japanese dialogue from *Dear Mr. Emperor II.*

51. Ozawa Shoichi played Chinese characters several times in his career; these included a drug-ring boss in *Rainbow Pistol* (*Niji no kenju*, 1961) and a Chinese restaurant cook in *Winter Flower* (*Fuyu no hana*, 1977).

52. Yûkichi Shinada, "Yamada Yoôji, jiden to jisaku o kataru," in Cinema Bi-weekly, ed., *Sekai no eiga sakka: Yamada Yoji, Kato Tai* (1977), 186. In this 1977 interview Yamada said that he moved from Harbin to Hoten (present-day Shenyang) and finally to Dairen before finally repatriating to Japan in 1948.

53. Pachinko is a pinball-like game of chance that uses steel balls.

54. Hobsbawm, *The Age of Empire*, 5.

55. Mainichi Shinbun, Oct. 29, 2003. The full quote says: "[Japan] most certainly did not militarily invade [Korea]. Rather, it was because the Korean peninsula was divided and could not be consolidated that by their own collective will [the Koreans] chose between Russia, China [*Shina*], and Japan. They sought the help of the modernized Japanese people who shared the same facial color as their own, and annexation was conducted by a consensus of the world's nations. I do not intend to justify Japanese annexation 100 percent. From their [Koreans] emotional point of view, it probably was annoying, maybe even humiliating. But if anything, it was the responsibility of their ancestors." The seventy-one-year-old novelist-politician's remarks show a marked change in the political climate regarding statements about Japan's former colony compared with just eight years earlier. At that time former Cabinet Minister Eto Takami was forced to give up his post after saying Japanese colonization had some positive effects on the Korean people and then Prime Minister Murayama Tomiichi sent a statement to South Korean President Kim Youngsam admitting that the bilateral treaty for annexation was signed on an unequal basis between Japan and Korea and that Japan would not forget the mental anguish it caused the Korean people.

56. Tojo Yuko, granddaughter of Tojo Hideki, in an interview with Associated Press reporter Nicholas Kristof. See http://www.ishipress.com/tojo.htm. Tojo Yukiko, "Sofu Tojo Hideki "issai kataru nakare!" *Bungei shunshu* (2000); Tojo Yukiko, *Tojoke no boshigusa* (Kobunsha, 2003). Yamamoto Sharin, *Manga: Kenkanryu* (Shinyusha, 2005) and *Manga: Kenkanryu 2* (Shinyusha, 2006). Kobayashi Yoshinori: *Shin gomanizumu sengen supesharu: Sensoron* (Gentosha, 1998); *Shin gomanizumu sengen supesharu: Taiwanron* (Gentosha, 2000); *Shin gomanizumu sengen supesharu: Sensoron 2* (Gentosha, 2001); *Shin gomanizumu sengen 10* (Gentosha, 2001); *Shin gomanizumu sengen supesharu: Sensoron 3* (Gentosha, 2003); and *Shin gomanizumu sengen supesharu: Okinawaron* (Gentosha, 2005).

57. "Japanese Film's Role Reversals: In 'Pride,' Gen. Tojo Praised, Americans Mocked." *Washington Post*, May 25, 1998. See Chester Dawson (Tokyo AP) "Japanese Film Glorifies War," Associated Press, Aug. 6, 1998, http://www.asiaweek.com/asiaweek/98/0612/feat1.html. The advertising tagline for the film promised viewers that they would "[l]earn the truth about the 'Tokyo Trials' as portrayed through the struggle of Tojo Hideki, the man."

58. In 2002, *2009 Lost Memories* was one of the most expensive South Korean feature films ever produced, costing an estimated US$6 million. It was the fourth highest-grossing film (foreign and domestic) of 2002 and stayed in the top ten for six weeks, gaining a total of 2,263,800 paid admissions nationwide. Box-office figures from the Korean Association of Film Art and Industry and the Korean Film Commission (KOFIC) at http://hyunfilm.tripod.com/2002.htm.

59. Feature film examples include: *Asako in Ruby Shoes* (Sunaebo, 2000); *Seoul* (2002); *KT* (2002); *Run 2U* (*Ron tu yu*, 2003); and *Hotel Venus* (*Hoteru biinasu*, 2004); as well as numerous television drama collaborations such as *Fighting Girl* and *Sonagi*.

60. Sakagami Jun, "Ajia o mikaeta atarashii eigazukuri no daippo," in *Torai no subete* (Kinema Junposha, 2002), 90–95.

61. Shimada Akiko, "Oda Yuji no Chugoku deno ninki," in *Torai no subete* (Kinema Junposha, 2002), 32.

62. Koichi Iwabuchi, *Recentering Globalization: Popular Culture and Transnationalism*, (Durham, NC: Duke University Press, 2003), 132.

63. Sohn Chang Min, *Torai no subete* (Kinema Junposha, 2002), 54.

64. Joseph Straubhaar, "Beyond Media Imperialism: Asymmetrical Interdependence and Cultural Proximity," *Critical Studies in Mass Communication* 8, no.1 (1992), 39–59.

65. Said, *Culture and Imperialism*, 12.

66. *Eizo no shogen: Manshu no kiroku*, Ten Sharp Collection, 1995, 30 vols. On the "discovery" of these films, see "Kyu Manshu eiga marugoto Nihon ni," *Asahi shinbun*, June 9, 1994; Ishii Kaoru, "Maboroshi no eiga o motomete," in *Manshu no kiroku* (Shueisha, 1995), 246–247.

Selected Bibliography

Journals and Almanacs

Bianco e nero (1937–1943)
Eiga (Film)
Eiga gaku (Film Study)
Eiga gijutsu (Film Technology)
Eiga hyoron (Film Criticism)
Eiga junpo (Film Bi-weekly)
Eiga nenkan (Film Almanac)
Eiga no tomo (Film Friend)
Eiga sozo (Film Creation)
Eiga to gijutsu (Film and Technology)
Eiga to ongaku (Film and Music)
Eigakai (Film World)
Eigashi kenkyo (Film History Study)
Film Daily Yearbook
Firumu kenetsu jiho (Film Censorship Bulletin)
Firumu kenetsu nenpo (Film Censorship Annual)
Harrison's Reports & Film Reviews
Hollywood Reporter
International Motion Picture Almanac
Katsudo shashinkai (Moving Picture World)
Kinema junpo (Cinema Bi-Weekly)
Kinema rekodo (Cinema Record)
Kokusai bunka shinkokai, 1938 (Cinema Yearbook of Japan 1938)
Kokusai bunka shinkokai, 1939 (Cinema Yearbook of Japan 1939)
Kokusai bunka sinokai, 1937 (Cinema Yearbook of Japan 1936–1937)
Manshu eiga (Manchurian Film)
Moving Picture World
Nihon eiga (Japanese Film)

Books and Essays

Place of publication for Japanese entries is Tokyo unless otherwise indicated.

Abe Mark Nornes, *"Dawn of Freedom."* In Abe Mark Nornes and Yukio Yukushima, eds., *Nichibei eigasen: Media Wars Then & Now*, 260. Yamagata: Yamagata International Documentary Film Festival, 1991.

——. *Japanese Documentary Film.* Minneapolis: University of Minnesota Press, 2003.

Aikawa Haruki. *Bunka eigaron.* Kasumigaseki Shobo, 1944.

Akazawa, Shiro, ed. *Bunka to fashizumu.* Nihon Keizai Hyoronsha, 1993.

Akiyama Kuniharu, *Nihon no eiga ongakushi.* Tabata Shoten, 1974.

Amakasu Masahiko. "Making Films for the Manchurians." *Eiga junpo*, Aug. 1, 1942

Anderson, Benedict. *Imagined Communities.* London: Verso, 1993.

Anderson, J. L. "Spoken Silents in the Japanese Cinema, or, Talking to Picture: Essaying the *Katsuben*, Contextualizing the Texts." In Arthur Nolletti, Jr. and David Desser, eds., *Reframing Japanese Cinema: Authorship, Genre, History*, 259–311. Terre Haute: Indiana University Press, 1992.

Anderson, Joseph L., and Donald Richie. *The Japanese Film: Art and Industry.* Princeton, NJ: Princeton University Press, 1982.

Baskett, Michael. "Dying for a Laugh: Japanese Post-1945 Service Comedies." *Historical Journal of Film, Radio, & Television* 23, no. 4 (Oct. 2003), 291–310.

Benali, Abdelkader. *Le cinema colonial au Maghreb.* Paris: Editions du Cerf, 1998.

Bernstein, Matthew, and Gaylyn Studlar, eds. *Visions of the East: Orientalism in Film.* New Brunswick, NJ: Rutgers University Press, 1997.

"Boken Dankichi no koto." In Shimada Keizo, ed., *Boken Dankichi.* Vol. 2, 186–187. Kodansha, 1967.

Boulanger, Pierre. *Le cinema colonial de "L'atlantide" a "Lawrence d'arabie."* Paris: Editions Seghers, 1975.

Brownlow, Kevin. *The Parade's Gone By.* New York: Knopf, 1968.

Brunetta, Gian Piero. *L'ora d'Africa del cinema.* Rovereto: Materiali di Lavoro, 1990.

Castle, Kathryn, ed., *Britannia's Children.* New York: St. Martin's Press, 1996.

Chen Fei-bao. *Taiwan dianying shihua.* Beijing: Zhongguo Dianying Chubanshe, 1988.

Cheng, Jihua, Li Shaobai, and Xing Zuwen. *Chugoku eigashi.* Trans. Morikawa Kazuyo. Heibonsha, 1987.

——. *Zhongguo dianying fazhan shi.* Beijing: Zhongguo Dianying Chubanshe, 1980).

Cho Hee Moon. "A Study of Early Korean Film History: Introduction and Reception of Motion Pictures 1896–1923." PhD diss. Chung-ang University, 1992,

Chosen Sotokufu Kinema. Chosen Sotokufu Kanbo Bunshoka, 1938.

Convents, Guido. "Film and German Colonial Propaganda." In *Prima di Caligari*, 58–76. Pordenone: Biblioteca dell'Immagine, 1990.

Crafton, Donald. *Emil Cohl, Caricature, and Film.* Princeton, NJ: Princeton University Press, 1990.

Davis, Darrell William. *Picturing Japaneseness: Monumental Style, National Identity, Japanese Film.* New York: Columbia University Press, 1996.

Del Mundo, Cloduoldo. *Native Resistance: Philippine Cinema and Colonialism, 1898–1941.* Manila: De La Salle University Press, 1998.

Dower, John. *Embracing Defeat.* New York: W. W. Norton, 1999.

——. *War Without Mercy.* New York: Pantheon Books, 1988.

Duus, Peter. *The Abacus and the Sword.* Berkeley: University of California Press, 1995.

———, Ramon Meyers, Mark Peattie, eds. *The Japanese Informal Empire, 1937–1945.* Princeton, NJ: Princeton University Press, 1989.

———. *The Wartime Japanese Empire, 1941–1945.* Princeton, NJ: Princeton University Press, 1995.

Eiga bunka tenrankaiki. Dainippon eiga kyokai, 1940.

Eiga Haikyusha Nanpokyoku Chosabu, ed. *Higashi Indo no eiga jijo.* Eiga Haikyusha, 1942.

Enomoto Yasuko. *Gakunin no miyako-shanhai.* Kenbun Shuppan, 1998.

Fell, John L. *Film and the Narrative Tradition.* Berkeley: University of California Press, 1986,

Friedrichsmeyer, Sara, et al., eds. *The Imperialist Imagination: German Colonialism and Its Legacy.* Ann Arbor: Michigan University Press, 1998.

Fu, Poshek. *Passivity, Resistance, and Collaboration: Intellectual Choices in Occupied Shanghai, 1937–1945.* Stanford: Stanford University Press, 1996.

Fujiwara Sakuya, and Yamaguchi Yoshiko. *Ri Koran: Watashi no hansei.* Shinchosha, 1987.

Gili, Jean A. *L'Italie de Mussolini et son cinema.* Paris: Henri Veyrier, 1985.

Gluck, Carol. *Japan's Modern Myths.* Princeton, NJ: Princeton University Press, 1985.

Goodman, Grant, ed. *Japanese Cultural Policies in Southeast Asia during World War 2.* New York: St. Martin's Press, 1992.

Greene, Martin. *Dreams of Adventure, Deeds of Empire.* New York: Basic Books, 1979.

Hake, Sabine. "Mapping the Native Body." In S. Friedrichsmeyer, ed., *The Imperialist Imagination,* 163–187. Ann Arbor: University of Michigan Press, 1998.

Hansen, Janine. *Arnold Fancks Die tochter des samurai: National-sozialistische Propaganda und Japanische Filmpolitik.* Weisbaden: Harrassowitz Verlag, 1997.

Harley, John. *World-wide Influences of the Cinema.* Los Angeles: University of Southern California Press, 1940.

Harootunian, H. D. "A Sense of an Ending and the Problem of Taisho." In H. D. Harootunian et al., eds., *Japan in Crisis: Essays on Taisho Democracy,* 3–28. Princeton, NJ: Princeton University Press, 1974.

Hay, James. *Popular Film Culture in Fascist Italy.* Princeton, NJ: Princeton University Press, 1987.

Hazumi, Tsuneo. *Eiga gojunenshi.* Masu Shobo, 1942.

———. *Eiga to minzoku.* Eiga Nipponsha, 1942.

Headrick, Daniel. *The Tools of Empire.* New York: Oxford University Press, 1981.

High, Peter B. *The Imperial Screen.* Madison: University of Wisconsin Press, 2003.

———. *Teikoku no ginmaku.* Nagoya Daigaku Shuppan, 1995.

Higson, Andrew, and Richard Maltby, eds. *"Film Europe" and "Film America": Cinema, Commerce and Cultural Exchange, 1920–1939.* Exeter: Exeter University Press, 1999.

Hirano, Kyoko. *Mr. Smith Goes to Tokyo: Japanese Cinema Under the American Occupation, 1945–1952.* Washington DC: Smithsonian Institution Press, 1992.

Hobsbwam, Eric. *The Age of Empire, 1875–1914.* New York: Vintage Books, 1989.

Hosokawa Shuhei. "Seiyo ongaku no Nihonka-taishubunka 42." *Myujikku magajin* (Sept. 1992), 153.

———. "Seiyo ongaku no Nihonka-taishubunka 43." *Myujikku magajin* (Oct. 1992), 146.

Hu, Chang, and Gu Quan. *Manying: Guoce dianyin mianmian guan.* Beijing: Zhonghua Shujuchu, 1990.

———. *Manei kokusaku eiga no shoos.* Trans. Yokochi Takeshi and Aida Fusako. Gendai Shokan, 1999.

Hung Ya-wen. "Nihon shokuminchi shihai ni okeru Taiwan eigakai ni kansuru kosatsu." MA thesis, Waseda University, 1997.

———. "Taiwan sotokufu ni yoru eiga seisaku." *Eiga gaku,* no. 12, 1998, 116–149.

Ichikawa, Sai. *Ajia eiga no sozo oyobi kensetsu.* Kokusai Eiga Tsushinsha, 1941.

Iijima Tadashi. *Kagaku eiga no shomondai.* Hakusuisha, 1944.

———. *Nihon eigashi.* 2 vols. Hakusuisha, 1955.

———. *Senchu eiga: Shiki.* M. G. Shuppan, 1984.

Imamura, Miyoo. *Nihon eiga bunkenshi.* Kagamiura Shobo, 1967.

Imamura Shohei et al., eds. *Koza nihon eiga.* Vol. 4: *Senso to nihon.* Iwanami Shoten, 1987.

Imamura Taihei. *Manga eigaron.* Daiichi Geibunsha, 1941.

Ishimaki, Yoshio. *Sekai no eiga kokusaku to Nihon.* Kokusai Eiga Tsushinsha, 1933.

Iwabuchi, Koichi. *Recentering Globalization.* Durham, NC: Duke University Press, 2002.

Iwamoto, Kenji, ed. *Eiga to daitoa kyoeiken.* Shinwasha, 2004.

Iwasaki, Akira. *Eiga no zensetsu.* Godo Shuppan, 1981.

———. *Negishi Kanichi.* Tokyo: privately published, 1969.

Kasza, Gregory. *The State and Mass Media in Japan, 1918–1945.* Berkeley: University of California Press, 1988.

Kawakita Kazuko. *Eiga hitotsujini.* Kodansha, 1973.

Kawamura, Minato. "Taishu orientarizumu to Ajia ninshiki." In Oe Shinobu et al., eds., *Kindai Nihon to shokuminchi.* Vol. 7: *Bunka no naka no shokuminchi,* 107–111. Iwanami Shoten, 1993.

Kobayashi Hideo. *The Literature of Lost Home.* Stanford, CA: Stanford University Press, 1995.

Koga Futoshi, ed. *Hikari no Tanjo Lumière!* Asahi Shinbun, 1995.

Koide, Hideo. *Nanpo engeiki.* Shinkigensha, 1943.

Koizumi, Goro. *Waga seishun to man'ei.* Lantosha, 1982.

Kokusai Koryu Forum, ed. *Ajia eigashi hakkutsu shirizu.* Vol. 2: *Kankoku no sairento eiga to katsubenshi no sekai.* Kokusai Koryu Kikin, 1996.

Komagome, Takeshi. *Shokuminchiteikoku Nihon no bunka togo.* Iwanami Shoten, 1996.

Komota, Nobuo et al., eds. *Shinpan Nihon ryukokashi.* 3 vols. Shakai Shisosha, 1995–1996.

Kono Kiyoichi, ed. *Kigeki eiga no osama: Saito Torajiro kantoku.* Akita: Self-published, 1989.

Koppes, Clayton R., and Gregory Black. *Hollywood Goes to War.* Berkeley: University of California Press, 1987.

Kubota Tatsuo. *Bunka eiga no hohoron*. Daichi Bungeisha, 1940.

Kunzle, David. *History of the Comic Strip*. Berkeley: University of California Press, 1973.

Kurata Yoshihiro. *Nihon rekodo bunkashi*. Tosho Sensho, 1992.

Kushner, Barak. *The Thought War: Japanese Imperial Propaganda*. Honolulu: University of Hawai'i Press, 2005.

Lebra, Joyce C. *Japan's Greater East Asia Co-Prosperity Sphere in World War II*. New York: Oxford University Press, 1975.

Lee Yong-il. "Nitei shokuminichi jidai no Chosen eiga." In Imamura et al., eds. *Koza Nihon eiga*. Vol. 3: *Tooki no jidai*, 313–314. Iwanami Shoten, 1986.

Lee, Yong-il, and Choe Young-choi. *The History of the Korean Cinema*. Trans. Richard Greever. Seoul: Jimoondang International, 1988.

Lee Yong-il, and Sato Tadao. *Kankoku eiga nyumon*. Gaifusha, 1990.

Lippit, Seiji. *Topographies of Japanese Modernism*. New York: Columbia University Press, 2002.

Lu Xun. "Preface to *Call to Arms*." In *Lu Xun: Selected Works*. Vol. 1. Beijing: Foreign Languages Press, 1956.

Machida, Keiji. *Tatakau bunka butai*. Hara Shobo, 1967.

Mackenzie, John M. *Imperialism and Popular Culture*. Manchester: Manchester University Press, 1986.

——, ed. *Orientalism: History, Theory, and the Arts*. Manchester: Manchester University Press, 1995,

——. *Propaganda and Empire*. Manchester: Manchester University Press, 1986.

Mainichi Shinbun, ed. *Ri Koran: Futatsu no sokoku ni yurareta seishun*. Mainichi gurafu bessatsu, 1991.

——. *Nihon nyusu eigashi*. Mainichi Shinbun, 1977.

Marchetti, Gina. *Romance and the "Yellow Peril."* Berkeley: University of California Press, 1993.

Masumoto Kinen. *Jinbutsu-shochiku eigashi*. Heibonsha, 1987.

Mitchell, Richard H. *Censorship in Imperial Japan*. Princeton, NJ: Princeton University Press, 1983.

Miyata, Setsuko. *Chosen minshu to kominka seisaku*. Miraisha, 1985.

——. *Soshi kaimei*. Akaishi Shoten, 1992.

Monma, Takashi. *Ajia eiga ni miru Nihon I: Chugoku, Honkon, Taiwan*. Shakai Hyoronsha, 1995.

——. *Ajia eiga ni miru Nihon II: Kankoku, kita Chosen, tonan Ajia*. Shakai Hyoronsha, 1996.

Muto, Tomio. *Manshukoku no danmen: Amakasu Masahiko no shogai*. Kindaisha, 1956.

Myers, Ramon, and Mark Peattie, eds. *The Japanese Empire, 1895–1945*. Princeton, NJ: Princeton University Press, 1984.

Naimusho Keihokyoku, ed. *Firumu kenetsu jiho*. 40 vols. Fuji Shuppan, 1985.

——. *Firumu kenetsu nenpo*. 4 vols. Ryukei Shosha, 1984.

——. *Kakkoku ni okeru eiga kokusaku no kikyo*. Tokyo: self-published, 1933.

Narangoa, Li, and Robert Cribb, eds. *Imperial Japan and National Identities in Asia, 1895–1945*. London: Routledge, 2003.

NHK Shuzaihanhen. *Dokyumento showa*. 4 vols. Kadokawa Shoten, 1986.

Noma Seiji. *Noma of Japan: The Nine Magazines of Kodansha*. New York: Vanguard, 1934.

Norindr, Panivong. *Phantasmatic Indochina*. Durham, NC: Duke University Press, 1997.

Oe Shinobu et al., eds. *Kindai Nihon to shokuminchi*. Vol. 7: *Bunka no naka no shokuminchi*. Iwanami Shoten, 1993.

Ogawa Chikagoro. *Ryukoka to sesso*. Nihon Keisatsu Shinbunshahan, 1941.

Oguma, Eiji. *Nihonjin no kyokai*. Shinyosha, 1998.

———. *Tanitsu minzoku shinwa no kigen*. Shinyosha, 1995.

Okano Kaoruko. *Kagaku eiga ni kaketa yume*. Soshisha, 1999.

Orr, James. *The Victim as Hero: Ideologies of Peace and National Identity in Postwar Japan*. Honolulu: University of Hawai'i Press, 2001.

Park, Chan-ho. *Kankoku kayoshi, 1895-1945*. Tokyo: Shobunsha, 1987.

Peattie, Mark. *Nanyo: The Rise and Fall of the Japanese in Micronesia, 1885–1945*. Honolulu: University of Hawai'i Press, 1988.

Reeves, Nicholas. *The Power of Film Propaganda*. London: Cassell, 2000.

Richards, Jeffrey. *Imperialism and Juvenile Literature*. Manchester: Manchester University Press, 1989.

———. *Visions of Yesterday*. London: Routledge, 1973.

Robertson, Jennifer. *Takarazuka Sexual Politics and Popular Culture in Modern Japan*. Berkeley: University of California Press, 1998.

Rogin, Michael. *Blackface, White Noise*. Berkeley: University of California Press, 1996.

Rousso, Henry. *The Vichy Syndrome: History and Memory in France Since 1944*. Cambridge: Harvard University Press, 1991.

Sadoul, Georges. *Le cinema pendant la guerre, 1939–1945*. Paris: Denoel, 1954.

Said, Edward W. *Culture and Imperialism*. New York: Vintage Books, 1993.

———. *Orientalism*. New York: Vintage Books, 1979.

Sakuramoto, Tomio. *Bunkajin no daitoa senso*. Aoki Shoten, 1993.

———. *Daitoa senso to Nihon eiga*. Aoki Shoten, 1993.

Sasaki Jun et al., eds. *Utaeba tengoku*. Tokyo: Media Factory, 1999.

Sato Tadao. "Hariuddo no Nihonjin tachi." In Imamura Shohei et al., eds, *Koza Nihon eiga*. Vol. 1: *Nihon eiga no tanjo*, 267. Iwanami Shoten, 1985.

———. *Kinema to hosei*. Riburopoto, 1985.

———. *Nihon eigashi*. Vol. 2. Iwanami Shoten, 1995.

Shabana Bontaro. *Hokushi sensen-kaisoku heichan butai: Totsugeki!* Nakano Shoten, 1937.

Shibata, Yoshio. *Sekai eiga senso*. Hokuryukan, 1944.

Shimada, Keizo. *Boken Dankichi*. 4 vols. Kodansha Bunko, 1976.

Shimizu, Akira. *Shanhai sokai eiga shishi*. Shinchosha, 1995.

Shimizu Kogakko Eiga Kenkyubu, ed. *Eiga kyoiku no jissai*. Tokyo: Self-published, 1941.

Shohat, Ella, and Robert Stam. *Unthinking Eurocentrism: Multiculturalism in the Media*. London: Routledge, 1994.

Silverberg, "Remembering Pearl Harbor, Forgetting Charlie Chaplin, and the Case of the Disappearing Western Woman: A Picture Story." *Positions* 1, no. 1 (Spring 1993).

Stephenson, Shelly. "Her Traces Are Found Everywhere." In Yingjin Zhang, ed., *Cinema and Urban Culture in Shanghai, 1922–1943*. Stanford, CA: Stanford University Press, 1999.

Sun Yu. *Dalu zhihua*. Beijing: Yuen Liang Chubanshe, 1990.

Tagawa, Suiho. *Norakuro jijoden*. Kojinsha, 1983.

———, ed. *Norakuro mangashu*. 4 vols. Kodansha, 1975.

Takashima, Kinji. *Chosen eiga toseishi*. Keijo: Chosen Eiga Bunka Kenkyojo, 1943.

Takasaki Takaharu. *Senjika no zasshi*. Fubosha, 1976.

Tamanoi, Mariko, ed. *Crossed Histories: Manchuria in the Age of Empire*. Honolulu: University of Hawai'i Press, 2005.

Tamura, Shizue. *Hajime ni eiga ga atta*. Chuo Koron Shinsha, 2000.

Tanaka Junichiro. "Koya no adabana Manshu eiga." In *Bessatsu ichiokunin no showashi: Nihon shokuminchi*. Vol. 2, 286–290. Mainichi Shinbunsha, 1978.

———. *Nihon eiga hattatsushi*. 5 vols. Chuo Koronsha, 1980.

———. *Nihon kyoiku eiga hattatsushi*. Kagyusha, 1979.

Tanaka, Stefan. *Japan's Orient*. Berkeley: University of California Press, 1993.

Tanikawa Yoshio. *Nihon no kagaku eigashi*. Yuni Tsushin, 1978.

Taylor, Richard. *Film Propaganda: Soviet Russia and Nazi Germany*. London: I. B. Taurus, 1998.

Thompson, Kristin. *Exporting Entertainment: America in the World Film Market, 1907–1934*. London: British Film Institute, 1985.

Tonoshita Tatsuya. "Senjitaiseika no ongakkai." In Akazawa Shiro, ed., *Bunka to fashizumu*. Nihon Keizai Hyoronsha, 1993.

Towa Shoji, ed. *Towa shoji goshikaisha shashi*. Tokyo: self-published, 1942.

Tsuboi, Hitoshi. *Manshu eiga kyokai no kaiso*. Tokyo: self-published, 1984.

Tsuji, Hisaichi. *Chuka denei shiwa: Ippeisotsu no nichu eigakaisoki*. Gaifusha, 1987.

Tsumura, Hideo. *Eiga seisakuron*. Chuo Koronsha, 1943.

———. *Eigasen*. Asahi Shibunsha, 1944.

Tsurumi, Patricia. *Japanese Colonial Education in Taiwain, 1895–1945*. Cambridge, MA: Harvard University Press, 1977.

Tsurumi, Shunsuke. *An Intellectual History of Wartime Japan 1931–1945*. London: KPI, 1986.

Uchikawa, Yoshimi. *Masu media tosei*. 2 vols. Misuzu Shobo, 1975.

U.S. Department of Commerce, Motion Picture Division, ed. *Review of Foreign Markets*. Washington, DC: U.S. Dept. of Commerce, 1938.

Utasaki Takahiko, ed. *Shogen Nihon yogaku rekodoshi senzenhen*. Ongaku no Tomosha, 1998.

Utsumi, Aiko, and Murai Yoshinori. *Shineasuto kyoei no showa*. Gaifusha, 1987.

Vasey, Ruth. *The World According to Hollywood, 1918–1939*. Madison: University of Wisconsin Press, 1997.

Virilio, Paul. *War and Cinema: The Logistics of Perception*. New York: Verso, 1984.

Walsh, Michael. *The Internationalism of the American Cinema*. Madison: University of Wisconsin Press, 1998.

Ward, Robert S. *Asia for the Asiatics? Techniques of Japanese Occupation*. Chicago: University of Chicago Press, 1945.

Yamagata International Documentary Film Festival, ed. *Daitoakyoeiken to eiga*. Yamagata: Yamagata International Documentary Film Festival, 1997.

Yamaguchi, Kaoru. *Zensen eishatai*. Matsukage Shorin, 1943.

Yamaguchi Katsunori et al., eds. *Nihon animeshon eigashi*. Yubunsha, 1977.

Yamaguchi, Takeshi. *Aishu no Manshu eiga*. Santen Shobo, 2000.

———. *Maboroshi no kinema man'ei*. Heibonsha, 1989.

Yano Toru. *"Nanshin" no keifu*. Chuo Koronsha, 1975.

Yomota, Inuhiko. *Nihon no joyu*. Iwanami Shobo, 2000.

———. *Ri Koran to higashi Ajia*. Tokyo Daigaku Shuppankai, 2001.

Yoshida Chieo. *Mohitotsu no eigashi: Katsuben no jidai*. Jiji Tsushinsha, 1978.

Yoshida Yoshishige et al., eds. *Eiga torai–shinematogurafu to [Meiji no Nihon]*. Iwanami Shoten, 1995.

Yoshimoto Sanpei. *Pokopen Taisho*. In *Shonen kurabu* (Dec. 1934).

Young, Louise. *Japan's Total Empire: Manchuria and the Culture of Wartime Imperialism*. Berkeley: University of California Press, 1998.

Index

References to illustrations are in **boldface**.